GEORDIE

GEORDIE
SAS FIGHTING HERO

GEORDIE DORAN WITH MIKE MORGAN

FOREWORD BY CHRIS RYAN

First published in 2007
This edition published in 2011

Spellmount, an imprint of
The History Press
The Mill, Brimscombe Port
Stroud, Gloucestershire, GL5 2QG
www.thehistorypress.co.uk

Reprinted 2016

British Library Cataloguing in Publication Data.
A catalogue record for this book is available from the British Library.

ISBN 978 0 7524 6053 6

Typesetting and origination by The History Press
Printed in Great Britain

CONTENTS

FOREWORD

Geordie Doran is a legend to all soldiers of the Special Air Service (SAS). Few men have gone through so many famous conflicts in Britain's history. From active service in the Paras in the Suez crisis of 1956, through the humid and steamy jungles of Malaya, to the burning deserts of Oman and the Yemen and many other hot spots, he became an inspiration to his comrades and those who have followed in his footsteps.

In the SAS, there are, and have been, many brave men, but Geordie was always in a class above in modern times.

His personality is deceptive. He has always had a quiet, modest, dignified manner while at the same time being very tough and hardy, and possessing a fine sense of humour. But in action he was always fearless, fiercely determined and never frightened to sacrifice himself to help a fellow comrade.

I first heard of him in 1976 as a 15-year-old when I was introduced to C Squadron 23 SAS by my cousin. This squadron, which had been formed by Geordie several years previously, all held him totally in awe as a vastly experienced regular of the SAS. Although it was completely unofficial, as I was not old enough to be attending the selections, I still took part. Geordie set out all the routes, which he himself had planned, and oversaw the process. At the end I was the only one left out of the whole selection course! But I was too young, so they told me to come back the following year, when I duly passed. I was well versed in the process of selection by then and knew all the routes and rendezvous (RV) points. I then joined 22 SAS in 1984.

One of these points – Geordie's RV – is still used on the Otterburn training area selection course north of Hexham, which runs to the Scottish border, where Geordie used to sit on a bridge as a Permanent Staff Instructor overseeing hundreds of potential recruits from all over the north and then supervising their selections. These selection courses are exactly the same as the famous current ones for 22 SAS at Hereford, only they were run over weekends rather than a six-month block process.

Geordie always treated the Territorial Army (TA) soldiers in his care hard but fair, and never made us feel like weekend soldiers. I myself was in the TA SAS for six years before joining the regular SAS.

Such was Geordie's reputation, among both the ranks and officers alike, that his exploits and persona were an inspiration to men he had never even met. His quiet courage, confidence and unmatched experience set a standard that everybody tried to reach. Not all succeeded, but the cream of the best were generally found and nurtured by Geordie's tried and tested methods. He is one of a select number of legendary figures who all inspire SAS soldiers even to this day – David Stirling, Paddy Mayne, Johnny Cooper (who Geordie served memorably with in the Yemen) – and many more unforgettable soldiers, all the cream of the best that Britain can produce.

When SAS troops go into action today in places like Afghanistan they know they are part of the most famous regiment in the world and that they have standards to live up to, as set by legends like Geordie, which their own self-discipline tells them they have got to meet, even when they are at the point of exhaustion.

I and others like me in the modern SAS would truthfully find some of the operations people will read about in this book hard to complete successfully today, even with all our modern weapons, technology, intelligence and back-up. In fact, some of the operations that Geordie and others pulled off were almost impossible: they were going into uncharted territory in terms of survival and operations. For instance, they were going deep into the jungles of Malaya with inadequate food supplies, the men sleeping in trees, living on their wits and courage, and fighting a very competent enemy, the Communist guerrillas, who were used to living and fighting in the jungle. And yet they won! The same applies to the famous desert campaigns of Oman and the Yemen.

All tactics used by the SAS today stem from the hard experience learned in the jungle – for example, the four-man team, each man capable of covering for the others. Nowadays the basics needed are exactly the same and can be modified for the desert, an urban environment or virtually any other campaign or terrain.

As well as being a superb soldier, with a formidable and almost unique length of service in Special Forces in so many danger spots the world over, Geordie is genuinely a very decent, honourable man who will always have my respect and that of countless other former and current members of the regiment.

There have been many fine members of the SAS, but Geordie himself has no idea how much of an effect he has had on so many lives or of the number of lives saved by his thorough and dedicated training of younger members of the SAS. In fact Geordie and soldiers of similar calibre devised a lot of the tactics that I and many others fell back on and used in the first Gulf War of 1991.

In this timely and historic book, co-authored with Mike Morgan, whose own father, Corporal Jack Morgan, was a founder member of the elite 2nd SAS Intelligence Section during the Second World War, Geordie richly deserves to take his place among the true legends of the regiment.

CHRIS RYAN

Chris Ryan is an international best-selling author and holder of the Military Medal, awarded for his outstanding courage in his famous solo escape back to Allied lines during the Bravo Two Zero SAS raid in Iraq in the first Gulf War in 1991.

Acknowledgements

I would like to pay tribute to my friend and Special Forces author and co-writer Mike Morgan for the tireless amount of work and expertise he has put into this book regarding its content, editing, format and layout over many months of hard endeavour. After asking Mike to view and vet my original manuscript, he expressed firm confidence in the project from the beginning. Ours has been a very happy and harmonious working relationship, and long may our friendship continue.

I also thank Chris Ryan, a former member of the TA SAS and a famous SAS soldier and author in his own right, for his excellent foreword which puts my life story into a very clear, concise nutshell at the start of this book.

My loyal wife, Ann, has offered me unstinting support over a long and happy marriage, as have my daughters Frankie (Frances) and Jackie (Jacqueline). I owe them all a debt of gratitude for being there when I have needed them most. In fact Frankie was the inspiration for this work as, one day – it seems like an age ago now – she asked me to put down my memoirs on paper as a family record. As you can see, I got rather carried away! This book, in its refined form, is the result, and I hope general readers, military veterans and serving soldiers alike will enjoy it for what it is – a true record of some of the key campaigns and experiences that have helped shape Britain's postwar history.

Lastly, I sincerely thank all my former Army, Para and SAS comrades without whom my book, *Geordie*, could not have been written. In a very real sense it is also very much *their* story, and I dedicate it to every one of them.

GEORDIE

ABBREVIATIONS

AFD	Airborne Forces Depot
BAOR	British Army of the Rhine
CO	Commanding Officer
CQB	close-quarter battle
CSM	Company Sergeant Major
CT	Communist terrorists
DCLI	Duke of Cornwall's Light Infantry
DF	defensive fire
DLI	Durham Light Infantry
DZ	drop zone
EAPC	East African Pioneer Corps
FF	free fall
FFR	fit for role
GP	Garrison Military Police
GPMG	general purpose machine gun
HALO	high-altitude low-opening
HE	high explosive
KAR	King's African Rifles
KL	Kuala Lumpur
KOYLI	King's Own Yorkshire Light Infantry
LG	Life Guards
LMG	light machine gun
LRDG	Long Range Desert Group
LZ	landing zone
MG	machine gun
MP	military police(man)
MTO	motor transport officer
NCO	non-commissioned officer
NF	Royal Northumberland Fusiliers

OBLI	Oxfordshire and Buckinghamshire Light Infantry
OC	Officer Commanding
OP	observation post
PDC	*parachutiste de choc* (French)
PE	plastic explosive
PJI	parachute jump instructor
PSI	Permanent Staff Instructor
QM	Quartermaster
RA	Royal Artillery
RAOC	Royal Army Ordnance Corps
RASC	Royal Army Service Corps
RE	Royal Engineers
REME	Royal Electrical and Mechanical Engineers
RF	Royal Fusiliers
RQMS	Regimental Quartermaster Sergeant
RSM	Regimental Sergeant Major
RTU	returned to unit
RV	rendezvous (point)
SAF	Sultan's Armed Forces
SEP	surrendered enemy personnel
SLR	self-loading rifle
SMG	sub-machine gun
SQMS	Squadron Quartermaster Sergeant
SSM	Squadron Sergeant Major
TA	Territorial Army
WO2	Warrant Officer 2nd Class
WP	white phosphorus

PROLOGUE:
ASSAULT ON HELL MOUNTAIN

GEORDIE DORAN is widely regarded as one of the truly memorable founding veterans of the modern-day postwar Special Air Service (SAS), writes Mike Morgan, author of Special Forces books *Daggers Drawn: Real Heroes of the SAS and SBS* and *Sting of The Scorpion: The Inside Story of the Long Range Desert Group* (The History Press).

Few front-line soldiers of the Paras and SAS have survived as many danger-packed campaigns throughout worldwide history as this quietly spoken but teak-tough veteran, who went on to transmit his hard-won skills and train new generations of Special Forces soldiers, the latest successors of which have performed with ultra-professional heroism in Afghanistan and Iraq. But, as he recalls his long and distinguished SAS career through the vivid actions described in this book, he admits that one of these campaigns in far-flung lands – the crucial battle to capture the Jebel el Akhdar, a towering mountainous plateau in Oman – could easily have spelled the bloody demise of the SAS Regiment not long after it had recovered from disbandment following its tremendous initial successes in the Second World War. The famed Malayan campaign against Communist insurgents in the late 1950s had recently been successfully waged, but there were many doubters in High Command who found it hard to believe that the SAS could operate – and win – in different environments around the world, and they were within an ace of ordering a second, final disbandment of the SAS if the ambitious attack in Oman failed. Now a vastly outnumbered SAS force was ordered to defeat a rebel enemy *six times* its size, well dug in at least 5,000 feet higher up the treacherous slopes of what the locals called the Green Mountain, owing to the vegetation that sprang miraculously from its dizzy heights in the midst of mile upon mile of barren, waterless wastes. It was obvious that the odds were stacked high against the SAS on this momentous occasion – but, as past heroics had proved, that was exactly the way the SAS liked it . . .

The hand-picked but vastly outnumbered SAS veterans of A and D Squadrons went about their warlike business with cool, confident efficiency as they prepared for their historic assault on the rebel fortress, almost impregnably sited on top of the towering Jebel mountain which loomed from the desert wastes in front of them like a dark, forbidding colossus.

The assembled British forces consisted of well-armed and superbly trained SAS ground forces, backed by helicopters and the pinpoint air supply and strike airpower of the RAF. Britain, having signed a treaty with the Sultan of Muscat and Oman in the 1950s, had to come to the Sultan's aid when his interests were aggressively challenged by Sulaiman ibn Himyar, chief of the Bani Riyam, his nominee the Imam Ghalib ibn Ali and the latter's brother, the powerful Talib. The ambitious and cunning Talib raised a powerful army of expatriate Omanis in Saudi Arabia and brought them to the Jebel, declaring himself master of central Oman and openly independent of the Sultan. The ancient fortress seemed impregnable to attack, and Talib was able to impose a stranglehold on the vital communications between the interior of the country and the coast. Action had to be taken to defeat him, but the Sultan did not have sufficient military might to solve the situation himself, and so he asked the British Government for urgent help. This was not a job for conventional forces and so, in turn, the British Government turned to the SAS Special Forces to do the job, using their experience, adaptability and skills.

The SAS commanders on the ground were, fortunately, able and experienced. They were led by their Commanding Officer (CO), the highly respected Lieutenant-Colonel Anthony Deane-Drummond, a former Para Red Devil of Arnhem fame – a soldier who, rather than surrender to the Germans in that heroic and highly costly debacle in 1944, had hidden in a cupboard in an enemy-occupied house on the battlefield for 11 days to enable his eventual escape. Earlier in the war he had taken part in the first British parachute raid, at the Tragino aqueduct in Italy; although captured by the Italians he made a daring escape to Switzerland.

The SAS plan to defeat the Omani rebels was sound, but it carried a considerable portion of risk. The SAS attackers, each carrying around 100 pounds in weapons and equipment, would have to scramble up the treacherous slopes to the plateau above cloaked only by the protection afforded by the hours of darkness – without being seen or heard – and, once on the plateau, have to rout a powerful, well-hidden and fanatical foe. However, the window of opportunity to achieve success was dangerously small, and the thought of the SAS men being caught helpless in the dawn light and decimated piecemeal on the exposed mountainous slopes below by the rebels' heavy machine guns, snipers and mortar fire was an unthinkable option.

Geordie, then a Lance Corporal in charge of two mortar teams, says of this mission, one of the most memorable earlier SAS actions which he describes in detail later in this book:

I arrived with around sixty to seventy of D Squadron SAS in November 1958. There were estimated to be at least 600 rebels dedicated to overthrowing the Sultan on the heights above. We were vastly outnumbered.

So we contained them, carried out reconnaissance and waited for reinforcements. A squadron arrived direct from Malaya in January 1959, which brought our strength to around 120–140 SAS. But there were still more than 600 heavily armed rebels in strength above us with many heavy machine guns, rifles and 82mm mortars. A few of them even had the old pre-First World War Martini-Henry rifles left over from earlier British colonial campaigns!

Many of the rebels lived full time on the Jebel, up to around 8,000 feet, but their main forces were on the plateau below at around 5,000 feet, well dug in and hidden in caves. It was an imposing natural fortress, last conquered by the Persians in 1256.

There were no qualms about it. We believed it could be taken, and we were all confident. We knew they were confined to that area, and we had to assault it to get them out. We had an ace up our sleeve, in that a diversionary attack was going to be mounted by some of our SAS boys just as we went in.

We were relying on detailed preparation, fitness, surprise and a cunning deception plan. News was leaked to our donkey handlers, who we knew could not be trusted with information and would almost certainly feed it to the rebels, that the main assault was going to be in a different place from the one we had planned. That seemed to work a treat, and the rebels moved a lot of men to where they thought the attack was going to come in.

The final assault was at 8 p.m. It was pitch-black, but the moon came out, which helped us. We all carried our own gear, weapons and ammunition, but each soldier also carried spare rocket projectiles for a bazooka-type rocket launcher, which was among our heavier weapons.

Around 110 men, including myself, took part in the main assault, with around 30–40 men from A Squadron SAS carrying out a diversionary attack in the Aquabat area of the mountain. They just went in hard and created as much noise and mayhem as they could.

When we got started on the main push it was very difficult climbing, on broken ground and with much scrambling over rocks in the dark. We had to balance the need for stealth and quietness with the pressing need to make solid progress to reach our objective at the plateau above before first light. If we didn't, we were dead. It was as simple as that. It was very cold and got colder the higher up we climbed, and the air was thinner. Some men found it hard to breathe with all the exertion and the 100lb packs, and one or two actually flaked out under their heavy bergen packs as they climbed. We had all trained hard to acclimatise by constantly moving up and down the steep terrain for several weeks, and most of us completed the climb without a problem, but it was tough.

We got to the top at about 4 a.m., just in time before daylight was due to flood the area, giving away our audacious advance. When we got to the top many of the enemy positions were unmanned, with the rebels preoccupied by our diversionary attack on the other side of the mountain. All the positions had to be thoroughly checked. Some of the rebels were found asleep near their weapons and had to be killed where they lay.

The men made good use of their reliable SLR rifles and and 7.62mm Brens, and my section was following up with the mortars, which could engage the rebels at long range, saving quite a few casualties among our SAS forces. Although we had .303 Lee Enfield sniper rifles, the SLR in particular did not have a long range and was pretty useless if the opposition was holed up in rocks at a distance – you just couldn't reach them.

But the masterplan worked out by our commanders worked like a dream, and we only had two casualties in A Squadron – caused by a stray bullet hitting a hand grenade one of the troopers was carrying in his bergen pocket. This exploded, badly wounding that man and the one nearest him. Both wounded soldiers were flown out by helicopter but, sadly, died later.

Many people did say before this assault that we had a massive disadvantage in the height that had to be climbed, combined with our vastly inferior numbers of troops. Many said that it could not be done, and, in all honesty, if the troops employed had not been SAS and had not been so fit and well trained and disciplined, it probably would not have been possible at all in the limited time span available. It had no right to be anything like a certainty, given all the factors apparently overwhelmingly against. But everything was meticulously planned, our knowledge of the ground was comprehensive and nothing was left to chance.

Our one big advantage was that the rebels did not know exactly where we were going to climb up and attack them. We kept them guessing, and it worked like a charm. However, it could so easily have gone horribly wrong, and if we had been caught cold in the daylight, it would have been a suicidal bloodbath.

In the event, as soon as we reached the rebel stronghold we found that the majority had been lured away by our diversionary attack, so we took up defensive positions, waiting for a counter-attack that never came. The rebels were routed, ran away and were completely dispersed, and we solved the problem for the Sultan, who was extremely grateful. We went round the villages in the area for about a week looking for any sign of the enemy, but they had just vanished. The rebellion was beaten and over, and the area secured for the Sultan.

It was a tremendous victory for the SAS Regiment, which had successfully operated in the jungles of Malaya, but this was a totally different desert environment. It proved beyond doubt the adaptability of the SAS. It saved the regiment's bacon, because the powers that be were at that time seriously thinking of disbanding it again, as they had in 1945 at the end of the Second World War. But this spectacular success literally ensured the survival of the SAS Regiment as it is today.

But then, survival was second nature to Geordie Doran. He was born a survivor on the tough streets of Tyneside and later survived, more or less intact, through some of the most famous – and notorious – Para and SAS campaigns that Britain waged through the 1950s, 60s and 70s, eventually playing a key role in training hundreds of SAS recruits right through to the early 1970s, recruits whom he honed to perfection, and who in turn trained many of the best-known SAS characters of today.

The reader will soon discover for him- or herself the unique capabilities of this extraordinarily self-reliant soldier.

But it is now appropriate for Geordie to take over the narrative himself to describe in pin-sharp detail the early influences that forged and shaped his character, and how his tough upbringing helped him become one of the most indomitable and respected – and talked about – veterans ever to serve in the elite ranks of the SAS.

Chapter 1

A Tough 'Jarra' Lad: Forged from Hardship

I believe it's a fact that no one seems to know exactly where the term 'Geordie' has come from. But over the centuries it has become widely accepted that it refers to a person born on Tyneside – not just the city of Newcastle, but in any of the towns that lie along the banks of the River Tyne. This Geordie, as I became known in the SAS Regiment and later far and wide, was born in Jarrow, pronounced 'Jarra', in 1929, the year of the infamous Wall Street 'stock market crash'. I was later confirmed in the Catholic faith in the full name of Francis William Joseph Doran, but have always been known to my family as Franky. However, the instant I joined the Army my comrades dubbed me Geordie – and the name has stuck to this day and is the one by which I will be referred to throughout this book.

The north-east of England, where I was born on 23 February of that fateful year of 1929, was to be devastated by worldwide economic depression. It bred poverty, crushing unemployment, desperation – and some of the toughest breed of survivors and fighters known to man.

I first saw the light of day, or rather the dim light of my parents' bedroom, in their upstairs flat in Hope Street, Jarrow-upon-Tyne. Catherine Cookson, the late famous novelist, lived about 2 miles away at the time, and I have to admit that I later became an untypical, but avid, fan of her dramatic, romantic works.

The fifth of eight children, I had two brothers and five sisters, of whom only two sisters now survive.

Hope Street, like most other streets in Jarrow, was terraced. There were no front gardens – just a backyard, usually shared with another family, in which the toilet and water tap were situated. Pa, who was also called Francis, used to hang our tin bath on the wall out there as well. We didn't have a bathroom; the accommodation was so small and cramped – two rooms –

there was just no space for such luxuries. It was so crowded at times that whenever someone wanted to leave to visit the outside toilet, or 'netty' as we called it, everyone else had to stand up to let them out!

I was born a second-generation Englishman. In the 1880s my paternal grandfather travelled over from Ireland to find work in the Tyneside shipyards. Both he and his wife, whose maiden name was Quinn, came from Mayo Bridge, a small village in County Down on the slopes of the Mourne Mountains.

My mother, Dorothy, whose maiden name was Blythe, had Scottish ancestors. Her dad died before I was born, as did both my dad's parents, so I knew only my maternal grandmother, also called Dorothy. I was 8 years old when my grandma died, and I missed her very badly. She was a lovely woman and had a large family, so I had lots of uncles, aunts and cousins.

Sunday afternoon was visiting time when Mother would take us little ones to see an aunt or two, but we would always end up at Grandma's at tea-time. Grandma would always have a big, roaring fire going, with a huge, black cast-iron kettle on it to boil water for the tea. She would give us all a king-sized mug of char with some of her beautiful home-made scones to go with it.

My earliest memories are of dimly lit rooms in the house where we lived and of figures huddled around the fire. My parents often had to use candles for light when they couldn't afford a penny for the gas.

The Wall Street stock market crash in New York caused an unprecedented worldwide depression of cataclysmic proportions. In Britain it generated a vicious slump which hit the north-east particularly badly, especially Jarrow, where there was only one main industry: building and repairing ships. Few ships could be built or repaired any more, because there wasn't the cash or credit available to pay for them. What work there was went to the bigger yards further up the river, or to other parts of the country. Most of the men in Jarrow were consequently thrown out of work. My dad was a shipyard riveter, so he was also forced onto the dole queue and had to find casual work doing anything whenever and wherever he could. It was an increasingly hard existence, but my family was very close-knit and stuck together and made the best of it.

When I was about 3 years old the family moved to Stanley Street, a carbon copy of the salubrious surroundings of Hope Street.

One of my more dangerous games involved a fresh fish shop across the road. I used to love to run over, touch one of the fish, which were laid out in an open window, and then run back again as a dare. Crossing the street then wasn't the hazard it is now: there was just the odd horse and cart or coal lorry. But I nearly copped it one day, though, when I ran out in front of the coal lorry and the driver managed to stop just inches from me!

Just before I was 5 years old we moved to Caledonian Road, which was near the centre of town. We occupied no. 33 at first, next door to Dad's sister Annie in no. 31. Later on we moved into no. 31 after Aunt Annie and her family went south to Luton. Caledonian Road was exactly the same as the other streets, except the houses were mainly single-storey. There was a pub at one end of the street – The Cottage Inn – and Meggie Colwell's little sweet shop at the other end.

We were desperately poor at this time, but even though we were dressed mainly in hand-me-downs and old shoes we never went seriously hungry. I remember having porridge nearly every morning. On Wednesdays we would have shepherd's pie. Mother was a dab hand at making broth with just spare ribs. She used to make it in a massive black pot. You could smell it cooking half a mile away – everybody around knew when the Dorans were having broth for dinner! We used to get fat dripping from the butcher's in a jam jar to spread on bread like butter, and it was delicious. Saturday was 'pease pudding' day. Mother used to send me to the pork butcher's for a jug of pease pudding, which was always hot and liquid. The jug used to be so heavy that I had to carry it with both hands. I would quite often stop and have a sip – it was lovely. Our family always had a decent Sunday dinner of roast beef and Yorkshire pudding, with spuds and cabbage, followed by semolina or sago pudding. A big bag of broken biscuits (cost, one old penny) was a special treat. I don't think I had a whole biscuit until 1953, when sweets were de-rationed eight years after the Second World War ended.

Every day at school all the children whose dads were on the dole or on very low income were entitled to free milk and a dinner. We had milk at school but had to go to the public baths for our dinner. They put boards over the pool, and the place became a dining hall. It was only used for swimming in the holidays.

Once a week the Salvation Army, which had a hall in the next street, would give out free loaves of bread to the needy. To qualify for that handout locals had to go into the hall, listen to some preaching and join in the hymn-singing. The hall didn't have a lot of room inside, and so it paid to get in the queue early. There was always a crowd of ragged kids attending these sessions, usually including myself and one or two of my sisters. The Salvation

Army staff, to their great credit, never asked any questions about which religion anyone belonged to. They simply handed out the bread regardless. As soon as the Dorans got their loaves we would run home and give them to our mother, who didn't ask any questions either!

This tough regime of hardship and daily survival on the streets, living by our wits and luck, continued more or less unabated until the outbreak of the Second World War. I grew leaner, fitter, stronger and ever more streetwise, but never lost sight of the strong family values which became my permanent anchor throughout my adventurous life.

Money may have been extremely short at this time, but there were some things in Jarrow that the locals had more than enough of – and that included vermin of all kinds. Rats, mice, beetles and cockroaches were liberally distributed throughout the town – and some families specialised in extras, such as fleas and bed bugs! Most of the houses suffered from damp, as there were no damp-proof courses or cavity walls then. I recall that beetles and cockroaches thrived in such conditions, and the first one out of bed in the morning would hear their tiny feet scurrying away to hide. Mousetraps were essential pieces of equipment in every household. What made matters worse sometimes was that a lot of people used to stick wallpaper on with a mixture of flour and water. That was fine until the damp caused the wallpaper to peel and, usually through the night, drop off. Mice would then home in on it for a snack. The rats were not quite so numerous, but they were exceedingly bold. One day I was walking down our street when I spied a big rat squatting on its hind legs in the gutter. It was chewing on a lump of something which it held with its front paws. As I drew level it stopped chewing and looked right up at me. It seemed to be saying, 'Who the hell are you, and what do you think you're doing walking down my street?' Even the rats were tougher than anyone else's.

When I was 5 years old my mother asked me if I would like to stay at home or go to school. As I had a lively, enquiring mind, I readily chose school and started at St Bede's Roman Catholic Infants' School in Monkton Road, Jarrow. I can't recall much about my time at that school. The priest would take confession and then give absolution and a penance – usually a few prayers which had to be said later. I can't remember on that initial occasion having any sins to confess. I was only a nipper, when all was said and done. If I went back today it would be a very different story: the priest would need a secretary to write it all down and I would be excommunicated on the spot!

Our family was strict Roman Catholic. Besides going to Mass on Sundays and so on we had to say our prayers every night before going to bed. All of us children would kneel down and say our prayers together. Pa would usually be listening to make sure we said them correctly and didn't miss anything out.

Religious fervour and young boys don't mix very well, however; I was much more interested in going out to play with the other lads in our street. We were too busy climbing, fighting and playing games to worry about saving our little souls. No one could afford a football, so we played with old tin cans, each boy guarding his own back door and at the same time trying to score in another. Tin cans are dangerous missiles, and I've got a scar on my chin to this day to prove it.

Paper aeroplanes were another popular pastime. The type of paper used in the manufacture of an aeroplane is crucial to the quality and performance of the finished product. Pages from mail-order catalogues were the best: they were glossy, strong and stiff enough to hold their shape for long periods of active flying.

Another popular use to which catalogue pages were put in those days was as toilet paper. Hard and glossy they may have been, but they were free. Newspapers and proper toilet paper cost money. A good, big catalogue could last a family for a month or so, especially when economy was practised, whereby each page was torn into at least four pieces to make it go further.

I still remember the names of some of my back-lane playmates. There was Ginger Ambrose; Freddy McLellan; Reggie Jarvis, whose dad was killed in the Merchant Navy during the war; Philip McGee, whose cousin, with the same name as myself, Francis Doran, was killed at Dunkirk; 'Tich' Clinton; Tommy and Billy Henderson; and Franky Dixon and his brother Donald, who, until May 1997, was the Labour MP for Jarrow. All good lads and good friends. We all knew much poverty, hardship and grief in those days: poverty and hardship, because of the economic plight of Jarrow in the 1930s; grief, because so many of our pals, relations and family members suffered and died in the war or from illnesses and diseases, most of which are easily prevented or cured now.

Donald Dixon would probably be surprised to discover that, considering my background, I now vote Tory. I have gradually become disillusioned with the Labour Party, which most of my compatriots supported ardently.

As we grew older our back-lane gang ventured further afield. We would often play down by the Tyne ferry landing and downriver at Jarrow Slake, an old anchorage area mainly silted up by then but still with enough water in it to be attractive to children. Also there was always an area somewhere in town where old houses were being demolished and the occupants housed elsewhere by the local council – in the 1930s that was the start of council house estates. Those places, plus the old pit workings where there was a deep pond, were very dangerous to play around in and were often patrolled by the police. If the cops, or 'slops' as we used to call them, managed to catch us, we would get a kick up the arse or a good clip around the ear. Some of the cops used to put pebbles in the fingers of their gloves to make them heavier, and when you had a clout you really knew about it. It was no good going home to complain, because the chances were you would get another clout from Pa for getting into trouble. That made sense, because several children were drowned or injured in those workings. But kids will be kids, and we went and played there anyway.

Another area was the slag heap just outside town: a very large, flat-topped mound of leftover moulding material from the local metal foundry. It had been built up over the years until it covered an area of about 3 acres and was 60 or 70 feet high, perfect for playing cowboys and indians on! But our gang had to take great care if we trespassed on the territory of a local rival gang. Our street and the next one, Charles Street, had a long-standing feud with Ferry Street and Queen's Road, and we had many pitched battles with sticks, stones and fists. In one memorable clash we used clothes props as lances. But even though the street gangs were all rough and ready and fought hard, they had a certain code of honour. We didn't pick on girls or smaller children, and if there was a stone-throwing battle going on between gangs and some girls or little kids wanted to pass by, then both sides would hold their fire. If anyone failed to observe the temporary ceasefire, there would be a yell from one of the gang leaders: 'Hey, stop hoying them bluddy bricks, there's lasses and bairns trying ti get past, man!' Also, if the police arrived on the scene and participants had to make a run for it, any member of any gang was always given fugitive status while hiding in an 'enemy' street from the common foe. I didn't realise it at the time, but it was perfect preparation for the real war situations I was to be involved in many times during later years when my life, and that of many other comrades, was regularly to be placed on the line in hair-raising, real-life action. Meanwhile, as a growing, energetic youngster, this was fun and part of the early glimmerings of manhood. Gang warfare tactics and armament varied. I remember just before the war when *Robin Hood*, the film starring Errol Flynn, came to a cinema in Jarrow. All the kids went to see it, and within days we were all armed with home-made wooden swords and bows and arrows. Caledonian Road met Queen's Road in mortal combat on an old building site. We fired arrows in the air and clashed swords. No one thought about throwing stones: it was all Robin Hood and the Sheriff of Nottingham doing battle. There were some casualties on both sides and a quantity of blood flowed, but nothing serious. I can't remember which side won, but it was very exciting while it lasted! The Law arrived eventually and chased us all away.

I left the infants' school aged 7 and attended St Bede's Junior. By now I hated school and often played truant. On those days I would go for long walks, sometimes with a companion or two, but mostly on my own. My fellow truants and I would think nothing of walking 10 to 20 miles in a day. A favourite route would be to cross over on the Tyne ferry and walk on to the coast at Whitley Bay. We then had to pass through Cullercoats Bay en route where, if we had any money, we would buy a bag of winkles to eat. Whitley Bay was a popular seaside resort, with pebble and sand beaches and a funfair, but it has now seen better days. Of course as truants we never had any money for the funfair, but we always enjoyed ourselves on the beach. Another favourite walk would be south to Usworth aerodrome, 7 miles each way. We went there to watch the aircraft taking off and landing. It was pretty awesome. When the war started Usworth became an RAF training base. Also, after a couple of years the Americans came in on our side and established an anti-aircraft position there. It was great talking to the Yanks and cadging chewing gum from them. We sneaked into their kitchen one day and pinched some slices of ham. I had never tasted anything so delicious in my life before! We were always ravenously hungry on truant days, because we couldn't go home until tea-time. I would be so hungry, I remember eating orange peel and bits of mouldy bread that I'd picked up from the ground – kissing it all up to God first, of course. I sometimes ate caramel toffee wrappers from the gutter, as I could taste the caramel on the paper. I even ate worms and slugs when there wasn't anything else! To quench our thirst we would drink straight from streams or horse troughs.

I don't know about now, but in the 1930s and up to the mid-50s, a lot of Tyneside housewives used to bake large, disc-shaped loaves of bread which were about 12 inches across by 2 inches thick and known locally as 'stottie cakes'. (The name 'stottie' came about because if the bread went hard and was dropped on the ground it 'stotted' or bounced.) If it was a fine day when the stotties were first brought out of the oven, they would be put on an outside windowsill to cool. A backyard sill was favoured, away from roving dogs and hungry children; but now and then a few stotties could be seen on a front window. Several times I or my truant pals would snatch a stottie to satisfy our hunger. It was lovely bread, the like of which you don't often get these days.

We learned a lot about hunger, thirst and fatigue on our truant trips. Years later, when I was in the Army, I suffered those three things many times. I think my days as a youngster doing our walks toughened me up and helped me to withstand it all. Also, playing in the muck and eating things off the ground probably gave us a certain amount of natural immunisation against some diseases. I'm sure it did.

Quite a lot of my school and back-lane friends did die from various illnesses, though. Tuberculosis, pneumonia, diphtheria and meningitis, to name but a few, were usually killers if contracted. Many children and young adults were crippled with poliomyelitis too. Rickets was mostly wiped out among the poor by the free issue from health clinics of malt and cod liver oil mixed in a bottle. Mother used to give us a big spoonful every day. Dried-milk food was also provided for children under 5 years. What with those health supplements, plus free dinners and milk at school, we were kept quite fit and well, although most of us were still fairly stunted in growth when compared with the children of today.

Family outings were a treat to look forward to. We had lots of trips to the seaside. The nearest sandy beach was at South Shields, a town at the mouth of the Tyne. From where we lived it was 4 miles to the beach, and the whole family, usually without Dad, because he'd be either busy in his allotment or working part-time somewhere, would set off walking early in the day to get a good spot on the beach. We had to walk, as the bus cost too much. Mother would be pushing a pram with my two younger sisters in it, plus a load of sandwiches, a teapot, brew kit and old jam jars to be used as cups. Just before reaching Tyne Dock, a town halfway to Shields, our party would trudge past the bottom end of Catherine Cookson's street. (That street is long gone now; an industrial estate now occupies the site.) Once established on the beach Mother would organise the tea and sandwiches. Boiling water for tea could be had at several stalls at a penny a pot. After that it was ice cream cornets and maybe a ride on the fair as a special treat. The outbreak of the Second World

War put an end to our family's seaside jaunts, however. All beaches that the Germans could have used for an invasion were closed off and guarded, and most were mined as well. They were not open for public use again for almost six years.

Our family lived at 31 Caledonian Road until 1955. At first we had four rooms: two bedrooms, a living-room and a kitchen. The kitchen and the room above it had been built onto the original dwelling, and when my two eldest sisters went away to work in Luton the house seemed almost spacious. I used to sleep in the bedroom above the kitchen with my older brother, Matty. It wasn't long, though, before that part of the house had to be demolished, as it was poorly built and unsafe. I had my second early brush with death at that time, when I ran out of the back door just as one wall of the extension was being felled. It missed me by inches. In place of the extension the landlord built us a scullery with an inside water tap, a sink and a gas cooker. We felt quite posh with our inside tap, because most of the other houses in the street still had outside taps. When their outside supply froze in the winter they would come to us for water. As with every other house, though, we still had an outside toilet. The flushing systems were very noisy, and outside, on a still morning or night, all you could hear was the sound of chains being pulled as people paid their first or last visits of the day.

After the extension was demolished we only had one bedroom for seven people. My parents slept in a double bed. I, together with my three sisters, slept in another double bed in the living-room cum dining-room. We slept feet to feet, me at one end and those three at the other. I can't remember where my brother Matty slept – probably on a couch in our room or the bedroom. Before going to bed, especially in the winter, we would be desperately, miserably cold. All the family would huddle around the fire, and to cheer ourselves up we sang songs, told stories or looked in the fire to see who could make out the shape of a face or something in the burning coal embers. Actually, I think I'd much rather do that now than watch some of the rubbish they put on TV these days! Our first radio, a ten-valve accumulator battery set, was still many years ahead.

First one up every morning was Mother. She would rekindle the coal fire, which had been banked up with coal dust the night before, and put a big black kettle on it for tea. Next she would start the porridge off, so that it would be ready for breakfast before we went to school. It used to take ages to make porridge then. If Dad had a job to go to, he would be up early with Mother.

Lastly we young ones rose to get ready for school. Getting ready didn't take long: just plimsolls, short trousers and a shirt or jersey for me. If it was winter, I might have a pair of boots. Very often I had no socks, and I didn't have any underwear until I was issued with it in the Army in 1952, six years after joining up. My sisters always wore frocks, blouses and sandals, or, if they were lucky, proper shoes. Very rarely did we have warm coats to wear, unless they were hand-me-downs or even hand-me-ups, either too big or too small. My ambition, one day, was to own a pilot's leather hat, which some of my mates had, and a pair of wellies. I never did get a pilot's hat, and I didn't get any wellies until 1967, when my wife bought me a pair for Christmas.

In 1936, when I was 7 years old, my brother Matty died. He died at home from meningitis, aged 19. My parents, big sister Rose and a priest were all round the bed praying. When he died they laid him in his coffin in the bedroom, and we all went to see him. It was the first dead body I'd seen. After the funeral Dad came home and found me lying on the couch crying. 'Never mind, Franky,' he consoled me. 'If you don't cry, Matty will come walking back through the door one day.' I was young enough to believe him, and that helped me to get over my grief. But I'll never forget my big brother. My mother had a baby son, Cuthbert, a few months after Matty died. She was so pleased, I remember her asking me to run up and down the street telling all her friends. I had a bad dream some months later: I dreamt that Cuthbert was lying in one of the big drawers of our sideboard, and he was dead. Tragically my bad dream came true not long after that. Cuthbert died, aged 6 months, from pneumonia. The family was devastated – two brothers gone in less than a year. I cried and cried. Very often now I think about what my brothers would have been like if they had lived.

It was about this time, in the mid- to late 1930s, when the economic depression really started to bite. The town was full of unemployed men just standing around in groups on corners. The dole was next to nothing, and there was a 'means test', which meant that some families who possessed items considered surplus to requirement had to sell them or else take a cut in their dole money. We Dorans got a lot of tramps and street buskers around in those days. The buskers used to walk slowly along the streets singing or playing a musical instrument – it was illegal to stand still and busk then. My mother would often take a tramp or busker into the house and give them a cup of tea and a bite to eat. She was a kindly soul and couldn't bear the sight of those men and women out of work and trudging along the street in the rain singing for coppers. Our family didn't have much to spare food-wise, but they would at least get a cup of tea, a slice of jam and bread and a warm by the fire. I can still picture my mother as she sat talking to those unfortunate people, her kindly eyes twinkling and her hands, all red and shiny from work, lying in her lap.

On one day during that period there was a riot in the middle of town. I was near the scene when the riot started, at the top of our street. What the cause was I don't know, but it involved a large group of unemployed men and the police. All of a sudden there were lots of men and police milling around, shouting and yelling. Stones and bin lids started to fly through the air. Shop windows were broken and police helmets knocked off. Some men were arrested, others fled. A while later the action died down, but there was a heavy police presence in town for a few days afterwards. In order to try to stir things up a bit the Labour MP for Jarrow, Ellen Wilkinson, together with some of the town councillors, organised a marching crusade to London. The object was to lobby Parliament and present a petition from the people of Jarrow asking for jobs to be created in the area. I watched nearly 200 men set off from Jarrow on 5 October 1936, and they marched all the way to London. Dad didn't go: he couldn't afford to leave us. I stood with the cheering crowd at the side of the road watching them set off. It was a peaceful march, no trouble. A good proportion of the men had been in the forces in the First World War, so the discipline was there. It was tramp, tramp, tramp, but all to no avail. They walked into history as the famous 'Jarrow Marchers'.

In that same year our monarch, King George V, died. The Prince of Wales, whose story is well told elsewhere, decided to abdicate instead of becoming the next king, Edward VIII. Instead, his brother, the Duke of York, was crowned King George VI in 1937. We had a big party in our back lane on Coronation Day. There was loads to eat, and the back-lane walls were painted red, white and blue. Individual commemorative photographs of every pupil were taken at school. The next year the King and Queen came to visit Jarrow. We had the day off school so we could line the route and cheer as they went past. I don't think their majesties would have been favourably impressed if they'd known that one of their subjects was a persistent truant! Sometimes I would sneak out of the school gate at playtime or, as was most often the case, I wouldn't go in at all. One day I didn't even leave home to go to school: I hid on the top shelf of our pantry. As I crouched up there Mother opened the pantry door to get something but didn't see me. After she closed the door again there was a long wait, and I was beginning to wonder how long I could stick it out. Eventually my sister Dorothy opened the door, reached up to the top shelf and saw me. Her mouth dropped open with surprise, but at first she couldn't make a sound; then she let out a yell, and Mother came running to see what was wrong. So it went on – a couple of days at school, then a day's truancy. One snag with truanting, of course, was that I couldn't go for a school dinner: there was always a teacher in attendance, and I would have been captured.

By this time, however, I had begun to develop what would become a life-long love of reading. Being a member of the public library I was able to indulge this love by drawing out a book to take with me while playing truant. I would spend many happy hours lying in a field on a nice warm sunny day, reading, and could forget about everything while immersed in a good book. Even hunger and thirst didn't seem to bother me so much in those times as I indulged my vivid imagination. But eventually my stomach, ever a reliable clock, reminded me when to go home for tea. As I lay reading I would drift off to sleep now and then, lulled by the sounds of cattle in the next field and the constant calls of birds, especially skylarks. There were lots of skylarks then, unlike now. I could see them rising and falling in almost any direction I looked. Truanting in the autumn wasn't very good for reading, but it was much better for feeding. There were always loads of blackberries in the hedges, and plenty of apples and pears waiting to be picked off someone's trees. I used to sneak into Pa's allotment occasionally and pull a few radishes and carrots to eat raw. During the autumn, also, I and several others would go spud-picking for cash, no questions asked.

When the war started I didn't have to play truant: they closed the school down until air raid shelters were built for us in the playground. During that time we had to go in small groups two mornings each week to a teacher's house for lessons. Of course, this suited me fine, because it gave me and my pals more time to walk and explore. We used to go and watch the soldiers guarding the beaches. They were well dug in, with trenches and coastal artillery. A German invasion was expected at any time. Also, there was the newly formed Home Guard, which we would follow around to watch them doing their exercises. This world war, ironically, would provide full employment for all after the crushing economic depression of the 1930s.

I used to go with Dad sometimes on his expeditions looking for scrap metal. One of the places we went to was behind the metal works foundry. It was there that all the waste slag, consisting mainly of sand and lumps of iron from the castings, was dumped. We would rake among this stuff seeking the lumps of metal and put them in our barrow. This took place in all weathers, hot or cold, rain or snow. We didn't possess raincoats, so we used to wear hessian sacks on our heads which were folded in such a way that they gave protection to the head and the shoulders. Sometimes the slag recently out of the foundry would still be hot, and we could warm our hands. We were never alone at that site: there would always be lots of other men and boys there too. All you could see were hunched figures, arms raking like mad and chucking metal into barrows. There was very little talk, just the frantic sound of the rakes going and the grim faces looking downwards all the time. Nearby was a railway line which carried the coal wagons to the foundry. If there wasn't much scrap metal about, my dad and I would go along the line with our barrow looking for bits of coal that had fallen from the wagons. Both activities were illegal, but the police didn't bother anyone very much. When the barrow was full it was my job to wheel it home, a distance of about 2 miles. My dad would carry on raking and get another pile ready for when I returned. It was backbreaking work for a few shillings. I remember taking a heavy load one day. I was nearly home when a bigger boy whom I didn't know came up to me, pushed me out of the way and tipped the scrap onto the road. He then gave me a few wallops for good measure. I fought back furiously, but he was too big and I couldn't get a punch in anywhere. Trying to kick him would have been difficult, because my plimsolls were too large and would have flown off. My attacker was about 15 years old and was easily 10 inches taller than myself. I never did find out who he was, nor why he had picked on me. But just then a woman came along, comforted me and helped me put the scrap back into the barrow. This was two more useful lessons in life – one about cruelty and the other about kindness, both from complete strangers. I was 8 or 9 years old at the time.

We had very few toys in those days. One Christmas I had a little red car, and about three years later I had a tiny model fort with knights on horseback. Another Christmas, at a charity party for 'poor' children, I was given a humming top. But my main playthings were small blocks of wood and flat-headed screws. I built forts with the blocks and the screws were soldiers. Steel screws were baddies and brass screws were goodies. When the war started steel was German and brass was British.

One of our most welcome visitors was the gas man, whose job it was to empty the meter each month. He was my favourite. I loved watching him counting up the pennies, then putting them into piles. When he had finished he would give Mother a certain percentage rebate, and she would immediately give each of us kids a penny. It was off down to Meggie Colwell's then for sweets. A man selling fresh fish came round once or twice a week, his cart piled high with different kinds of fish, but mainly 'collared' herring. Last but not least there was the rag and bone man. He had a little cart with old car wheels on, and it was pulled by the tiniest pony I'd ever seen. 'Rags-'n'-woollens!' he would shout. 'Balloons for knickers – fetch your ma's old bloomers out an' I'll give you a balloon. Fetch your old woollens an' get a goldfish!' went his cry. 'Give us some of your pa's old socks an' get two goldfish!' Some kids would go straight into their homes and nick things for the rag man. Many a dad came home for tea to find a couple of goldfish swimming around in a jam jar on the table and later on discover that half his socks were gone!

On 3 September 1939 the Second World War broke out. Britain's Prime Minister, Neville Chamberlain, had given Hitler a final warning over Germany's threats to invade Poland. Hitler flouted Chamberlain's last-minute ultimatum, and so Britain was involved in a world war against Germany for the second time in just over two decades. I was 10½ years old. On the day war started, a Sunday, I was outside playing in the back lane. At about half past eleven that morning I heard someone shouting out, 'War declared!' They had just heard it on the radio. It was very exciting for young lads like us, as we all wanted to join the Army and fight the Germans. But I was still too young when the war finished six years later. There was one way in which we could help the war effort, though. The town council had organised a scrap metal centre, and we went round houses with barrows collecting bits and pieces. The council also had every metal railing in town cut down and sent them off too.

It wasn't long before food rationing was introduced. Many items were on ration, like meat, eggs, butter and sugar. Some things that had to be imported, such as bananas and oranges, we didn't see again until after the war. Sweets and chocolate became almost non-existent. Each family was issued with ration books, and we had to be registered at different shops for particular items – the butcher's, baker's, grocer's and so on. Whenever a person bought a rationed item a coupon would be marked or torn out of their book. The weekly rations were quite meagre, but that didn't affect us at first because, being poor, we couldn't afford much anyway. It wasn't until later, when a lot of our supply ships from the USA were sunk by German submarines, that we began to feel the pinch. The rations shrank, and so did we. People's clothes started to appear ominously slack on them. A thriving black market soon developed. A lot of shopkeepers and suppliers kept extras of some items 'under the counter' for their friends or other special customers. If everyone had been getting their basic entitlement, it would have been OK, but the rations were so tight that someone's extras usually meant that some poor bugger further down the line had to go without. Queues became the norm for everything. The only place without a queue was the pawn shop, as no one had anything left worth pawning. My mother spent half the day in queues, sometimes to no avail because the shop would have run out of stock before she was served. It paid to have several members of the family in different queues. That way we could be reasonably sure of getting something.

Other wartime activities, some of them much more important than our ration problems, were taking place – the evacuation from Dunkirk in June 1940 and the Battle of Britain during the summer of that year, to name but two. Meanwhile the evacuation of children to relatively safe areas in the country was in full swing. I remember seeing children from our town being taken away on buses and trains. Most of them had a few belongings packed in pillowcases. I desperately wanted to be evacuated – not because I felt scared, but just because I wanted to live in the countryside. I had my pillowcase packed ready for ages. Inside were crammed a toy car, some wooden blocks and a coat, these being my total possessions. However, my parents wouldn't let any of their children go. Most evacuees returned home within months anyway – they were homesick.

The warning siren sounded for Jarrow's first air raid not long after the war started. It was a false alarm. The German Air Force came over, but it was about 100 miles from us. After that, to prevent too much disruption of work, the siren was sounded only when the enemy bombers were definitely heading our way. We had air raid wardens whose job during a raid was to assist people in taking cover. They wore steel helmets and armbands with ARP on them. They blew warning whistles and shouted, 'Take cover, air raid!' The ARP also carried big wooden rattles, of the ratchet type used at soccer matches, to warn of a gas attack. We had all been issued with gas masks and were supposed to carry them with us at all times. Our first real air raid took place about nine months after the war started. I was playing in the back lane when the siren went but carried on playing, thinking that nothing was going to happen. Then there was the sound of a heavy aircraft flying quite low. Anti-aircraft guns opened up next. All this had happened so quickly that I was rooted to the spot with surprise. I looked up and saw a huge aircraft straight above me; three or four black objects fell from underneath it as I watched. Bombs! I made what seemed at the time a slow-motion leap through our back doorway and into the air raid shelter. The bombs exploded a few seconds later. The rest of the family were already in the shelter, and we stayed in there, emerging only after the all-clear sounded. We went out into the lane and looked towards where the bombs had fallen. There were huge clouds of smoke rising from about three or four streets away. Later on I went to the top of our street and saw lots of people coming from that direction. These were the people whose homes had been hit, and they were being moved to temporary accommodation. They were carrying a few belongings and blankets with them. Most of them were covered in dust and looked completely stunned. The children were crying and clinging to their parents. It was a pathetic sight. I can't remember how many had been killed in the raid, but it was quite a lot, and there were many injured. The Queen Street area just near the gas works – which was probably the intended target – had been hit. That was just half a mile from our street. Over the next couple of years it got much worse. We didn't get it as bad as London and some other places, of course, but it was bad enough. The Germans were obviously having a go at the shipyards and heavy industry which stretched out down both sides of the Tyne – a nice big fat target, and we were right in the middle of it.

The air raids happened mostly at night, psychologically the worst time because of disturbed sleep, and they seemed more terrifying in the darkness. The air raid shelters, which had been built by the council, had thick walls with 6 inches of concrete on the roof; they were always cold inside, even in summer. During a raid the family would be huddled together, not only in fright but also for warmth. After the wailing of the siren the throbbing drone of approaching aeroplanes was the first sound we would hear. Next the anti-aircraft batteries would start hammering away – bang, bang, bang. Then there would be the worst sound of all: the horrible whistling scream of falling bombs. Some of them seemed as if they were going to land right on top of the shelter, and Mother would cry out, 'Oh my God, this one's for us!' That would be followed by earth-shaking thumps as the bombs landed. We were lucky: Caledonian Road didn't get hit at all, or only by lumps of shrapnel from the anti-aircraft shells bursting overhead, though they were sufficient to knock holes in the roofs.

To try to relieve the food situation the Government started a 'Dig for Victory' campaign, encouraging everyone to cultivate as much land as possible to grow vegetables. A gang of lads from my street got permission to start an allotment on future building land near the town cemetery. It kept them busy for a good while trying to prepare the ground, but it was thick, hard clay and no use for the purpose. They never grew anything in it, not even a decent weed – they didn't get the chance. One morning they went there and viewed with astonishment what was left of their allotment: it was a gigantic crater about 30 feet wide, 20 feet deep and half-filled with water. The night before there had been an air raid, and we had heard a few big thumps in the distance. One of those thumps had been a bomb right on our allotment. Hitler was really starting to panic: he must have realised that once the gang got a few rows of spuds and cabbages going, his days were numbered! In desperation, therefore, he had ordered the vaporisation of our allotment. I'm grateful he didn't bomb during the day, though, otherwise we would have been vaporised as well. Anyway, the bombers missed the best target – my old man's allotment, which was in full production on the other side of the cemetery.

After the untimely demise of the local allotment, I was determined to strike back at Hitler and so joined the Sea Cadets, which I really enjoyed. They were a good bunch of lads who met twice a week in a little hut in a field down by the river. Part of the field was marked off in the shape of a ship, with white rope on small posts, a small wooden hut in the middle representing the bridge. For first and last parades we had to line up for inspection in our 'watches' forward of the bridge. I was in starboard watch. We were taught morse code, semaphore signalling and the intricacies of knots, some of which I still use today. Sailor suits were issued with HMS displayed on the hat bands. Sometimes our group would go for a march on Sunday mornings. We cadets had a small band and would march behind it into town. We once went over on the Tyne ferry and marched to the town called Wallsend, where Hadrian's Wall ended, and then came back over the river to base. That was the only time our Sea Cadet unit went on a real boat! One activity I enjoyed very much was when we practised shore raiding. Rifles were issued for this, but fortunately for us, and anyone else within range, none of them were capable of being fired, as they were all antiques. Anyway, we'd dash all over the field shouting and yelling, making shooting noises and looking extremely ferocious. Hitler would have been very concerned if he could have seen us! I left the Sea

Cadets after a year and started roaming the streets again with the gang. It was the summer of 1942, and I was 13 years old.

It wasn't long before I was in trouble with the Law. All of my gang smoked – cigarettes if we could get them, cinnamon sticks if we couldn't. We would stroll into a tobacconist's shop, buy a Woodbine fag for a halfpenny in old money and then get a free match to light it. When the shopkeeper's back was turned some of the gang would pinch anything handy. They even pinched some boxes of snuff one day, but when they tried it they couldn't stop sneezing for about two hours. Another gang dare was to go into Woolworth's and steal something from the back of the counter. It didn't matter what it was so long as it was from the back, the most difficult and dangerous place to reach. I once snatched a ball of silver wool. Inevitably one of the gang got caught; he didn't want to take the rap alone and so he split on the rest. When the gang went to court I was considered to be the ringleader, being the oldest, and was singled out for the harshest punishment: two years' probation and a £1 fine. My dad had to pay the fine, but ironically I repaid the debt many years later when I was in the Army and my dad was caught illegally raking on a tip. I coughed up the fine, as my dad was hard up at the time.

After my brush with the Law I kept out of trouble. I realised that I had been stupid and I learnt my lesson. Every weekday I had to report to the probation office at 4 p.m. Mr Porter, the probation officer, used to ask me if I'd been a good lad and then let me go. He was a very nice man, never bullied anyone or gave long lectures, nor did he look down on me. One strange coincidence about all this was that on some of our gang's pinching raids we used to nick things from allotments, such as fruit and rhubarb. One of those allotments we reached by crawling through a big conduit which went under the road from the council rubbish tip and came up into the allotment itself. One day, during my probation, I was walking past that particular allotment and I glanced in. There was Mr Porter digging away: it was *his*! Luckily no one found us out on that one.

By winter 1942/3 the war was at its height. Many of the older lads in the street had been called up into the forces. I knew only one of them well: John Flowdy, who was in the Royal Navy and was lost on a convoy to Russia.

With the war came full employment, and Pa got a job in a metal foundry making bomb cases. It was extremely hard and dirty work. When he came home from his shift he would be filthy and still covered in sweat. (Coincidentally the factory where he worked was the same one that we used to rake outside for scrap in the Depression.) What with Dad coming home knackered from work, Mother having to struggle so hard to keep us fed and clothed and seven of us living in two rooms, we had lots of family rows. My sisters and I had many battles. When I was in the wrong, which was nearly always, Mother would yell at me, 'You bad bugger, you'll grow up to hang!' I've been in the wrong many times since, but I haven't been hanged yet. My sister Rose threw a fork at me once, and it stuck in my head just above my right eye – I've still got the scar. But I loved Rosie most of all – she was good right through. She died in 1987, and if there is a heaven she'll surely be in it.

Because of night air raids a blackout had been imposed. Street lights were switched off, and all the windows had to have blackout curtains. ARP wardens patrolled at night, and if they saw the tiniest chink of light appearing from a window they would bang on it or the door and shout, 'Blackout!' During the long nights of winter, especially when there was no moon, it was a bit dicey moving around outside. There were few torches, and batteries (which didn't last long anyway) were in short supply. The town council had obstacles such as kerbs and lamp posts painted white, which helped a bit, and small luminous badges were available for people to wear. All vehicles had to have headlight screens. These obscured the lights so much that in the big towns and cities where there were a lot of vehicles many accidents occurred.

By this time Dunkirk and the Battle of Britain were history. On everyone's lips now was the victory at El Alamein by Monty's 8th Army, Allied thousand-bomber raids on Germany and the savage battles on the Russian front. But all that didn't make it any easier on the home front, where not only was food strictly rationed, but also fuel and clothing were desperately short. Rationing of clothing made no difference to us, however, because we had no spare money for extra clothes. My first pair of long trousers, which I was given in 1942, were hand-me-downs. Dad kept our footwear in reasonable repair, but leather was also scarce. We were still getting quite a lot of air raids, and my second-eldest sister, Peggy, had a narrow escape one night. She was being escorted home from work by her fiancé, Billy, when the siren went. Enemy aircraft were soon overhead, so they took cover in a nearby public air raid shelter. Shortly afterwards the street outside was hit by several large bombs. A man standing in the shelter doorway was killed by flying debris, and the shelter itself was half-buried in rubble. Peggy and Billy were badly shaken but unhurt. My eldest sister, Dorothy, who was married shortly before the war started, now lived just across the road from us. Her husband, Tommy, worked in a shipyard and was also an ARP warden; he was unfit for military service, having only one good eye. I used to hide in their house sometimes when I was on truant. They would both be at work, and my mother would have their kids at our house. I would lie on the settee for long periods listening to their radio. A lot of classical and light classical music was on the radio then, and that's how I came to like that type of music. I also liked to listen to the big bands, like Glenn Miller's.

My poor mother used to work very hard then. On top of everything else she had clothing to wash, a long and tedious job. First she had to heat the water on the kitchen fire, then put it in a big tub out in the backyard, together with the clothing. The soap used was grated bars of carbolic – very fierce stuff – and a material called 'blue' which was supposed to be good for the whites. Once everything was in the tub it had to be pummelled around with a 'poss stick' or 'dolly stick' as some called them – a weighty length of round wood with a handle on one end. The clothing had to be possed for quite a long time and then rinsed. After that, to get the maximum water out, it went through the 'mangle' or 'ringer', a set of rollers on a stand and worked with a turning handle. Very often I would do a bit of possing and turn the ringer handle for Ma while she shoved the clothes through. After that, of course, the clothes had to be hung to dry.

Towards the end of 1942 I joined the Army Cadets and stayed in them until September 1945. As with the Sea Cadets, I enjoyed every minute. We had proper battledress uniforms and rifles, although the rifles were modified to prevent them being fired, and they didn't trust us with bayonets either. We did, however, get to shoot small rifles on an indoor range. These were .22in calibre, light to handle and with no recoil. The unit had field manoeuvres every weekend, and on one night each week there was foot drill and weapon training in the town drill hall. We also went to camp for one week every summer. Camp was in the same place every year, a big Army barracks at Barnard Castle about 40 miles away. Lots of my school mates were in the cadets with me, and we really enjoyed the week away together. It was a tank training camp, and we were thrilled to see real tanks trundling around. On route marches we would sing at the top of our voices marching songs such as 'It's a long way to Tipperary'. We would also make a hell of a racket in the billet at night. Very often the soldiers nearby would complain about the noise, because they couldn't get to sleep. Later, when I was in the Army myself, I appreciated their point of view.

Once a month we held a drill hall dance, to which everyone connected with the unit was invited. Lots of women and girls would turn up for these dos, and we always had a good time. We learned quite a few dances, but our favourite was the 'Bradford barndance'. In the barndance all the couples formed a circle around the hall, and then, after dancing a series of steps, everyone changed partners. What made that dance so popular was that eventually we danced with every female on the floor and, eventually, you would find yourself holding the one you fancied, with the chance to chat her up. I took several girls home from our jigs after asking them during the barndance. For refreshments we had a tea and cake bar. How different from later years! I used to meet my mates there and we would compare notes on how we were doing with the girls. There was a side room off the main hall, and some of the girls would go in there. We called it the 'kissing room' because there was always a big queue of boys by each girl waiting to kiss her. We would emerge after a session in there looking all hot and bothered, with faces covered in lipstick.

In our Cadet Company there were three platoons, two Protestant and one Roman Catholic. I think that was wrong, because it aggravated religious differences. We should have been mixed. Left to themselves, though, the boys mixed together OK.

At Easter 1943 I left school – officially, this time. I remember, the day before going, that one of the parish priests came to talk to all the children who were leaving St Bede's. Among other words of advice the priest cautioned us to beware of 'The Devil, the World and the Flesh'. We couldn't wait to get out there and take our chances! There was one thing he told us, though, that has stuck in my mind ever since. He said, 'Always love your family and stick by your family, because the family unit is the most important thing in the world.' I think he was quite right: there isn't anything more important, or precious, than the family unit. As for my truanting, I must say right now that the teachers at my school were, all of them, OK. I just didn't like school. I couldn't stand being cooped up in a classroom all day long. I'm a free spirit; I like to roam at will. But another thing I must also say is that I was wrong in playing truant. It's not an activity I would recommend.

I was still on probation, so when I checked in to Mr Porter I told him about leaving school. 'All right, Franky,' he said. 'See me tomorrow and I might have a job for you.' I duly turned up next day, and he told me that I could start work after the Easter holiday. He had got me a job in a ship repair yard in the next town, Hebburn. The yard was called Hebburn Palmer's, as it was owned by a family called Palmer. They didn't get nationalised until 1948. It wasn't much of a job, just a labourer in a shipyard, but it was as good as I could expect with no educational qualifications and having been a naughty boy. I had hoped to get an apprenticeship to be a joiner or a carpenter. I had enjoyed woodwork classes at school, woodwork day being the only one when I made sure that I went. But jobs of that sort were relatively scarce and were more or less handed down from father to son. Never mind, labourer I was. It was honest work at least. My parents bought me second-hand overalls, boots and a cap, and I was ready for work. Dorothy's husband Tommy, who was employed in the same yard, promised to take me there on the day I was to start and show me where to report to. The working hours were 7.30 a.m. to 5 p.m., Monday to Friday, and 7.30 a.m. to noon on Saturday. So, on the Monday after the Easter holiday 1943 I strode off down the street with Tommy to catch the bus to work. I had my overalls, boots and cap on; I had a couple of fags in my top pocket and money to buy a dinner in the canteen. I was a working man aged 14 and a bit. For me, childhood was over . . .

But I was too young and too full of rebellious spirit to knuckle under, despite a variety of typically tough manual jobs. In the shipyards my first task was to tighten nuts and bolts that had already been put on by someone else. My starting wage was 13s 6d or 67½p, for a 48-hour week. Much harder jobs followed, including manhandling 200lb girders through machines in the construction of Bailey bridges for the Army. Finished prefabricated sections were reassembled on the banks of rivers or ravines by the Royal Engineers, allowing troops, tanks and lorries to pass over. These bridges were especially crucial in the invasion of France after D-Day, 6 June 1944, enabling the Allies to ford numerous rivers and obstacles. But just after my sixteenth birthday I had a big row with my foreman and told him exactly what I thought of him. I was sacked on the spot. Within a week I had a job at another shipbuilding yard, Hawthorn Leslie, and began a five-year apprenticeship as a ship's caulker. This involved making ships watertight by splitting the metal plates and forcing them against the plates underneath, forming a watertight seal. I also had to use an acetylene burner to cut holes in the steel plates where pipes had to go through and cut away damaged metal from ships sent to the yard for repair. I stuck this hard graft for another ten months. It was dirty, dangerous work carried out in rain, hail, snow or shine. However, one day someone on the gang threw a heavy rivet from the top of a ship at one of the yard policemen – a notoriously unpopular character. Fortunately it missed, but I – though innocent of any crime – was blamed, as I was working in the area at the time. Someone had to carry the can, and so yours truly was given the boot again for misconduct. There was no dole at that time, so I signed on at British Steel in Jarrow as a shift worker making steel ingots. It was red-hot, hard work which soon built muscle and toughened sinew. Later I transferred to the flat strip mill and had to wear steel-rimmed wooden clogs in which I walked the mile to work and back each day. I was still in the Army Cadets and continued to train in my spare time in the evenings and at weekends.

Finally I was put on the straightening machines, a good piece-work job with a light and cool environment. Everything went fine with this job so long as the rolling mill was kept going. If it stopped, the whole factory ground to a halt. During one such long stoppage with nothing to do I and a few working colleagues decided to drift off to the canteen to play cards. We reasoned that we could see through the window if the mill started up again, but we were spotted by the enraged foreman. All of us were sacked, with me at first being let off with just a warning, but someone complained that this was unfair, and so I got my cards too. So there it was – on the dole for the third time within my short working life. It was August 1946 and I was still only 17½. If I carried on this way, I was destined for big trouble sooner or later. It was high time to join the Army and get some real discipline . . .

Chapter 2

FACING WORLDWIDE THREAT:
GERMANY, GREECE AND CYPRUS

After spending a few days mooching at home and wandering the streets pondering what to do next I developed an irresistible urge to join the Armed Forces. The idea hit me with unmistakable clarity and my mind was soon made up – as usual. After all, I had enjoyed my time in the Army Cadets immensely, and it was obvious that Civvy Street didn't want me. I was tired of being made to feel like a reject, so why not join a professional unit where I could learn to become a team player and see the world at the same time? The nearest recruiting office was at City Road, Newcastle, a half-hour away from home on the No. 6 bus. I was turned down by the Royal Navy recruiter for my lack of education and didn't fancy the RAF as it was 'too elitist', and so I approached the cheerful recruiter in khaki. They were hard up for soldiers then because of having so many worldwide commitments – India, the Far East, the Middle East and Germany (the British Army of the Rhine or BAOR) to name but a few. I was fixed up with a medical for the next day, which to my surprise I passed. The standard must have been 'If he's warm, breathing and walking, he's OK.' I was 5ft 6in tall, thin, wiry and weighed little more than a wet dish-cloth. Several weeks later, on 3 October 1946, I was duly sworn in to His Majesty King George VI's service as a soldier. The terms of service were five years with the colours and seven years on the reserve. On my attestation form I was 19033387 Private Doran FWJ, General Service Corps. It was the start of a long and eventful Army career which was to lead to illustrious service in many famous regiments in addition to the Paras and Britain's most elite Special Forces regiment, the SAS.

On joining up I was asked which part of the Army I wanted to serve in after basic training. I was keen to join my local regiment, the Durham Light Infantry (DLI), a leading north-east unit. There were about 40 recruits in my intake at Brancepeth Camp near Durham, and during our first six weeks' training in the autumn of 1946 we were taught how to fire and maintain rifles and light machine guns (LMGs), plus we endured a lot of physical training to get fitness levels up to scratch. Eventually we were issued with .303 bolt-action Lee Enfield rifles, effective at more than 1,000 yards in the hands of a trained soldier. These were exactly the same weapons as those issued to British soldiers during the Second World War. My weekly pay was a princely 28s (£1.40), and from that I regularly sent an allowance of 7s (35p) home to my mother in Jarrow. My father was unable to work, following an industrial accident for which he got no compensation, and my sisters were all in low-paid jobs. The family was yet again in one of its many struggling phases, and I did not think twice about helping out.

After subsequent corps training at the Light Infantry Training Centre at Cove Camp, Farnborough, basic training was duly completed. I hoped for a posting to join the DLI, then stationed in exotic climes in India. But, to my great disappointment, in typical Army fashion I was taken off the DLI draft and told I would be joining the King's Own Yorkshire Light Infantry (KOYLI) instead, to serve as a peacekeeper in postwar Germany. The reason for the change was that India was classed as an 'active service' station, and I, at 18, was too young to take part, 19 being the minimum age. India at that time (early 1947) was a very troubled spot. It was just before the country received independence from Britain, and the different religious and political factions were really at each other's throats. Germany, in contrast, was a relatively peaceful posting, as the Cold War with Russia had not yet got off the ground. It was hardly two years since the end of the Second World War, and the Germans had other problems to contend with – like trying to survive. So once again I had to say farewell to some good friends. Not one of my squad came with me: they all went to India, and I learned later that a few of them were killed there. I was given ten days' pre-embarkation leave. Within a week my new draft was marched down to Farnborough station to travel by troop train to Hull to board a troopship bound for Cuxhaven in Germany. As, for the first time, I watched the shores of England fade into the distance I wondered what could be in store for me next. It took 36 hours to reach Cuxhaven, which meant one night on board ship.

Arriving at Cuxhaven on 10 April 1947, we were sent to a nearby transit camp to await transport to our units. Special orders that applied to BAOR were issued. The orders stated that the soldiers must wear uniform all the time and must indulge in no fraternisation with German civilians. This meant we were not allowed to even talk to anyone, except on official business. The non-fraternisation law was soon broken, however, as the men quickly found ways and means of meeting up with women and visiting pubs for a drink of schnapps.

Soon after the Second World War ended in Europe, Germany was divided up into four controlling zones – British, American, French and Russian. Berlin, which was in the Russian zone, was also split into four zones. To reach their Berlin zones the Western forces had to use strictly controlled air, rail and road corridors through the Russian zone. The Russians at that time were busy getting a stranglehold not only on their zone of Germany but also on the countries occupied by their forces, such as Poland. Free travel from Eastern Europe was brought to a complete halt. Later Winston Churchill coined the phrase 'Iron Curtain' when he made a speech in which he said, 'An iron curtain has descended across Europe, dividing East from West.' In the Western zones Control Commissions ran the country until a German government could be elected to take over. My comrades and I were schooled in all these intricacies at Cuxhaven, so that by the time we moved from there we were well genned up on the tricky political situation.

From Cuxhaven, we moved south by train to Bielefeld and into another transit camp. After four days at Bielefeld we boarded a train for the 30-odd-mile journey north-east to Minden, the final leg of our journey to join the 1st Battalion KOYLI, where they operated from ex-German Army barracks. The buildings were brick-built and grouped around a central barrack square, with the troop accommodation down each side, and HQ, gymnasium, cookhouse, etc at either end – a very good, well-organised set-up. Troop accommodation was first-class. Each block was three storeys high, plus a basement and an attic. All the rooms were centrally heated and had the double-window type of double glazing, with one set opening in and the other opening out.

Not far from their camp at Vogelsang the soldiers toured the remains of one of Adolf Hitler's Aryan 'stud farms', from which he had hoped to breed his planned Master Race of pure Aryans. We were allowed to visit this place, which was within walking distance. The 'farm' was not entirely ruined, and I spent some time there investigating the various buildings, which I found extremely interesting. It was at this establishment, and others like it, that Hitler attempted to propagate his idea of the Master Race, which would be composed mainly of blond, blue-eyed Aryan-type men and women. Toward that end people of the required appearance and physique from Germany and the countries occupied by Germany during the war were rounded up and sent to these stud farms to breed. Once there they were paired off, any surplus women went to German soldiers at the camp, mainly SS. All were ordered to produce children. When the offspring of these couplings were barely days old they were taken away and put into special nurseries, there to be brought up as members of the hoped-for perfect Aryan Master Race. To the British soldiers the Vogelsang stud farm looked as if it had been a well-organised set-up. There were sports fields, swimming pools, a games arena and what had obviously been excellent accommodation. On the walls surrounding the games arena prominent murals had been painted which depicted the ideal Aryan men and women. The figures were all completely naked and obviously designed to encourage the occupants in their patriotic labours. For the German military personnel who were sent there to father children it must have seemed an infinitely more preferable posting than the horrors of the Russian front.

In November 1947 my unit was told that the KOYLI was being moved to Malaya, where Chinese Communist terrorists had started a long and bloody campaign (in which I was later to be closely involved with the SAS). However, I was still too young to be sent to an active service station and so, along with around 50 others who were either too young or scheduled for demob, I was transferred yet again – this time to the 1st Battalion Oxfordshire and Buckinghamshire Light Infantry. The OBLI, or 'Obbly Gobblies' as they were called in the ranks, were then stationed at Lüneburg, about 25 miles south of Hamburg, then only 20 miles from the border with East Germany and Russia and the now massively deployed Cold War forces of the Eastern Bloc. Lüneburg Heath, a vast area of scrubland, is where Field Marshal Montgomery accepted the German surrender to give victory in Europe on 3 May 1945. I was posted to B Company. It was 3 December 1947. At this time in BAOR some units, including the OBLI, were engaged in an operation called Woodpecker. The task involved large-scale pine timber felling in the forests. Most of this timber was shipped back to the UK to be used mainly for pit props down the coal mines. It was hard work in all weathers, and to compensate for that the troops were on double rations. The camp at Lüneburg had a large sports field with a running track, and our Company Commanding Officer, who was a keen athlete, had us running and playing sports every chance he got. The Officer Commanding (OC), a Cornishman named John Tresawna, an ex-Para, was also a very good cricketer; he taught us how to play the game properly, explaining the rules and tactics clearly and with great patience. Major Tresawna also made our everyday infantry training extremely interesting. He was an exceptional man and a good officer. I was to meet him again five years later, in very different circumstances (as described in Chapter 3).

One day in early April 1948 the company set off in trucks for what we thought was going to be field training. We were dressed in battle order, with weapons and live ammunition. After a while the trucks stopped and the Company Sergeant Major (CSM) ordered the soldiers out. 'Sit down, eat your haversack rations and pay attention to Major Tresawna,' he instructed. 'Right,' said the OC. 'You're all dressed and equipped for action, which is exactly what we might be engaged in before long.' We all looked askance, sandwiches poised, not understanding. He continued: 'Just down this road, a few hundred yards away, is the border with East Germany. We are going to patrol the border and might have some trouble with the Russians.' The OC then went on to explain that the Russian troops, who lived mainly off the land, had stripped the country bare in their area and were now sneaking over the border into the British zone to steal cattle and pigs and livestock. The Germans living on the Western side had asked for help, and that's where our mob came in. It would soon be my first taste of real action. The CSM told us to be ready to move in half an hour. There was a great oiling of rifle bolts and checking of weapons. It concentrates the mind when you think you might be going into action shortly, maybe even coming under fire for the first time.

When we marched off towards the border it was with full magazines on (plus one up the spout), butterflies and fast-beating hearts. We came to a barrier across the road; this was the border. In those days, before the Berlin Wall, the big fences and the watchtowers, the border was just a fence or a stream. There were two Russian soldiers standing on their side of the barrier watching as we approached. They were dressed in baggy brown uniforms, with knee-length boots and a peaked cap. Both were armed, one with a rifle and the other with a 'burp' sub-machine gun (SMG), so called because its high rate of fire sounded exactly like a burp. Just before we reached the barrier we turned to the right off the road and started to follow the border, which was a fence, across country. As we did so the Russian with the burp-gun mounted a bicycle and pedalled away quickly down the road on their side. We carried on alongside the fence, not seeing anyone until we came to where a track bisected the border. At that point there was a Russian with a burp-gun and bike watching us. This threatening behaviour happened all day. Every time we reached the point where a track came up to the border there would be a Russian soldier, complete with burp-gun and bike, standing and watching. We would wave and say hello, and they would wave back. The first two men at the barrier had obviously reported us, and they were shadowing our progress.

Stopping for a break at one Russian checkpoint, I happened to be quite near, so I strolled over and offered the soldier a cigarette. He accepted, smiled and we both lit up. We couldn't speak each other's language, but after a couple of puffs he waved his fag, smiled again and said something which I took to mean 'Good'. There we were, the flesh-and-blood end of two opposing political systems. He seemed to be a pleasant, ordinary type of bloke, yet within a short while we might be doing our best to kill each other.

Another 10 or so miles further on we found ourselves in a small village with a farm nearby. We slept in the farm that night because that's where the targets were – livestock. The night was pitch-black, and when I did my two hours' guard I was shit-scared: every little sound was a Russian sneaking up on me. But for the moment nothing happened, and next day we carried on patrolling. This time we saw a lot more Russians watching us, and we guessed, rightly, that it meant trouble ahead. We stopped at another farm that night, but this time we dug shallow, fox-hole defensive positions. About 1 a.m. I was awakened by urgent shouts from the sentry. He had heard suspicious noises coming from the direction of the border and loosed off a Very light flare. By its brief illumination the sentry had spotted Russian troops creeping around on our side of the border. Just then the Russians started shooting in our direction. They were firing high: I could clearly hear the crack of bullets passing overhead. I was on the LMG (a Bren gun) that night, and by this time I was kneeling up in my fox-hole behind the weapon ready for action.

Someone gave the order to return fire and, despite the shock of being under enemy fire for the first time, all the rigorous training paid off, and I found myself operating the LMG quite calmly: two-round bursts, double tap. I couldn't see much to aim at, though, except the flashes of the Russian weapons. The action lasted for about three hours. It was a good ding-dong shoot-out. I could hear bullets ricocheting off a wall to my right and thudding into a tree on the left. Then, not long before dawn, the Russians stopped firing. They must have got fed up with it and realised there was no plunder to be had that night. I hope the bastards went hungry next day. I don't know if we did any damage to the Reds, but we had no casualties. I was highly chuffed. I had come through my baptism of fire OK. For days after that we thought the Third World War would break out, but nothing happened. Stalin must have realised that he wouldn't get far against the British Obbly Gobblies!

Our unit kept up the patrolling for months, but there were no more dramatic shoot-outs. One of my comrades was captured, but the Russians released him after a spell of parleying. In November 1948 I was promoted to Lance Corporal and sent on a course to the Military Police (MP) training school at Bielefeld. I and a couple of hundred blokes from BAOR were sent on the same course to receive a month's training, after which we would be selected to become Garrison Military Police (GP) – their task being to assist the MP's Red Caps. This was not to my liking at all, but there was nothing I could do about it. At the end of the course there was a big passing-out parade, and I was asked if I would like to be an MP. 'No thanks,' I replied. 'Anyway, I'm half an inch too short to be an MP.' They still kept me temporarily, though, because I found myself and two other lads, one from the Black Watch and the other a Gordon Highlander, posted to an MP detachment at Blankenese, a suburb of Hamburg. Our tasks there were manning the telephone and accompanying the MPs on their patrols. We had to have blancoed belt, gaiters and shoulder strap but were allowed to keep our regimental insignia and berets.

At this time the Berlin Airlift was in full swing. The Russians had closed all rail and road links from the West to Berlin, which meant most of the fuel and food needed in the British, American and French sectors of the city had to be flown in. A constant stream of aircraft was landing and taking off at Hamburg airport. The Airlift went on for months, the Reds eventually backing down after a real cliffhanger. Stalin's purpose, it was thought, was to force the Allies to abandon Berlin. He failed, narrowly, but it came to the brink of all-out war.

I deliberately began getting into trouble, hoping to get a return to action. I went out with some mates on the razzle in the big city one night and got thoroughly drunk. Staggering around the streets we saw a party going on at a house, so we went in and started dancing with some women. Then after a while we headed for Winkle Strasse, a notorious brothel street. There was a huge sign at the entrance of the street declaring it was 'Out of bounds to all British Forces'. So in we went! It was a fantastic place. There were scantily clad women with come-hither looks sitting in shop windows and twirling keys on their fingers. We sauntered along inspecting them. In each window there was a hole cut, probably for the woman to give her key to a client. I put my hand through one and had a stroke of a thigh. Just then there was a shout: two MPs were running towards us. We ran the other way, giggling and laughing. Whistles started blowing, and when we ran round a corner it was straight into the arms of two more Red Caps. That, at last, was the end of my career as a GP. After being demoted and receiving two weeks' jankers (confined to barracks), my pal and I were both sent back to our units. It was the end of February 1949, and I had just turned 20.

The OBLI had moved from Lüneburg to Göttingen, a small town on the northern edge of the Hartz Mountains. It was a pleasant spot almost untouched by the war. In April that year, 1949, NATO was formed. Two months later I rejoined the OBLI. The regiment was sent home on 28 days' leave and told to report afterwards to a camp near Crowborough in Sussex, from where the battalion was to go to Greece. Within two weeks the battalion was aboard the troopship *Dilwara*, bound from Southampton to Greece. I was philosophical, as always. On the evening we sailed I stood at the aft end of the ship drinking a big mug of tea and watching the English coastline fade away into the distance. Once again I asked myself, I wonder what's going to happen next. It was mid-June 1949.

We arrived at Salonika in northern Greece. Our task was, if called upon, to support the Greek Army, which was then busy fighting Communist invaders from Bulgaria. Our camp was about 3 miles from Salonika, facing the sea and with a splendid view of Salonika Bay. In the distance beyond the bay rose beautiful, snow-capped Mount Olympus, which is, according to ancient Greek legend, the home of the gods. Not long after arriving in Greece I was transferred to the battalion mortar platoon. We trained hard every day. Forty-five seconds was the maximum time allowed for a three-man team to unload their mortar plus ammunition from a vehicle and be set up ready for action. We had one minute to load up again after a shoot, the 15 extra seconds being because the mortar baseplate might be stuck in the ground. But it wasn't all work. We had nights out on the town, mostly in the NAAFI club, which had a balcony overlooking the harbour. Food and drink were cheap. Leaning against the jetty wall one night, where I had gone for a breath of fresh air, I was picked up by a beautiful prostitute. She had been standing close by, and I noticed how voluptuous she was. She was very attractive. She came alongside, grabbed my hand and in a loud whisper said, 'Come on, Johnny.' I thought it impolite to refuse. Along the waterfront and up a side alley we went. I was watching for any MPs and preparing to run. It was dark in the alley, and I became apprehensive. I had heard tales of pros luring blokes into places like this and then them being robbed by waiting accomplices. I didn't get undressed, because I had also heard about blokes getting their clothes nicked while they were on the job. One old soldier told me that he used to put his clothes into a small pack which he wore while performing! Afterwards I kissed my little Greek girl goodbye. She was very nice, and I felt a bit sorry for her, because even though she had a beautiful smile she had sad eyes. In the poor economic state suffered by Greece then it was probably the only way she had of making a living.

Not long afterwards my unit was informed that it was being transferred to Cyprus. I was in the advance party which travelled down to Athens by public ferry for the first leg of the journey, to be completed by Royal Navy frigate. It was mid-December 1949. The land around Waneskeep camp was flat and uninteresting, and when it wasn't muddy after rain it was ankle-deep in dusty silt. Nicosia was a charming old city and very interesting, but of the Greek Cypriots whom I encountered there, excluding the elderly and the young who were all very friendly, I did not like or trust a single one. They were mostly unfriendly men, both in speech and actions. In a bar one evening a group of us encountered a show of hostility from some Greek Cypriots which almost developed into violence. They were muttering and scowling in our direction. I thought we were going to have a battle when one of them pulled a knife, but after some posturing he put it away. We also saw signs of Communist propaganda in cafés, such as hammer-and-sickle posters with pictures of Joe Stalin. I doubt, though, that they would have preferred to have had the KGB there instead of us.

In March 1950 the platoon was relocated to Dhekelia on the south coast, not far from the port of Larnaca, in camp huts right by the sea. Our Platoon Officer was dead keen, working us hard on mortar training, plus live firing on nearby ranges. He would also send us out, singly, on initiative tests. We had to find our way around, without a map, collect certain items here and there and return to camp by a set time. One especially memorable aspect of the training was at the rifle range. There the butts where we handled the targets and indicated fall of shot were merely shallow depressions. The butts men were forced to lie down all the time, as standing or kneeling could have proved fatal. While lying there you could hear the bullets cracking only inches overhead. It was excellent training for being under fire.

This businesslike existence abruptly came to an end one day when I fell out with my Platoon Officer, though it was mostly himself to blame. This resulted in the loss of my stripe and in my being posted to B Company, based near Limassol on the south coast, the actual camp being at Polymedia a few miles inland, where a much more sedate life was led. About this time, mid-1950, the situation in the Canal Zone of Egypt was heating up, with Nasser increasingly causing trouble. The Korean War started in June, in Kenya the Mau Mau terrorist organisation was emerging and the Malayan emergency was in full swing. We were certain that our unit would be sent to one of those trouble spots. But no, the top brass must have thought that the Obbly Gobblies would have sorted things out too fast and spoiled everything, so we were left to soak up the sun in Cyprus. A few of us regular soldiers in B Company put in for transfer to other light infantry regiments but were turned down. The main reasons given were that it was too much trouble, both economically and administratively, to post individuals around the world to where they wanted to serve. In those days of troopships it was easier to move whole units.

In September, B Company was moved to Dhekelia camp. The mortar platoon had been transferred from there to Famagusta. After a few weeks there I was glad to be posted back to the mortars again and rejoin my old mates.

Again the dedicated training by our Platoon Officer got underway, training that was soon to stand me in fine stead during many years of Special Forces operations. Our Platoon Officer was still keen on initiative exercises. As 'escaped prisoners of war' we had to trek over half of Cyprus with sketch maps, no compasses and little food or water. Travelling mainly at night we had to steer by the stars – a specific example of something that served me very well when I joined the SAS some years later. In early 1951 we moved back to Dhekelia to make room for elements of 16 Parachute Brigade, which was staging in Cyprus before going on to the Canal Zone in Egypt. Not long before that a letter had appeared on our noticeboard asking for volunteers for the Parachute Regiment, but stipulating that a man had to have at least twelve months still to serve in the Army. Alas, I only had six months to go and, if I couldn't join the Paras, had no plans to sign on again. Little did I know it then, but I was to be retained for ten extra months, the Army was so severely stretched worldwide to cover all its commitments. National Servicemen were kept in for six extra months. In April I went home on end-of-tour leave. It meant goodbye to the Obbly Gobblies, because after four weeks' leave I would be posted to another light infantry unit. The troopship *Empress of Australia* sailed from Famagusta with me on board for the ten-day journey to the UK. From the rear rail, bound for Southampton, I watched Aphrodite's 'island of love' slip astern.

We awoke one morning and there was the English coast, a beautiful sight. From Southampton I went straight home. I neared our front door, heart pounding and knees trembling. As I went in through the door – nobody locked their doors then – my eyes started to fill. Two years is a long time away from home, even if it was just a humble, overcrowded house in a poor area of Tyneside. Mother didn't recognise me at first, but then her tears came too. It was May 1951. Eventually I had to report to Cowley barracks, the OBLI depot in Oxford, after my leave. From Oxford I was posted to Kiwi barracks, Bulford, on the edge of Salisbury. (During the Second World War a New Zealand regiment had been stationed there, and they carved a huge kiwi out of the chalk hillside nearby.) My new unit was the Duke of Cornwall's Light Infantry (DCLI). Again I was put in the mortars and shortly afterwards was told I had to serve an extra ten months with the colours, which meant demob in August 1952. Every Saturday morning at Bulford we had a battalion cross-country run. If you didn't finish on time you jeopardised your chance of a weekend pass. The DCLI was a very fit battalion indeed. In November we were sent on a week's leave, after which the unit was to be based in Minden, Germany, an old haunt of mine. Once there the DCLI would be part of the 6th Armoured Division. I must admit I was far happier to be nearer the action again.

January 1952 dawned, and our training carried on apace. Joe Stalin ignored the message of 'Peace on earth, goodwill toward men' and was intent on ramming Communism down our throats. We faced a massive military threat from the Eastern Bloc countries, where the largest army the world has ever known was poised to invade the West. The Cold War was really hotting up. The only thing that gave the Communists serious pause for thought was the certainty of obliteration from British and American nuclear weapons if they attacked. But the Lefties in Britain and America, especially those who had climbed onto the back of the Campaign for Nuclear Disarmament (CND), were doing their best to nullify our nuclear shield. Fortunately for the West they failed. In February 1952 King George VI died, and the troops learned that his daughter, Elizabeth, was their new Queen, although the Coronation was not to be held until June 1953. There were no more livestock anti-rustling patrols on the border, however. The Russians had built a fence all the way along it, and the only people who came across now were those desperately trying to escape from the Communist 'Utopia' to the free West.

Meanwhile in their wisdom the chiefs had made me up to Lance Corporal again, and I had managed to pass parts three and two of the Army certificate of education. So there I was, with a head full of knowledge and a bit of 'birdshit' on my sleeve, just in time to get demobbed after doing my extra ten months. Alternatively, if I signed on again my prospects of promotion seemed excellent. But other events in other theatres of war were about to intervene and push this soldier of misfortune once more in an entirely different direction.

Chapter 3

FIGHTING REAL WARS:
TOUCH AND GO IN KOREA

I must admit that I was by now a very fit and muscular young man indeed, well trained and ready for action. Under the rules of National Service I was sent back to England in August 1952 for demob. I went first to Bodmin Castle in Cornwall, the DCLI HQ, and from there to the demob centre in Woking, Surrey, where I handed in my uniform and was fitted out with civilian clothing. This could well have been the point where I parted with the Army for good, but I had already decided that Civvy Street was far too tame for my tastes now. When I arrived home in Jarrow I had already made up my mind to enlist again, but first I intended to have a few months' holiday and live off my savings. I enjoyed going to St James' Park football ground on Saturday afternoons with a few of my old school mates to watch Newcastle legends Jackie Milburn and Joe Harvey. But most of my days were spent on punishing, self-imposed walks and keeping fit. I had several different routes and would keep up a steady 6 miles an hour pace for three or four hours at a time. The restlessness was obvious to my family and friends.

I also spent a fair bit of time doing physical exercises at home. I kept to the routine that the physical training instructors drilled into us in the Army, i.e. arms, shoulders, trunk and legs. I was so fit I had muscles in me snots!

After a couple of months I had had enough of the 'easy' life and gladly went to the recruiting office in Newcastle to sign on for three years to serve with the DLI. A few weeks later I was sent instructions to report to Brancepeth Camp – the same place where I had first joined in 1946. From now on I would be thrown into the midst of one hot spot after another. I knew full well this would be the case. It was a clear, conscious choice, taking me from the realms of the 'amateur' boy soldier to the lofty ranks of the true professional.

The DLI had two battalions then. The 1st Battalion was serving in Korea, so I asked to be sent there. I had a feeling at the time that I was being foolish, putting myself in harm's way. But I thought, if you want to be a soldier, then why not do what soldiers do? Besides, I agreed with the reasons why we were fighting in Korea – to stop the spread of Communism. If there are those who would doubt the wisdom of that, just look at the mess that North Korea is in today, building up its own stock of nuclear weapons and huge conventional forces.

After several weeks the draft, much swollen by this time, was moved to Southampton, where the soldiers boarded the troopship *Dunera*. It was a cold, wet, miserable day in early February 1953 as the troops sailed away and the shores of England soon faded from sight. I was just a few weeks short of my twenty-fourth birthday. The journey to Japan, where we were to stay for a while before going on to Korea, took almost five weeks. To start with, the Bay of Biscay and the Atlantic down by Spain and Portugal were both calm, and my guts stayed in their proper place. The Mediterranean was like a mirror. Five days from Gibraltar we moored up in Port Said to await passage through the Suez Canal. Port Said was, and still is, a very busy harbour. Besides the *Dunera* there were several oil tankers and cargo ships either at the docks or waiting to go through the Canal. Among the big ships there were lots of smaller craft darting here and there, with much shouting and tooting of horns. The town of Port Said itself appeared to be drab and dirty, with various aromas drifting from there across the oily water towards us – and not all of them pleasant. It wasn't long before the notorious Arab 'bum boats' were swarming alongside, trying to sell trinkets and souvenirs to the troops. One time a group of us were idly leaning over the rail watching this activity when one of the lads cried out, 'Look, down there in the water – is that what I think it is? It looks like a cock and a pair of balls!' We all stared in the direction he was pointing, and sure enough that's what it was, a penis with the testicles still attached floating gently along. Somebody must have caught a rival lover with his missus or girlfriend and taken revenge with a knife, we reasoned. It brought on a dreadful shudder all round.

The ship passed through the Canal and Bitter Lakes to Suez, and then out into the Red Sea. The daily routine included physical training and shooting from the rear of the ship at balloons tied on lengths of string: good practice which kept the soldiers' eyes zeroed in.

It was on this trip that I first met up with the SAS – at this time a little-known and very secretive force. One day I came across a small group of blokes playing cards in a corner. They had an unfamiliar Winged Dagger cap badge in their red berets. I asked them what regiment it was, and they told me unconcernedly, saying that they would be leaving the ship at Singapore. The SAS was then based in Malaya, fighting Communist terrorists (or CTs). If I had been going anywhere dull and unexciting, I would have put in for a transfer to the SAS there and then, but I was heading for a full-scale war in Korea and soon forgot about them, until I ran into them again later. Some new passengers boarded at Singapore, among them a Fijian Army rugby team. It was the first time I had seen any Fijians. They were huge, broad-shouldered men with dark, glistening skin. Some of them were handsome and some quite ugly, but they all had smiling eyes, with a gentleness in their manner and in the tone of their voices. Most of the lads took an immediate liking to them. I later discovered that the Fijians were formidable fighters, and I was to meet more of their kind many years later when some of them joined the SAS. The Fijians would sit on the open deck in a big circle, play their guitars and sing in beautiful deep voices. They would have an audience of hundreds, all sitting quietly and listening. It was sheer magic, that lovely Fijian music and singing, with warm nights, brilliant stars and just the gentle roll of the ship. Quite a lot of troops disembarked at Hong Kong. The British Army was being reinforced there to face down a threat from the Chinese who were playing silly buggers on the border with the New Territories on the mainland.

Next stop was Japan, where we were to stay for a while before going on to Korea in a smaller ship. The *Dunera* docked at Kure, just across the harbour from Hiroshima, where the Americans had dropped the first atom bomb, in 1945. The soldiers were told there were still problems with radiation, although it was now nearly eight years after the event. At Kure we were billeted in old Japanese Army barracks. Among the hundreds of troops waiting there to join their units in Korea were the DLI, the Black Watch, the Duke of Wellington's Regiment and various odds and sods including the Royal Artillery (RA), the Royal Electrical and Mechanical Engineers (REME) and the Royal Engineers (RE). We were issued with special clothing and equipment for service in Korea. This consisted of a thick, heavy-duty combat suit complete with peaked cap which no one ever wore, and a pair of 'boots, cold wet weather', with massive soles resembling cross-country tyres. Frankenstein's monster would have looked great in them! A heavy, ribbed pullover was also issued. Unfortunately these pullovers, although warm, had a tendency to shrink after getting wet and were also prone to the effect of dyes from other items of clothing. It was not unusual for a man to put his pullover on in the morning, be on duty in the rain and then find himself wearing a multi-coloured pullover so small it was difficult to get off! Another interesting item which we were given was a vest made of woven string. The theory was that all the little holes among the strands of string would trap body warmth and hold it there beneath the shirt. The theory worked – and they later became commercially successful – but it was like wearing a loose ball of parcel twine. To complete the underwear there was a hideous pair of baggy, ill-fitting long johns. The overall cover for this lot was a warm but non-waterproof parka which, when wet, weighed a ton and took a week to dry out. Our new webbing equipment, which went under the name of '44 pattern', because it was first issued in 1944, was dark green with metallic buckles and was very good, hard-wearing kit. Our personal weapons were sten guns and No. 4 .303 Lee Enfield rifles.

All the British units in Korea at this time were part of the Commonwealth Brigade, which included units from Australia, New Zealand and Canada and was itself part of the United Nations (UN) force committed to throwing the Communist invaders out of South Korea. On 14 March our DLI draft boarded a sea-going ferry and two days later docked in Pusan, Korea. The next leg of our journey, by train to Seoul, the capital, took ten hours and gave the lads plenty of time to study the hilly countryside, which seemed to have no cultivation other than rice paddy fields. One interesting sight on our slow trip north was a train full of Chinese POWs heading the other way – they didn't appear to be unhappy with their lot. Upon arrival at Seoul in the middle of the night we transferred to lorries for the final lap to the battle zone. I should mention here that by this stage in the war the fighting, mostly static, was all taking place north of the 38th Parallel, the border between North and South Korea. The DLI were in a rest camp when we joined them, a few miles from the front line. Another lad, Peter Welsh, and I were put into the mortar platoon. Peter, a National Serviceman, was to become one of my best mates until I lost touch with him about three years later.

Two days after our arrival the DLI moved up and relieved an American unit on Hill 355. That particular American outfit didn't impress me much. They appeared very slovenly, and they left the position – at least the mortar site, that is – in shit order. We found rubbish all around, overflowing latrine holes and even some abandoned weapons sticking out of the paddy where they had been carelessly flung. The Chinese, who were positioned opposite

Hill 355, must have known we had arrived, because they lobbed over some air-burst shells just to say hello. There wasn't much we could do about that except don our steel helmets and carry on setting up the mortars ready for action. Immediately after that we got stuck in and cleaned up the position.

Hill 355 had been a static position for several months and was well established. The mortars were in good, sandbag-lined pits, with plenty of room for manoeuvre and to store ammunition. Just a few yards away was a dugout shelter, a 'hoochi' in Korean, where the mortar crew could sleep and store their kit. We had beds made from two iron fence poles with telephone wire stretched between. There was about 2 feet of earth on the dugout roof, plus a sandbag blast-wall covering the entrance. There is not much doubt that without such protection we would have suffered many casualties. In addition to the hoochies there were slit trenches here and there in which a body could take refuge if caught outside by enemy flak. There wasn't a lot of time in between hearing the whistle of a mortar bomb or artillery shell coming in and when it landed, so you had to be pretty nippy. Whenever I moved about the location I always kept a mental note of where the nearest hole was in case I had to dive into it. One very useful piece of equipment that we had dotted around the position was called, in Army slang, a 'desert rose'. Desert roses usually consisted of a length of pipe or rolled-up corrugated iron placed into a hole in the ground at an angle, with rocks in the bottom for drainage. Desert roses were for peeing in and were located near to dugouts so that we didn't have to go all the way to the latrine. Necessity is the mother of self-preservation in battle zones.

The dugouts had been constructed by the RE. Many years later, at an SAS reunion in Hereford, I was talking to one of the blokes – Derek Dixon, who lives in Hereford – and it turned out that he had been with the RE on 355. A damned good job they were there, too. They saved our bacon more than once. The food we had in Korea was fabulous – mostly American rations, fresh meat and veg nearly every day, plus chicken, pork, turkey, and bacon and eggs. The troops established a cooking area, and one of the lads would volunteer to be chef. Two good meals were put away daily, and there was tea on the go all day long. There was no set routine except to start off shaved and with clean boots each morning. I used an American steel helmet as a wash bowl. All spare time, when not firing the mortars, was spent cleaning and improving the position. The site was on a slope, so steps were made with empty ammunition boxes, which proved invaluable in the wet weather.

Several times a week the troops had to restock with mortar bombs. The ammo truck dropped them off by the road at the bottom of the hill, which meant they had to be carried up to the mortar pits. To lighten the load the men would remove the bombs from their transit boxes and from the individual containers, leaving only a waterproof cover on the tail unit. The tail cover had a tape handle which enabled them to carry three or four bombs comfortably in each hand. With each bomb weighing 10lb, their usual load would be up to six in each hand. 'Busty' Towell, from Somerset, the platoon strongman, could carry twelve bombs in each hand – an amazing total of 240lb uphill! The troops would be engaged in this backbreaking chore for at least three hours at a time. We were in action every day and most nights 'posting metal over the hill', and there was a lot of ammo used. When not helping to repel any enemy action on our front, or supporting our unit's patrols, we could well find ourselves giving covering fire to units on our flanks. Also, on relatively quiet nights the mortars would be laid onto likely targets, then whoever was on guard would wander along and plonk a bomb down a barrel at odd times as 'harassing fire'. Every morning our Platoon Commander received a report from battalion HQ regarding the previous day's action. According to those reports we killed and wounded a lot of the enemy with our mortars.

Of course the Communists tried to nail a few of us too. Our position was stonked with mortar fire most days, sometimes just the odd bomb to annoy us, but at other times, especially when attacking our hill or the positions on our flanks, they would lay it on real thick. If we were firing our mortars at the time, we would have to carry on and hope we didn't get a direct hit, although sometimes, if we were doing a slow rate of fire, it was possible for one man to handle the mortar on his own while the other two sheltered behind a little blast-wall in the pit. I was caught out in a particularly heavy stonk one day while making my way back from the latrine. I clearly heard the deadly whistling noise. For the next 30 yards or so between me and the dugout I inspected the bottom of at least three slit trenches on the way. One bomb nearly got me, though, when it landed only a few yards away. Just managing to throw myself flat into a slight hollow I felt my eardrums being pushed in, as if a giant had banged me on the sides of the head with a couple of bin lids. My mate Peter thought I'd been hit badly and was on his way from our dugout to help me, but I yelled 'OK' and flew through the shelter door just before the next salvo came in. I was peppered with mud and small stones and suffered a slight cut on the leg, but I was otherwise all right. I was lucky: most of the shrapnel passed over me. But I had trouble hearing for several days afterwards.

But the luckiest bloke in the platoon was definitely the line repair man, Corporal Stokes. Radios were so unreliable in those days that the only sure way of communicating with the fire controller in the forward positions was by field telephone. Field telephones, powered by dry battery and connected with a thin black cable, had a range of about half a mile, but the worst problem with a land line was that it could be damaged by shell fire or cut by an enemy patrol. To help counter these drawbacks several separate sets of telephones could be used between two points, with the lines laid out on different routes, or more than one cable could be fixed to each set, laid out in parallel and joined to each other every 50 yards or so. Then, if one line was damaged, it would still be possible to get through via the joins. But communications were still regularly cut, and that is when Corporal Stokes unflinchingly went into action. When duty called, off he would run through shot and shell, night or day, carrying his repair kit. He was very lucky not to be killed or wounded on the way. He was an exceedingly brave man doing an unglamorous but highly essential job.

There was one thing that used to happen every now and then, and it was quite annoying. In front of us on the top of 355 there were a couple of Centurion tanks. Normally they would be positioned just below the crest of the hill so that the opposition couldn't see them, but occasionally one of the tanks would move to the top, loose off a few rounds at the enemy and then roll back down again. Every time that happened, back would come a few return shots from the other side. The enemy shells would fly over the hill and miss the tanks. Unfortunately, straight beyond them was our mortar position, and we would cop the lot. Years later, when I was in the SAS, I found out that a bloke in my squadron, Bob King, had been a crewman in one of the tanks. When I told him about what used to happen he just laughed like hell! It was enough to make anybody swear. But that's one thing I didn't do then. My friend Peter Welsh and I were both Roman Catholics, and some time before the tank incidents started we had agreed to stop swearing. We kept it up for a year, but when Peter went home on demob I started again. We also went to RC services when possible. One Sunday on 355 we attended a Mass at an RA heavy mortar site about a mile from us. Personal weapons and a bandolier of ammo had to be carried in case, not only because of any enemy encountered on the way, but also as protection against attacks from Korean civilians and Army deserters. Desperate for money and food, they roamed around the rear areas, and two unarmed Brits walking along the track would have been easy meat.

After Mass we stayed talking to the other lads for a while. As I chatted, I spotted a familiar face on the fringe of the crowd. I stood looking for some time trying to remember who it was and where I had seen him before. He was talking to someone and kept turning his head away, but finally I recognised him. The face belonged to Major Tresawna, who had been my OC in the OBLI at Lüneburg in Germany five years previously. Fancy that, I thought, Major Tresawna, here in the DLI! I wanted to go over and greet him, have a chat, but I didn't like to interrupt. As I waited I recalled all the good training he had given us – sports, including cricket, and infantry tactics. We had practised section, platoon and company attacks, day and night, until we could almost do them blindfold. 'Remember,' he had drummed into us, 'whatever size of formation, you always keep one foot on the ground. Don't move until your support fire is ready.' How right he was. It works all the way up, from just two men using the 'buddy system' to cover each other, to whole armies guarding each other's flanks. All that flashed through my mind in a moment. Just then Major Tresawna finished his conversation and turned to move away from me. I started forward, raising my hand and calling to attract his attention, but I was too far away and he must have been in a hurry, because both he and the chap he had been talking to set off at a brisk run. I had to leave then as well, but I thought, 'Never mind, now that I know he's with us I'll most likely get the chance to meet him some time.' Unfortunately it was not to be, because Major Tresawna was killed very shortly after that while out on patrol in no-man's-land. A great loss – he had been a father-figure to us young lads back then in 1948. He was an officer to look up to and a fine gentleman.

During this time, in spite of being in danger under enemy fire and attacks I was, paradoxically, very happy. I was doing a job that I liked and was with a fine bunch of blokes. About half of the mortar platoon was made up of National Service conscripts, but there were no moaners among them. They were all good lads who got stuck in and made the best of things. The Regulars in the platoon were reliable, professional soldiers and good friends too. They had a smattering of men from all the Light Infantry counties – Shropshire, Yorkshire, Somerset, Cornwall, Oxfordshire and Buckinghamshire, but most were from County Durham. In my crew were Peter Welsh from Leeds and Andy Dunkeld from Washington, County Durham. Among the others were Lenny Bowman from Spennymoor, Reggie Old from Gateshead, 'Gonker' Rowlands from Blaydon, 'Tatie' Hope and Lenny Wardle from near Durham, 'Topper' Brown from Hartlepool, the unit's trusty 'line man' Corporal Stokes, also from Durham, and 'Busty' Towell (as already mentioned), the platoon's strongman, from Somerset. They, and all the others whose names I can't recall, were just ordinary men. They didn't look like heroes and would have run a mile if you had called them heroes, but that's exactly what they were. It was a great privilege to have served with them. I can't remember much about our Platoon Officer. He was a nice enough bloke but seemed very aloof, only speaking to us in an official capacity and never socialising.

After four long weeks on 355 we were relieved by the Royal Fusiliers (RF), a southern regiment with white hackles proudly bobbing on their berets. Back safe in the rest area, the DLI was welcomed by the cooks with huge mugs of tea liberally laced with rum. As all of us soldiers drank deeply, we could feel the tension of the past few weeks draining away. I found I could laugh at anything, any silly joke that was cracked. The rest of the lads were exactly the same – we were almost hysterical. At the time these warning signs were routinely ignored as unimportant, but experts now recognise that prolonged exposure to enemy fire and shelling gives rise to combat stress, a definable medical condition which affects troops in varying degrees, sometimes rendering them completely incapable of future action. Others are luckier and seem to take it in their stride.

After a short period in the rest area, catching up on sleep and being issued with new clothing and equipment, my unit moved back to 355, taking over again from the RF. The DLI had by now been reinforced by a number of South Korean soldiers. These were known as 'Katcoms', the Korean Augmentation Troops Commonwealth Brigade. There was one allotted to each mortar crew. Mine was a Corporal Sin, and he proved to be a good soldier without any vices, despite his name. Meanwhile peace talks were being held at a place called Panmunjon, which was not all that far from the DLI's location. At the site of the talks a strong searchlight was shone straight up into the air every night. This was to ensure that no fire was directed onto the area. However, in spite of the peace talks the war actually hotted up quite a bit. The enemy started putting in some big attacks to try to gain as much ground as possible before peace was declared. We had no large-scale efforts against 355, but the positions on our flanks were given some stick. First the South Koreans on our right had a hammering, then, towards the end of May, the hill to our left, known as 'the Hook', was severely mauled. During both attacks the DLI also came under very heavy mortar and shellfire, no doubt in an attempt to keep our heads down. But despite that we managed to give support with our mortars. At the same time we were obliged to keep a sharp lookout to the sides in case the enemy had broken through and we were being outflanked.

The Hook was an important tactical position, at that time occupied by the Duke of Wellington's Regiment, or 'Duke of Boots', as they are more popularly known. Chinese troops put in a full-scale assault on the Hook but were repulsed with heavy casualties. The Duke of Wellington's were good old steady British infantry, a fine lot to have by your side. After our second month on 355 the ground on and all around the mortar site was pitted with craters, mainly from mortar bombs. Once again we were lucky and no one was injured, but it was close. One night I was trapped with Corporal Sin in a slit trench during a very heavy stonk. It was too dangerous to attempt a run for the dugout, so there we sat, hunched up, facing each other. I shone my torch on Sin's face to see if he was OK. He was shaking and whimpering with fright. 'Better try to calm him down,' I thought, 'otherwise he might jump out and run, and if he does he'll be killed for sure.' A shrapnel-damaged box of Bren-gun mags was lying on the side of the trench. I dragged it down and signed to Corporal Sin to help me sort them out and take the good rounds out of the damaged magazines. Five minutes of doing that and he looked all right. I felt a whole lot better myself too.

On another night our section of two mortars moved to a location about half a mile away to one side in order to reach a new target. We lobbed bombs from there for a few hours before retiring to a nearby bunker for a kip. The Chinese must have figured out where the flak was coming from, because they gave us it back for the rest of the night, with interest. First light and we crept out for a look: bomb craters all around, and my mortar had taken a direct hit, smashing the bipod legs!

Corporal Sin and his comrades were all very small men. They had been trained and equipped by the Yanks, but while they were with us they wore British uniforms. They were all pleasant, cheerful guys, but they had some funny habits, shaving their foreheads and putting footpowder on their faces being among the most peculiar! I think they were quite pleased to be with us, as in their own army they wouldn't have been treated so well. I had heard tales of how brutal life was in the Korean forces. One day I saw a group from the neighbouring South Korean unit move down into the valley on our right. The group stopped and formed a rough circle. In the centre, waving his arms around, stood what must have been the man in charge. Suddenly one of the men in the circle was grabbed by those on either side and dragged into the middle, where the chief started shouting and screaming at him. A few minutes later the unfortunate man was taken to one side and given a severe beating by his escort, using sticks, boots and fists. I reckon it must have been some sort of court martial, dishing out instant and violent punishment. Several more men were dealt with in a similar manner before the group moved off, the miscreants in tow looking very much the worse for wear. Some of our Katcoms had been watching the performance, and I noticed them whispering together, looking very serious.

The DLI's second month on 355 passed and the RF took over again. It had been a memorable two months, not only on account of the war, but because of other events which had been taking place in the world, especially some famous firsts. Mount Everest had been conquered for the first time by Sir Edmund Hillary and Sherpa Tenzing, and Queen Elizabeth II had been crowned on 2 June 1953. On Coronation Day, at the precise time of the crowning in Westminster Abbey, the boys and I gave the enemy a full five minutes' rapid mortar fire.

During the ensuing rest period the DLI were transported to a nearby Australian camp where a concert had been laid on, the highlight of which was a female singer who sounded like Olive Oyl on Ecstasy but generated a lot of heat by exposing plenty of bare flesh. The platoon spent the next few days camped by a river, where we just lay around or went swimming. Afterwards, on the march back to the main camp, we stopped by an RA 5.5in gun position to watch the unit carrying out a shoot. You will never ever see any better gun drill than that of the British RA. Each fire order was given and acknowledged clearly and precisely. Gun crews then carried out their various tasks in a smart, businesslike manner. No fuss, no frigging around, everything calm and orderly, then – CRACK! – off went the shell.

A mobile NAAFI had been established near our camp, so I went along to buy some chocolate and restock with razor blades. Every nationality in the UN force was represented there – Brits, Yanks, Turks, Greeks, Aussies, Kiwis and some Orientals who I couldn't identify. Soon after that we moved to occupy a position known as Hill 159. The Chinese were our opposition on this front. Quite near our mortar site was a reserve rifle company area. One day they were hit by a particularly heavy burst of shelling. During a lull we saw an American MASH (Mobile Army Surgical Hospital) helicopter come in to evacuate a wounded bloke. Next day the same thing happened. Both men died from their wounds. I knew both of them. It was the first time I had seen the MASH helicopters in action. MASH seemed to be a bit scatty as portrayed in the comedy TV series of the same name, but in reality they did a damned good job and saved many lives by their prompt actions.

As our mortar position was in a steep-sided inlet the Chinese could only get at us with their less destructive heavy mortars. But we suffered many stonks, once again being saved by strongly built dugouts. During those bombardments the noise would be terrific. One day our section was moved to a forward location. The powers that be were expecting a big attack either on the DLI, the US Marines on our left or the South Koreans on the right. Our position would enable us to give support on the flanks if necessary. The Chinese did attack but sooner than expected, catching us out in the open as we prepared our mortars. Shellfire rained down and, as we didn't have orders to carry on, we hastily took cover. Dashing for some dugouts nearby, my crew disappeared into one and I did a flying rugby dive into another. Lying there, winded, I heard a southern American voice drawl, 'Kinda hot out there, is it, boy?' Looking up, I saw a Yank sitting casually regarding me and smoking a big fat cigar. Feeling a right nit, I picked myself up. 'It is a bit,' I replied. We had a brief chat for a few minutes before I left after hearing our sergeant calling us back into action. The Chinese attack fizzled out that night.

The DLI unit stayed for a while longer and next day had the opportunity to view across to the Chinese positions. As we watched, the US Air Force was busy bombing the enemy lines, using deep-penetration bombs to reach down into the many caves and bunkers dug into the hillsides. The Americans also hammered the Chinese with napalm bombs. When napalm (jellied petrol) is exploded it becomes a burning mass reaching down into dugouts and trenches, sticking to everything. It is a truly terrifying weapon. We all felt sorry for the ordinary Chinese and North Korean soldiers suffering horribly for the sake of brutal Communist regimes, the leaders of which, we were convinced, cared not a jot about their fate.

After a month on Hill 159 the DLI moved to another rest area. We were due to take over our next position, the notorious Hook, at the end of July. Meanwhile we were looking forward to a peaceful week, sleeping on mattresses with mosquito nets, clean clothes and no work. It was not to be that way for long. On our third night we were rudely awakened and ordered to stand by ready for action. A briefing followed, and it became clear that the Chinese had launched a massive attack all along the DLI sector of the front. As we were due next on the Hook our immediate task now was to hold reserve positions behind. The briefing ended with the word 'Move!' Frantic loading of ammunition, mortars and then troops took place in hectic fashion, and we were ready in an hour from being woken. The order came and off we trundled. It was a pitch-black night, but no lights were to be used. I was lying on top of a lorry-load of mortar bombs. I tried to catch up on a bit more sleep but was kept awake by the thought of how many pieces of me would be found afterwards if a shell hit my truck. About an hour later the convoy stopped. We waited, but no orders came to unload. Then the word was passed to return to camp. The enemy attack had been halted – with no gains to them. The relief was immense. There was time for a short kip after unloading the trucks and then, later on that morning, all the troops were called together and informed that the war in Korea was over. It was 27 July 1953.

Apparently the Chinese had had one last attempt before the ceasefire came into effect to gain as much ground as possible in their attack the previous night. But they failed in their objective, losing a lot of men trying. The UN forces had advanced well north of the 38th Parallel, the geographical border between North and South Korea. The DLI's new location turned out to be right on that line, not far from the River Imjin. Daily dips in the river and taking things easy became the order of the day. Some men went on leave to Tokyo, but just before my turn to go one of the American transport aircraft which were used crashed, killing 129 US servicemen. All aircraft were grounded then. However, a leave camp had been established by the sea at Inchon, so a group of us were sent there for a week. There had been a terrific battle at Inchon three years previously, when British and US marines had landed behind the Chinese lines.

During our stay on the 38th Parallel I saw a lot more of the rest of the battalion. Among the officers there was one whom I was to meet again five years later when I joined the SAS: a certain Lieutenant de la Billière, later General Sir Peter de la Billière, Commander of the British Forces in the first

Gulf War. At the time we were told that his full name was Peter de la Cour, de la Billière. By the time I saw him again in the SAS it had been shortened down to DLB.

Towards the end of August the Sussex Regiment took over from us, and we moved down to Pusan to board a troopship for our next theatre of duty, the Canal Zone of Egypt. A farewell parade was held before we left the 38th camp, at which we were addressed by the Brigadier. At the end, as was the tradition, we gave three cheers and waved our berets in the air. The OC of the DLI gave the order 'Remove head-dress!' Our South Korean soldiers, who were on parade at the rear, didn't understand the order, but when they saw us take off our berets they did likewise. The OC then shouted, 'Hip-hip – hurrah!' We all cheered and waved our hats. This was repeated twice more, the Koreans cheering with us. The OC then gave the order 'Replace head-dress!', whereupon the Koreans gave another rousing cheer! Everyone, including the Brigadier, burst out laughing. It was a good note to end on.

On a more sombre and reflective note, at Pusan the troops visited the UN cemetery. Someone had draped Light Infantry green ribbon on the DLI graves so the lads could find their comrades more easily. There are 26 DLI graves at Pusan, five belonging to men I knew personally, buried in yet another corner of a 'foreign field'. Next day the DLI boarded the troopship *Empire Orwell* and set off for Egypt. What would fickle fate have in store for us next?

Chapter 4

TERRORISM:
EGYPT AND THE CANAL ZONE

The *Empire Orwell* was carrying a large number of ex-POWs who were bound for the UK. Most of them had been held in North Korean prisons for two years or more, where they had been very badly treated, suffering extremes of hunger, physical discomfort and mental torture, including 'brainwashing' with Communist ideology. A few POWs had indeed succumbed to the brainwashing, even to the extent of betraying their mates for various 'crimes' and often receiving extra food as a reward. When the war ended the Chinese gave the collaborators the choice of staying and going to live in China or being repatriated. Only one Briton, a Royal Marine named Conlon, chose to stay.

We weren't long at sea before trouble broke out among the ex-POWs. Several of the alleged collaborators were severely beaten up, and when the *Orwell* stopped at Hong Kong two or three of them were thrown over the side into the harbour. The captain, so we were told later, then decided to leave all the suspected collaborators in Hong Kong rather than risk a riot at sea. After that it was a peaceful trip to Suez, calling at Singapore and Ceylon (Sri Lanka), where we soldiers enjoyed some shore leave, then over the Indian Ocean to Aden. The weather was perfect, almost as good as you might hope for on a world cruise. The ship stopped at Aden for a while, but we troops weren't allowed ashore. Then, a few days later, after a pleasant trip up the Red Sea, we entered the Suez Canal. As we passed one point someone among a small group of British soldiers standing by the Canal shouted, 'Get your knees brown!' This brought forth a roar of derision from the troops lining the rails of the *Orwell*, especially when they could see that the man who had shouted was himself almost Persil-white. Perhaps the poor lad didn't know that 'Get your knees brown', intended as an insult to fresh troops just out from Britain, should have been called out to troopships going *down* the Canal, not *up* the other way when full of sunburnt warriors from the Far East!

Disembarking at Port Said the DLI were transported south to Fanara, which is about two-thirds of the way back down towards Suez and not far from the Great Bitter Lake. The name of our camp, which consisted of tented accommodation, was St Gabriel's. Very apt, I mused, as the bugles of the DLI were to be heard blowing there daily for the next twenty months. Fanara village, about a mile from the camp, consisted of a small huddle of mud-brick houses grouped around a bridge-crossing over the Sweet-Water Canal. Designed to provide irrigation the inaptly named Sweet-Water Canal winds its way eastwards from the Nile and then turns south with many offshoots, eventually emptying into the Red Sea. The name 'Sweet' was given to differentiate it from the saltwater ship canal. It is still sweet by name, but not by nature, the water being anything but wholesome. All along its length the canal was used as a sewer and a handy place to dump dead animals. Even human bodies could occasionally be seen floating gently by with the current. By most village bridges, which were built very low, my comrades and I would see an old man sitting patiently armed with a long pole. His job, it seemed, was to poke dead bodies under his bridge so that they floated on down to the next village and did not create a dam effect. At intervals along the canal bank there were small, beaten, level patches upon which the Arab men prayed. Before prayers the men would stand waist deep in the canal and wash. They would also gargle and rinse their mouths out! These people were immune to every disease going. We were told that if any of us were just to fall into the Sweet-Water, we had to report sick immediately and be given ten to sixteen different inoculations to counter the possible effects of the contaminated water.

But there were also spectacular sights. The land is flat in the area of the Suez Canal and, seen through the red-hot shimmering air, what appeared to be mirage-like ocean-going vessels sailing through sand were in fact ships travelling along the Canal. In the Canal Zone sand got in every crack and cranny. There were some 90,000 British servicemen and women stationed there then, and at any one time I estimate that they carried among them on their bodies enough sand to fill every bunker on every golf course in Britain! And to go with the sand we had the flies. There is no other fly to equal the Egyptian fly. It is the most annoying fly in the world. The first thing I was aware of in the mornings was flies on my nose, mouth and eyes. They simply adored me. They accompanied me to the toilet, then to the wash place. At the cookhouse they helped me out with my breakfast. During the day the Egyptian fly mingled with Zone dust on my body and stamped it in. They were extremely persistent. Any ordinary fly when swatted at would buzz off, at least for a while, but not the big E. Oh, no. He would move away just exactly enough for the swatting hand to miss, then immediately settle back onto the victim's skin. Nowhere was safe. I remember driving along deep in the desert and stopping for a break. Within a fraction of a second an E fly landed on my nose. What they found to feed on otherwise in the middle of a desert I could not imagine.

The reason for the huge British military presence in Egypt was to ensure that the vital Suez Canal remained open. Not only was it a lifeline for British outposts in the East, but most of Britain's oil from the Persian Gulf came through that route. It was because of these reasons that the Russians would at that time have relished the chance to take it from Britain. This became a real threat in 1956, when Nasser, Egypt's ruler, who was friendly with Russia, nationalised the Canal. There was every type of unit based in the Canal Zone – infantry, tanks, artillery and all the support units necessary to keep them maintained and equipped. Reputedly the largest ammunition dump in the world was at Abu Sultan, about 20 miles north of our camp. There was a huge ordnance depot just down the road the other way at Geniefa. Also there were numerous other similar, but smaller, establishments dotted here and there. So the whole Canal Zone was full of tents, barbed wire and sweaty blokes, all covered in dusty sand. One notable outfit, made up of men from the then British colonies of Kenya, Uganda and Tanganyika (now Tanzania), and stationed not far from us, was a unit of the East African Pioneer Corps (EAPC). Most of the officers and senior NCOs in the EAPC were British.

The first thing we did at St Gabriel's was to hand in our olive-green uniforms and get issued with khaki drill. This was supposed to blend in with the desert, but in practice it stuck out like a sore thumb: it was the wrong colour altogether. Every desert I have been in is a greyish, greenish, dull sort of pink, with the odd streak of white and black mixed in – a bit like the camouflage the Long Range Desert Group (LRDG) used to paint their vehicles with in the Western Desert when they were fighting Rommel in 1941. Also, I think by what I saw of the British Army uniforms worn during the Gulf War in 1991 that they finally got the colour somewhere near right. Anyway, there we were in 1953, sticking out like sore thumbs in Egypt. Most of the time we trained – that is, when we were not doing guard duty. There was no shortage of training areas: we just went out into the desert and trained, usually with live ammunition. There was a rifle range near camp which had a small sandhill at the far end to catch the bullets. Some of the local Arabs, ever mindful of buckshees, would hide behind this hill and, during a pause in the firing, run out and rake furiously in the sand for spent rounds to sell as scrap. They knew when to get behind the hill again because they could hear the orders being called out on the firing point. It was a very dicey way of making spare cash. Several of them didn't make it to cover in time and collected the bullet sooner than expected.

The guard duties were numerous. All military installations had to be guarded, including a water filtration plant that supplied water to the camps, a jerrycan factory and, last but not least, ourselves. Camp guard was a 24-hour job, but the others could be anything from a week to a month, and the whole battalion, less our camp guard, would be on duty if it was the Abu Sultan ammo dump. The army commander's house guard, a twenty-day effort, was the worst. The house was by the Great Bitter Lake. On the gate the sentry had to stand perfectly still, as per Buckingham Palace, in front of a sentry box. That wasn't a big deal, but some nut in the hierarchy had the bright idea that all vehicles, both military and civilian, proceeding past on the road should be saluted. The reason given for this piece of idiocy was that there might be an officer in the vehicle. I suspect that a lot of Egyptian taxi and truck drivers drove past just to get a salute and, more seriously, a sentry standing still in full view was also a fine target for any terrorist who fancied taking a potshot at him. On the large installations it was impossible to observe the whole perimeter, so we had to rely on barbed wire with loads of empty tin cans tied on to rattle when disturbed. At Abu Sultan part of the perimeter was also protected by a minefield. But the Arabs were crafty: they would send a donkey or a dog through first to blow a path. They had to be quick, though, because the guard would soon be on the scene, and we had orders to shoot to kill if an intruder failed to stop and surrender.

I remember one night when I was commanding a four-man guard at the water filtration plant. From the road the plant was reached by a loose railway sleeper bridge spanning a water-filled ditch. The ditch emptied into the Sweet-Water Canal about 30 yards away, and beyond that, over a bridge, was a small village. A not very bright perimeter light struggled to illuminate the ditch bridge. I was sitting outside the guard tent enjoying the cool, flyless air, when I noticed from the corner of my eye one of the bridge planks rise up, turn, go along a bit, then descend into the ditch. 'Bloody hell,' I thought, 'the cheeky bastards!' There must have been at least two men in the ditch lifting the sleepers and then floating them along to be collected by others further down. I waited for the perimeter sentry to come round and then told him and the others in the tent what was happening. I made a plan. The sentry and I would wait by the gate and then, when one of the others turned off the perimeter light, we would dash out and try to catch the thieves. The plan worked, up to a point, but we weren't quick enough. The Arabs were out of the ditch before we could get anywhere near them and speeding off towards the Sweet-Water Canal. I shouted the official order in Arabic to stop, but they ignored it, splashed across and disappeared into the village. They avoided the canal bridge, knowing we would catch them. As it was we couldn't risk going into the canal, and we couldn't shoot in case we hit someone in the village. Also, it would have been a waste of time trying to find them among the houses. On the way back I saw that only one sleeper was missing, and that would have been halfway to the Red Sea by then.

We heard some fantastic stories about the thieving that went on. There was one tale about a soldier who was sitting in a parked truck at Port Said. He was waiting to pick up some blokes from a troopship. The soldier had the cab window down and was resting his arm on the door. Suddenly an Arab dashed from a crowd of onlookers and, with a long heavy knife, cut off the soldier's hand. The Arab then tore the soldier's wristwatch off the stump and, keeping hold of the hand, which had a gold ring on one finger, fled back into the crowd. An accomplished Canal Zone thief – in other words, all of them – could nick the blankets off your bed while you were sleeping in it. They would gently tickle the sleeping man until he reacted by turning over, then roll the bottom sheet and top blankets after him. Next step was to tickle the sleeper on the other side to make him roll back again. The thief would then carefully lift the bedding and slink off.

I learned to drive in Egypt, both tracked and ordinary vehicles, plus 350cc BSA motorbikes. Driving in Egypt then was an adventure in itself, especially on motorbikes. Out in the desert tracked vehicles were fine, but trucks and motorbikes were too easy to bog down in the many patches of soft sand, or else they came to grief in the treacherous, rocky wadis. Driving on the roads also had its hazards. They could vary in width or even disappear altogether quite quickly because of drifting sand which piled up into hummocky drifts.

Arab terrorists posed another problem. One of their favourite tricks was to stretch a taut length of almost invisible piano wire across the road at neck height, the idea being to decapitate a motorcyclist or someone in an open truck. Most of the British trucks had a length of angle iron welded on the front to cut through any such wire, but on a motorbike riders had to ride with their chins down near the handlebars and hope for the best.

There were a few perks to lift the routine, though. We didn't get a lot of time off in between training and guard duties, but now and again we had the chance to visit the village of Fayid, a few miles away on the shores of the Great Bitter Lake. In Fayid, or 'Gungeville' as I used to call it, there were several sleazy bar-restaurants and junk-filled trinket shops. I had my first camel steak at Fayid. It looked like an ill-treated T-bone but was surprisingly palatable. The Arab beer was something else, a concoction called Stella which tasted like liquid grass. After a night on the Stella I had to mow my tongue next morning! The cinema was surrounded by a high wire fence, intended as protection against Arab terrorists throwing grenades or other missiles. Quite often we would hear shots being fired while we were waiting in the queue. Some would be quite close, and there would be the sound of bullets whizzing overhead. There were many camps in the area, and most nights the guards and intruders would crack off a few rounds at each other. I remember one night our camp guard let loose a whole Sten SMG magazine (twenty-eight rounds) at an intruder and missed with every one. Fortunately, because of the Sten's short range, all the bullets hit the desert before they reached the next-door camp, which, if I recall correctly, was occupied by a battalion of Grenadier Guards. I don't think they would have taken kindly to the DLI carrying out a cull of their unit.

Our toilets were holes about 20 feet deep, over which huts with doorless cubicles were placed. They were absolutely black with flies. One way of keeping them at bay was to light a page of newspaper and chuck it down the hole before you perched. The smoke would do the job. One day, however, someone must have overdone the burning-paper trick. I happened to be nearby when there came a terrific whooshing noise and a huge cloud of smoke billowed from the door. This was followed rapidly by several blokes, running as fast as they could with their trousers still down by their knees. Apparently there had been a build-up of methane gas down the pit, and the burning paper had provided ignition. It hadn't been severe enough to burn any arses, but the fire brigade had to come and put it out!

Our CO, Major Jim Loveridge, was a good bloke. He had a pendulous lower lip and was known affectionately as 'Jimmy the Lip'. He was a great one for personal and weapons cleanliness on inspections, and we would get picked up for the smallest scrap of dirt anywhere. 'Pay attention to detail' was his maxim – a strict but fair bloke, and we all liked him.

After a few weeks the RAF kindly invited groups of us to fly over the Canal Zone in their Valetta transport aircraft. We were flown around for about an hour. It was my first time in an aeroplane. (Little did I realise it then, but I would be jumping from Valettas into hair-raising situations two years later when I joined the Parachute Regiment.) I must say the Zone looked, and smelled, a damned sight better from the sky than it did on the ground. The mud houses of the villages appeared picturesque in their higgledy-piggledy way, and the cultivated areas seemed quite neat, with the workers moving around like ants. The lakes and canals glinted silver in the sun, while far to the east lay the pinkish grey of the Sinai Desert. It was the turn of the Royal Navy next, when a party of sailors spent a week in our camp and a dozen or so DLI men had a glorious, refreshing week's trip on a frigate. We sailed on the Red Sea first, then up the Canal to the Bitter Lake. A screen was rigged up on deck to show films. It was a strange sensation to be watching a show and then glance to the side and see the water scudding past. We were treated well on board, with plenty of food and drink, including a daily tot of rum. As I drank my tot, I remembered that when I was a lad I had always wanted to be a sailor. But I realised then that it wouldn't have been the right choice, as life confined on a ship would not have been right for me. As far as seeing the world is concerned sailors see the ports and possibly some of the immediate surroundings, whereas in the Army we experienced not only the ports but most of that particular country as well, including their food and customs.

It was in Egypt that I received my first personal and near-fatal experience of terrorists. These dangerous fanatics were working for Nasser, whose aim was to grab total power in Egypt. He had his wish when, in April 1954, he took over the premiership from General Neguib. The terrorists, however, continued their activities, including the murder of British troops, until the British withdrawal from the Canal Zone in the mid-1950s. In the worst month around fourteen men were killed in terrorist actions. One day an Arab decided it was my turn. I had been to the dentist's, which was about a mile or so from camp, and was walking back along the verge of the road. I heard a lorry approaching from behind, but as I was off the road I didn't take much notice. Just before the lorry reached me, though, something made me turn round. Maybe it was the noise of the engine – it sounded too near. This sixth sense saved my life. As I looked round I was just in time to see the wing mirror of the truck coming straight at my head. I managed, in the split-second of realisation, to move slightly away. But not, unfortunately, far enough, because the mirror hit me just above the ear. It was a deliberate attempt to kill me; either that, or he didn't like the way I wore my beret, because that went flying! I was dazed by the blow and didn't get a chance to notice any licence number on the fast-disappearing vehicle. Arabic numerals were just squiggly lines to me, anyway. I was very lucky and the wound healed up quickly, but I have still got a lump to show for it just above my right ear.

Shortly after March 1954 a War Office (now Ministry of Defence, or MoD) letter appeared on the company noticeboard asking for volunteers to join the SAS Regiment. The SAS were operating in Malaya fighting CTs. I immediately went to the office to volunteer. Frankly I had had enough of Egypt and fancied a bit of action with the SAS. But the Sergeant Major had other ideas, barking, 'If we let all those go who volunteered, we wouldn't have anyone left!' Persuasively he continued, 'I know what's wrong. You are fed up with this place and want a change. So listen, in a month's time you can go home on leave for six weeks.' That sounded OK by me. I couldn't pass up a chance like that and would have plenty of time later to get into the SAS, I thought. Later this hunch was proved correct. But for now the Kenyan emergency, caused by a terrorist organisation calling itself the 'Mau Mau', had flared up. The Mau Mau were murdering people (mainly white farmers) in horrific fashion, and the terrorists' object, they said, was to be free from British rule. In the months before the SAS letter came a few of my comrades had asked for a transfer to a Light Infantry unit which was serving in Kenya but were turned down. Anyway, the Sergeant Major was as good as his word and organised home leave, and I was made up to Lance Corporal again. Flights to the UK for leave were available provided that participants paid their own fare, which was £51. The aircraft were ex-RAF wartime York transport planes, roughly converted to passenger use. The magic day came, and I duly reported to RAF Fayid to catch my flight. On board I had a seat in the bomb bay. The pilot was ex-RAF – I hoped he wouldn't get carried away daydreaming and order 'Bombs away!' Once airborne it was absolutely freezing, as heating had not been part of the conversion, so all the passengers had to wear their overcoats for the whole journey.

Back home in Jarrow I discovered that the family had moved to Howard Street. The house, or rather upstairs flat, overlooked St Bede's School, which I had attended so many years previously – though more off than on – in my youth. My mother had told me in a letter that they now had an indoor toilet *and* a bathroom. This was luxury indeed. I looked forward to having a good soak. After an eight-hour journey on the train from London I arrived home knackered but happy to be reunited with my family – and got my hot soak. The town of Jarrow hadn't changed a lot. There were still plenty of slums and wide, open spaces where the rubble had been cleared from bomb sites, and there were the remains of old houses partly demolished before the war. I had lost contact with my old school mates and so spent most of my leave wandering around on my own, visiting museums and cinemas in Newcastle and going to my old haunt of South Shields on the coast. Then, all too soon, it was time to return to action. I was ordered to report to a transit centre in London to await a flight to Egypt. The centre was in a disused tube station at Goodge Street, with the sleeping accommodation about 500 steps below. I wryly suspected that, with devious Army logic, the place was deliberately chosen in order to get the troops fit again after their brief but 'soft' leave.

Landing back in Egypt I found the heat, dust and flies were all waiting. It was a truly grotty place, but I didn't care. I now counted myself a professional soldier, willing to put up with any conditions provided that I was fairly treated by those in charge.

I was promoted to full Corporal, in charge of company transport. My job was to supervise crews and daily maintenance and make sure the vehicles were ready for action at all times. There was a bewildering array of vehicles – light tracked carriers, Morris one-tonners, American Stuart tanks minus the turrets, which were used for towing the unit's 17-pounder anti-tank guns, and the pre-Land Rover, the Austin Champ. The Champ was a new, four-wheel-drive Jeep-type vehicle, with a Rolls-Royce engine and a completely reversible gear box. By moving just one lever, the Champ could be driven from first to top gear in reverse. Some of my drivers actually tried this at speed, with predictable results.

One good perk came with my new job: I had a tent to myself. I slept alone with only racks of vehicle spares for company. No snorers to keep me awake, and no guards. It was paradise. I procured a stone water jar called a chatti. These jars are made of porous stone; when they are filled, the water seeps through the sides like sweat. This has the effect of keeping the water in the jar cool, especially in a breeze, which I had coming through my window from the Great Bitter Lake.

But one duty I was still stung for was that of Regimental Orderly Corporal. This consisted mainly of clearing the NAAFI bar at closing time. Most nights it was OK, but once this big bloke, a known troublemaker, threatened me with a bottle. I would have rather let him carry on drinking, but orders were orders. Part of my dress on duty was wearing a bayonet, and so when this guy came at me I reached behind and withdrew it halfway from the scabbard. No way was I going to let him bottle me. If he had moved in, I would have given him it in the guts without hesitation. He must have guessed what I had in mind, because he suddenly backed off. After that I watched my back when walking in camp, but bottle-brain didn't try anything again. Like most bullies, he was a coward. Soon afterwards, on a train to Suez, my famed sense of premonition came to my aid in a potentially lethal situation yet again.

About mid-March 1955 the second attempt to murder me happened. Our company was escorting a trainload of East African Pioneers to Suez, from where they were due to sail home. Our task was to guard against terrorist attack, plus to make sure the Pioneers didn't cause any trouble on the way. I was alone in a compartment at the end of the train and, as we rattled along, I was standing gazing from the window and singing away to myself. I don't know how I knew, but after a while I felt that I wasn't alone any more. It could have been a slight reflection of movement in the train window or a slight noise or something – I don't know to this day. I swung round. Advancing slowly towards me, hands outstretched as if to grab my neck, was a huge Arab. He was dressed in baggy trousers and a waistcoat, with a dirty fez on his head. His fierce eyes were filled with pure evil. Quickly raising my rifle and pointing it at his chest, I eased the safety catch off. There was already a round up the breech. The Arab stopped abruptly. If he had had any kind of weapon, I would have shot him immediately, but he seemed to be unarmed, just gazing down fiercely into the muzzle of my rifle. He dropped his hands and pretended he just wanted to talk. 'Hello, Tommy,' he said. 'All right?' 'Yes,' I replied, looking him in the eyes and still keeping him covered. After a few tense seconds his gaze wavered at last and, turning slowly, he left. I sat watching the door for the rest of the journey, my rifle ready across my knees, but neither he nor anyone else appeared. When we arrived at Suez I had a quick look around, but that particular Arab was nowhere to be seen. He had simply vanished into thin air. Afterwards, when telling my mates what had happened, I realised just how lucky I was. Half a second later in turning round and I would have had my chips. My dead body, minus rifle, would have been discovered later, cast out of the moving train. Similar attacks had killed many other unwary British troops.

Not long after this episode we were informed that the DLI was being sent home to the UK in May of that year. It was good news: we had by now all had a bellyful of the Canal Zone. A few days before our departure from the land of the Pharaohs the battalion put on a farewell parade, the salute being taken by the Commanding General. We had rehearsed well for this occasion, and on the big day everything went like clockwork. To finish off the parade we first marched past the General in columns of threes and then, in traditional Light Infantry style, we marched past in line at the double, our band and bugles playing 'The Keel Row', the lyrics of which commemorate the keel men of the River Tyne, hardy men who used to transport coal down the Tyne in barges by sail and oar. Like the DLI, the keel men were tough, a breed apart. Some of the local Arabs gathered to watch. What they saw were good British soldiers of high morale. Nobody was kicking us out of Egypt; we were withdrawing with dignity on the orders of our Government. Several days later we moved by train to Port Said. We sailed back, entering Britain in June 1955, and it was 'Welcome home, Tommy' once more. At journey's end, Barnard Castle in County Durham, the men were put into the same camp in which I had spent two happy weeks with the Army Cadets in 1944–5. Some local women from the Women's Institute had laid on a welcome-home party. After that it was back on leave to Jarrow for a month, where my family were just about to move house yet again, this time into a semi-detached house with all mod cons, including a front and back garden, lounge and dining-room.

After leave, the boys and I settled down to a dreary, humdrum existence in camp. Very little training was done, nobody seemed to care and it was fantastically boring. In the canteen the same ancient piano was still there on a stage in one corner. Wherever I went in the world with the Army, even when in the SAS, NAAFI pianos all seemed to sound the same to me – ghastly. They must have employed a piano tuner whose sole job was to travel the globe and mistune all NAAFI pianos in sight. This, I suspect, was part of a conspiracy with the Army top brass, who didn't want the troops to hang about in the canteen for too long, as if the char and wads (tea and sandwiches) were not deterrent enough!

Yet another demob day drew near, and the Sergeant Major tried to get me to stay on again. 'I'll make sure you're promoted to Sergeant,' he promised. He was a nice man and I liked him, but I couldn't face the prospect of life in that camp. So, in early November 1955, I went and collected another demob suit. But as I gazed into my reflection in the large mirror by the door at the demob suit centre, looking yet again, in raincoat and trilby hat, like Humphrey Bogart in a rather gaudy Tyneside re-run of *Casablanca*, I was proud of being a soldier. But I was torn two ways, as I was desperately disappointed with my lot. I was plainly unfulfilled as a professional soldier and was still seeking real adventure.

Little did I know that I was soon to swap my spivvy demob suit for a jump smock and the coveted red beret of the Paras and land slap-bang in the midst of yet another historic conflict – Suez.

Chapter 5

THE PARAS:
CYPRUS AND THE SUEZ CRISIS

Searching around Jarrow for suitable employment I found myself in a succession of jobs that I eventually could neither settle into nor find fulfilling, ranging from factory work to a building labourer. It was a familiar pattern. These lasted from several months to as little as ten minutes in one memorable case, when I stubbornly believed I knew a better way to spread earth on a grass verge than the foreman in a local road-widening scheme. But a comment from a colleague in a steel-tube factory where I was relatively happy with my job on crane work crystallised my thoughts. One day one of my new mates said thoughtfully, 'You look like us now, Franky. When you first started you looked suntanned and healthy. Now you're pasty-faced with bags under your eyes, just like the rest!' An argument with the foreman followed about some safety aspect of the job which also ended in me collecting my cards. Next day I went to a textile factory about a mile from home and was offered a job starting the following afternoon on the two–ten shift. At five minutes to two I was waiting just inside the factory. I watched the six–two shift people still hard at it, pushing rolls of textile along on trolleys. They looked just like zombies to me. I thought, 'No, that's not for me. I'm off.' I went straight into the office and told the foreman, who didn't seem a bit surprised. Finally I had had enough of trying to fit in with civilian life. I had crossed my Tyneside jobs Rubicon for the last time.

Outside the factory gates I caught the bus to Newcastle, went straight into the Army Recruiting Office, gave them the details of my former service and expressed my fervent wish to serve Her Majesty the Queen as a soldier in the Parachute Regiment. While waiting for the decision I followed my usual routine of throwing myself into intense physical exercise, with lots of biking and route-march-type walking. I was fit and ready once more. Eventually a letter came from Army Records telling me I had been accepted and to report to Newcastle for a medical, which I passed. I then received instructions to report to the infamous Parachute Regiment P course at the selection centre at Aldershot.

On the day I left I said my goodbyes to the family yet again. Mother cried and didn't want me to go, but she realised that I would be happy. The old man just thought I was barmy. Arriving at the camp in Aldershot along with other trainee Paras I was issued with personal kit plus bedding and told that the P course would be starting the next morning. It was obvious we weren't going to be kept hanging about. As I settled down in bed that night I said quietly to myself, 'Well, here goes, shit or bust.' I had made a pact with myself that if I failed, I was going to desert and head for the Irish Republic, where I hoped it would be possible to get a job on the land or on the fishing boats. I was 27. It was early May 1956.

Two different groups of men were trying to get into the Parachute Regiment: direct enlistments from Civvy Street, who had to be trained as soldiers first; and ready-trained personnel from other units – infantry, gunners, REME staff, medical corps and so on who wanted to transfer. I, naturally, was in the latter group. Parachute training would follow for those who passed the P course, after which they would be posted into their particular unit within the brigade, infantrymen being sent to one of the battalions. The 16th Parachute Brigade, as it was then, was self-contained. It had all its own supporting units, with most of their equipment either air transportable or parachutable. About sixty of us paraded that first morning dressed in denims, boots and gaiters and steel parachute helmets with a number on the front and back. I was number eleven (legs). I remember hoping with some conviction that my little legs would last. We were split into groups, each with an instructor. Staff Sergeant Mike Reilly, Army Physical Training Corps, was in charge of my group. I was to meet Mike again some years later when I was in the SAS. He didn't waste any time. 'Right turn, double march', and off we went to the training area. This consisted of thousands of acres of heath and scrubland churned up into mud and loose stones by tanks, and with some deceptively low but really heart-breaking hills. Within the training area, also, was a large, knacker-splitting assault course. In between sessions on the tank tracks we did agility training in the gym by jumping over the horse and swinging on ropes and other back-breaking exercises. In the gym the dress was plimsolls and no helmets – not for our comfort, but just because they didn't want the gym floor damaged! Most afternoons were taken up on the assault course, nice and slow first time round, then full speed. We swung on ropes and clambered over walls, nets and ramparts with a jump at the end, and everywhere was thick, sticky mud. There was a high, horrific-looking tower made of scaffold poles and planks which we didn't use the first day, but it certainly gave us something to think about. I was a bit stiff-jointed in bed that night, although not too bad. My self-imposed fitness training was paying off. Some of the other lads were in a bad state, though, with blisters everywhere and seized-up muscles. Next morning the ranks had thinned somewhat, as several of the blokes had decided it wasn't for them and departed.

The runs became longer and the jumps higher. I liked it when we had to swing on a rope from a platform and let go to land on a semi-vertical net, which we then had to scramble up and over. One poor lad couldn't get it right: he kept dropping off the rope too soon and thumping into the ground. He looked the perfect type for a paratrooper, broad in the shoulder, narrow at the hip, handsome and muscular, but he was uncoordinated. He left that afternoon. This was a good thing too, because from there we progressed to the tower, where one of the most frightening tasks took place about 30 feet up, when we had to jump from one plank end onto another over a 6ft gap. By the end of the first week my stiffness had gone, I could run and hardly get out of breath, and I was actually enjoying it. In between the recruits were ravenous after their testing exertions. We were well fed in the cookhouse but still hungry enough for a visit to the canteen at night. We used to go to the Smith Dorrien canteen, not the NAAFI, where the food and especially the tea were of a much superior quality. (Smith Dorrien had been a general in the Boer War.) During the second week we had a lot of confidence tests and were more closely observed as individuals. 'Move your arse, number eleven, I'm watching you!'

There was a session in the swimming baths where, for starters, we had to jump naked from the high-diving platform. I had never been higher than the side of a swimming pool, and for me it was terrifying. But worse was to come when we had to swing from one high-diving platform on a rope and transfer, Tarzan-like, onto another rope which was swung towards us from a platform on the other side. When it was my turn I just managed to grab the other rope with one hand, but it wasn't a very good grip and I could only hang there holding onto each rope, legs splayed wide. Don't forget we were all naked – what a sight! Eventually I let go and plunged into the water, and water, from that height, is quite hard, especially upon exposed bollocks!

On the second from last day the recruits were put through the 'log race' test. This consisted of each team having to carry half a telegraph pole in a certain time around a set route on the tank tracks. Toggle ropes were used to carry the pole between the team members, with four men on each side. The route selected covered the most awkward ground, with a particularly difficult hill about halfway round. I was one of the rear pair, and on the way my companion tripped and got dragged along a fair distance, being cut and bruised before he found his feet again. It was all strain and pain, but the instructor merely heaped more curses upon our heads, urging us to greater and greater lung-bursting efforts. I was able to switch off a bit by thinking of something else. Looking down at the pole from the rear I felt it reminded me of the stagecoaches in western films when the hero, usually John Wayne, had to stop the panicking horses by jumping from the stagecoach seat onto a bar that hung between the animals. John then had to work his way along the bar until he could mount one of the leaders and pull his head up to stop him. I wondered what the instructor would say if I suddenly leaped onto the pole, worked my way along to the front bloke, jumped on his back and pulled his head up! I reckon I would have been heading for the Irish ferry the next day.

On the very top of the tower, which was about 50 feet high, there were two horizontal scaffold poles about 3 feet apart. As a confidence test each man had to climb to the top and stand upright with one foot on each pole. Then, staring straight ahead, which made balancing extremely difficult because there was no focus point for the eyes, he had to shout out his number, rank and name loud enough to be heard on the ground. If anyone looked down or failed to yell loud enough, they had to do it again. A couple of the lads couldn't manage that one and left that day.

The final physical test consisted of one-minute boxing matches between equal-sized pairs. This was called 'milling', and the idea was for the recruits to get stuck into each other as hard as they could go. The only rule was no low hitting. Neither I nor the other lad were any use at boxing, so when it came to our turn it was just a wild flurry of blows. The instructor shouted, 'Come on, you're like a couple of bluddy schoolgirls!' My opponent then managed to loosen one of my teeth, and I countered with a severe right to his left elbow. I was just lining one up on his nose when the bell went. Our efforts must have been OK, because we both passed. The final confidence test took place in the classroom, when each man had to stand on a stage and give a five-minute talk on any subject. I gave a lecture on sweeping brushes.

I had, since joining the Army, become something of an expert in these, having used a wide variety of brushes in many parts of the world – from the pathetic, broken-shafted and almost hairless models used in the sandy tents in Egypt, to the mighty brooms of Aldershot, resplendent with metal scrapers and hairs on them like a porcupine. Next day the group gathered in the classroom – about twenty men fewer than when we had started – to hear the course results. Each man's rank and name was called followed by 'Pass' or 'Fail'. By the time half the names had been called I was mentally buying my ferry ticket to Ireland, but then, after my name was called, I heard the magic word: 'Pass.'

After a weekend leave, which I spent in London, my group was packed off to RAF Abingdon near Oxford for a month-long parachute course. The motto of the parachute school is 'Knowledge dispels fear'. This proved true in my case, because the two-week pre-jump ground training which we were given instilled perfect confidence. Of all the RAF personnel whom I have encountered the Parachute Jump Instructors (PJI) were by far the best. They were true professionals, and nice blokes with it. The ground training took place in a massive hangar filled with aircraft mock-ups, parachute harnesses hanging from the roof, ramps to jump off and coconut matting covering the floor. After we had been split into smaller groups the first thing we were taught was how to adopt the parachuting position: 'The only one', according to our instructor, 'that is not in the Kama Sutra.' In the parachuting position, which has to be adopted well before landing, the feet and knees should be together, with feet parallel to the ground and knees bent, arms up with elbows in, and hands grasping the two front parachute lift webs, or risers. The head should be down, eyes scanning the ground. The basic reason for this position is that it minimises the chance of being injured when landing. In addition it makes it easier for the parachutist to perform a proper parachute roll on landing, which also minimises the risk of injury. Before we fitted a parachute on for the first time our instructor informed us that other, and some would say much more serious, injuries could be caused by a badly fitted harness. The leg straps came from the rear up under the crotch to fasten at the front. 'Make damned sure', the PJI warned in a grim tone, 'that you pull the family jewels well to the front and out of harm's way *before* adjusting your leg straps, otherwise you could be a eunuch by the time you reach the deck!' At the end of two weeks swinging in harnesses and landing and rolling on mats the squad was covered in new sores and blisters and more than ready to be airborne. We were scheduled to carry out eight descents, including one at night and two with equipment, with personal kit and weapon in a special container attached to the front of the harness. The equipment could be lowered on a 5m rope during descent to allow it to hit the ground first.

On the day we did all this for real the first two actual jumps were to be from a cage slung underneath a huge barrage balloon parked on the airfield at RAF Abingdon. I remember it was a beautiful, still and cloudless summer evening. The toilets were full right to the last minute. There is always a strong and frequent urge to pee just before a jump. 'Nervous pisses' they're called in the trade. It's natural – the body's way of preparing for action. A last-minute briefing and the first four men boarded the cage. I was with the next four. Up went the balloon, its anchor wire being let out from a big reel on a truck. At 800 feet, which was jumping height, it stopped. After a while we heard the faint sound of the PJI shouting, 'Go!' A small figure fell from the cage, and his canopy developed. Another three bodies came out and drifted away. Then we heard the ominous sound of the cable being wound in. Our turn was next. We filed into the cage. Last in, first out – that was me. Before we left the ground the PJI made sure that our static lines, which pulled the parachute out of its bag as you fell away, were fixed to the strong point above the cage. Up we went. It was a weird sensation, hanging silently beneath the big silver balloon. Still rotating slightly, the cage suddenly jerked to a halt. The PJI looked at us and grinned. 'Look,' he said. 'There's my house down there.' We all gazed hesitantly over the side. There were indeed a few houses, microscopically small, beneath us. I met the eyes of the bloke next to me. His face looked like a plate of porridge that had been standing for about two weeks. *Clang* went the safety bar when the PJI dropped it to clear the doorway for jumping. My guts tightened up another few notches. 'OK,' said the PJI, calm as you like. 'Number one, are you ready?' 'Yes,' I squeaked, when reason was telling me to say *no!* 'Stand in the door,' came the order. This is when all the training paid off. I moved immediately into the proper exit position, one hand on top of my reserve, the other on the edge of the door ready to push off and one foot forward on the door sill. 'Go!' – I went. My boots came up right in front of my face and then disappeared down again. There were a few small jerks to my shoulders and then I was floating free. I should have looked up to check my canopy was developing, but I had been so fascinated by the sight of my boots coming up that I had quite forgotten. I raised my eyes. There it was, blossoming nicely and no twisted rigging lines to kick out of.

I carried out the drill of all-round observation, essential when jumping from aircraft, as there could be many other bodies floating near to be steered away from. Then, at about 200 feet, I adopted the parachuting position and assessed my drift. Left, I reckoned, so I pulled down on the two right lift webs. Doing that made the canopy become distorted, and air spilled out of the left side, countering the drift. Just before landing I let go of the lift webs and performed what I believed to be a textbook side left roll on the ground. The chief instructor summed it up somewhat differently. 'Like a sack of bluddy shit,' he said with feeling. Anyway, I was on cloud nine. After that first jump we all wanted to go straight back up and do it again. But we had to wait our turn, and by that time the full terror of it had sunk in. However, on the second jump I was more aware and was actually praised for a 'reasonable' back right landing. Wahoo!

Next the squad completed their descents from aircraft onto the drop zone (DZ) at RAF Weston on the Green, just north of Oxford. The aircraft used were two-engine Valetta 'Flying Pigs' and four-engine Hastings. Both were noisy and uncomfortable, especially the Valetta. First time up in an aircraft and one man on the course refused to jump. I found this strange, as jumps from the balloon were all so silent and cold-blooded, whereas from an aircraft it was all noise, hustle and bustle, without time to look at the ground. At first the group regarded the man who had refused with contempt, but later, as they progressed and each was tested further, they realised that everyone has their own bravery threshold and that this 'poor sod' had merely reached his. In my opinion there is no such thing as conscious fearlessness. I believe that before you can be brave you first have to be capable of being scared, and that only idiots are fearless.

On the last day of the course the successful group paraded outside the training hangar to be presented with their Parachutists' wings and red berets. All of us in the squad were immensely proud and pleased, and I had another cause for celebration – being a Parachutist meant an extra few quid a week to top up my Army pay packet, and that would come in very handy indeed. It was now the end of June 1956.

Within three weeks of leaving Abingdon most of the recruits had returned to Aldershot, staying at AFD, the Airborne Forces Depot. We had some leave and then were kitted out for service in the Middle East, complete with inoculations against all known diseases. After that we boarded the troopship *Nevasa*, bound for Cyprus. Progress was via the Bay of Biscay and down the coasts of Spain and Portugal, with a day's shore leave in Gibraltar and another stop at Malta. In Cyprus we newly fledged Paras were told we would be taking part in operations against EOKA, the infamous Greek Cypriot terrorist organisation. After we disembarked at Famagusta a truck ride along the (to me) familiar road to Nicosia brought the troops to the Parachute Brigade camps. I noted that among the huge sprawl of tents and Nissen huts was the original Waneskeep camp where I had been with the OBLI. Because of my previous experience in action I was posted to 1 Para mortar platoon, which, I was pleased to discover, was 99 per cent made up of real genuine blokes, about two-thirds of them National Servicemen. The exception was one of the sergeants, who was known irreverently as 'Herman the German'. When I met him the dislike was immediate and mutual. In the Paras the men were then issued with '44 pattern' webbing kit, exactly the same as issued in Korea, including the familiar thick rubber-soled CWW boots which, although an improvement on leather and studs, were still very clumsy, especially on rocks. However, we had a new type of windproof trousers which kept the wind out well, even though they were far too baggy and had to be taped down for silent movement at night. Personal weapons were the familiar No. 4 .303 Lee Enfield bolt-action rifle and the 9mm Sten SMG. The No. 4 rifle was reliable and accurate, but the best thing that could be said about the Sten was that it was better than nothing. Stens were notoriously prone to stoppages and were very inaccurate beyond 20 yards range. At that time the safety catches on Stens were either non-existent or too easy to be accidentally released. A good illustration of this was when one of the soldiers clambering into the cab of a truck banged the butt of his Sten on the seat. Because the safety catch had slipped off the sudden jolt caused the working parts to go back, feed a round up the breech on return and, because the weapon was on automatic, fire off thirteen rounds, all of which hit another soldier already in the cab, killing him. Talk about unlucky for some.

My first two months in Cyprus were spent taking part in anti-EOKA operations, mainly in the mountainous country to the north of Nicosia. EOKA was a Greek Cypriot organisation devoted to the cause of 'Enosis'; that is, independence from Britain and union with Greece. At that time EOKA had two main leaders, Bishop Makarios of the Greek Orthodox Church, who many saw as EOKA's spiritual and political head, and 'General' George Grivas, who could be described as EOKA's military chief. In mid-1956 Makarios was in exile in the Seychelle Islands. Grivas had up until then eluded capture. The Turkish Cypriots, who made up about one-quarter of the island's population, were opposed to union with Greece. EOKA used terrorist techniques to boost their claims, including murder – usually of unarmed civilians and British service personnel – and intimidation. EOKA warriors rarely picked a fight with anyone who could fight back, such as a truckful of Paras travelling along, because we always had the canopies rolled up and our personal arms poking out over the sides ready.

As I lay in bed, the night before my first patrol, I felt happy and excited: at last, a bit of action! I knew it would be hard work, both physically and mentally, but I was looking forward to it. Searching for EOKA terrorists on the rugged, tree-clad slopes of the Kyrenian Mountains north of Nicosia was extremely arduous and time-consuming work. Besides tramping around in open country we also carried out house searches. First, a cordon would be thrown around a village to prevent any suspects escaping; then the search parties went in. When a house search was completed we had to obtain the resident's signature on a chit to say that nothing was damaged or stolen. I still have a page of signed chits in my photograph album. There was humour, frustration and tragedy on these operations. I remember once doing a metal detector sweep in a Greek church: EOKA sometimes hid weapons and explosives even under church floors. While I was working away the church door opened and in strode the General Officer Commanding Cyprus, General Harding himself, accompanied by several staff officers. They all stopped and watched. Just then I heard a signal in my headset. There was something under a flagstone right next to the General's feet. 'Bloody hell,' I thought. 'I've made a find and the General's watching!' With the help of the lad working with me I prised up the flagstone. Whatever we had expected to find – pistols, grenades or the like – bore no resemblance to what was actually there. Lying on the dirt in solitary splendour was a large, rusty, bent nail! Hurriedly dropping the flagstone down again before the General could see what was underneath we carried on sweeping.

One pitch-black night my platoon was in an ambush position on a mountain track. The troops were very keyed up, because enemy movement was expected. At first all was still and silent. Then, faintly to begin with, but definitely getting closer, we heard the sound of footsteps. Thumbs moved to safety catches and eyes strained for any hint of movement. I was one of those closest and so knew that we would have to let whoever it was get past me at least before starting to shoot. I waited, breathing silently through my open mouth, adrenalin pumping. A dark shape approached, feet scrabbling on the stony track. My finger slowly tightened around the trigger. The Paras had been given orders to 'shoot to kill', and a dusk-to-dawn curfew was in operation, so any movement meant enemy action. The figure was now level with the tense and waiting Paras when suddenly I saw a huge head with a long jaw and two big pointed ears on top. A bloody donkey! Those village donkeys knew their way home day or night; but we had to let it go through, as there could have been terrorists following with the animal in front to give warning of an ambush. If that was the case, then it worked, because someone in the platoon laughed and the donkey did a runner, braying like mad. But tragedy struck on another night patrol. Another ambush was in place, with other platoons in positions nearby. Suddenly there came a terrific burst of firing from one of the other ambushes, followed by some shouting and then silence. It wasn't until the next morning that our platoon found out what had happened. Apparently a patrol from another Para unit had accidentally blundered into one of their own ambushes and been shot up, several being killed and wounded. Someone had boobed big-time, but the lower ranks were never told who was responsible.

Each evening during operations, which usually lasted a week or so, the Paras met up with our platoon truck, which carried ammunition, extra food and water, plus small petrol cookers and the troops' sleeping bags. The latter were massive contraptions of wartime vintage, much too bulky to carry around. After a meal it was off to an ambush position or, on rare occasions, heads down for a kip. As always, ever the appreciator of the scenic outdoors, I enjoyed a night's sleep among the trees, where I could make a nice soft bed of pine needles and gaze at the stars. During day patrols we carried enough food to last the day and brewed tea in old biscuit tins on wood fires. It was very beautiful up in the Kyrenian Mountains, and on our brew stops I loved to sit under the shade of the pines with my mug of tea and listen to the silence. It sounds corny, but it used to get to me. If we were on the northern slopes there was frequently a fantastic view of the coast with the blue sea beyond. The idyll was soon to be shattered, however, by a historic military campaign which reverberates with controversy and ignominy to this very day.

While our Para force was engaged in our deadly campaign against EOKA, potentially world-shattering events were taking place not all that far away in the Middle East. In June 1956 President Nasser of Egypt had nationalised the Suez Canal, effectively putting it under his own control. Besides raking in all the fees of passage from international shipping, Nasser also had the final say on who used the waterway. It is widely accepted that Russia was the covert driving force behind Nasser's move. The Communist regime had already armed Egypt and dearly wanted to have a major say in Canal operations. Western European countries' short-cut to the Gulf for oil and for trade to the Far East was severely curtailed, forcing shipping to go via South Africa – not only a longer route, but also a far more dangerous one in time of war. Something just had to give. The great conspiracy theory at the time was that Israel would attack Egypt through the Sinai Desert, so giving Britain and France the excuse to invade Egypt, ostensibly to stop the Israeli attack but in reality to reoccupy the Canal Zone.

Whatever the outcome, 16 Para Brigade and other key British combat units were ordered to start intensive training. To start with, 1 and 3 Para were airlifted back to the UK for urgent extra parachute training. When we arrived back in Cyprus, where we still carried out anti-EOKA terrorist ops, training for the invasion of Suez began in earnest. We trained on the flat, dusty plains surrounding our camp area, which was most like the terrain we expected to be fighting over in Egypt. It was extremely hard work. We carried the mortars on our backs all the time because we had to assume that we would be parachuting in and might not have any, or not enough, vehicles. To give a sense of realism some of the exercises started from a DZ. We couldn't do actual jumps, so we had to leap off trucks moving over the DZ, just like the SAS used to in the Western Desert in 1941 against Rommel. On one memorable occasion, though, when trucks weren't available, the battalion travelled in civilian buses. Arriving on the DZ the drivers were ordered to take their buses over in formation like a flight of aircraft. Then, one after the other, we jumped out of the bus door, letting our kit go first to the extent of the rope to which it was secured and performing a parachute landing roll. The bus drivers must have thought we were mad! On those exercises we suffered severely from fatigue and thirst. No matter how much water we carried it was never enough. But just before the Suez op started I remember looking at the lads of our platoon and company, and what I saw was a bunch of tough, hard characters who would, I was sure, give a damned good account of themselves. In camp the rumours flew thick and fast about where and when we'd be going and what we'd be doing when we got there. During a visit to the camp loos, nicknamed 'Oasis', one day I heard a bloke saying he had got the true gen. 'We'll be dropping on Cairo first, to get Nasser,' he declared.

Most nights during the second half of October 1956, RAF bombers from the nearby base flew over the Paras' camp on their way to strike at Egyptian airfields and other targets to prepare the way for the main assault by sea and airborne forces. By this time also the French Paras, including the Foreign Legion airborne, were in Cyprus. These were highly experienced troops – hot action in Vietnam and Algeria had seen to that. By the end of October my brigade was packed and ready to go. It was then, to our great disappointment, that we were told that only 3 Para, including some Guards Para Company Pathfinders, would be dropping in by parachute. Both 1 and 2 Para would be going by sea. No reason was given for this decision, but it appeared that the proposed operational area was too small for more than one battalion group to manoeuvre in comfortably at a time. The British troops did not know it then, but the Israeli Army had already started its attack over the Sinai Desert. On 3 November 1 Para boarded tank landing craft at Famagusta. At this stage everybody in the world knew that we were about to invade Egypt. Reporters and TV crews swarmed around. My mother told me later that she had recognised me on one of the barges ferrying us out to the landing craft. How she singled me out from all the other red berets I don't know, but she did. However, off we sailed upon the deep blue sea, spending the next few days meeting up with other ships from Malta and forming a convoy.

In the early morning of 6 November our landing craft was slowly approaching Port Said with only about half a mile to go. There was a huge pall of black smoke hanging ominously over the city. The day before, 3 Para had dropped at El Gamal airfield just outside Port Said, and Royal Marine Commandos had landed on the beach near the harbour. At the same time French Paras had landed in the Port Fuad area on the other side of the harbour. On the way in we were watching some helicopters buzzing to and fro between ships and shore. Suddenly one of the helis flopped into the sea. It floated all right for a while but then began to sink rapidly. A few heads were clearly bobbing around the wreck. There was nothing we could do except watch helplessly. Eventually a small dinghy came screaming out from the shore and picked up the survivors. Our landing craft nosed into the quayside and lowered the bow ramp. Troops doubled out first, followed by trucks packed with spare ammunition, including mortar bombs. The Marines had already cleared the immediate area of enemy, so all we had to do was form up and start inland. Our objective was the west end of Port Said, towards El Gamal airfield, where 3 Para were engaged in a fierce battle. As well as our personal kit and weapons, we also carried the mortars. I, as a No. 1, had a baseplate, sights and aiming posts. My personal weapon was a Sten SMG. The all-up weight was in excess of 100lb. Plodding along we had the sea to our right, with the Marines occupying the buildings to our left. There was quite a lot of small arms fire going on in the city, and we could hear rounds whizzing overhead. Most of the buildings and beach huts along the shore had been badly damaged, and there was a lot of debris lying around.

Reaching our designated area we dug in on the beach and waited. We dug quickly, and a good job too, because just as we finished one of the ammunition trucks parked nearby was hit and caught fire. Bullets started going off with the heat and flew in all directions for about an hour. I thought that the Egyptians by this time would have started throwing some mortar and shellfire at us, or maybe even an air strike, but nothing happened. We didn't know it then, but the RAF had succeeded in destroying the Egyptian planes on the airfields, and their ground forces were in a state of utter confusion. A newspaper reporter suddenly appeared on the scene and started asking silly questions. He looked a bit of a berk to me and was being very sarcastic about our role in the operation. After a short while someone told him in no uncertain terms to 'Fuck off'. This he proceeded to do, and we didn't see him again. We were unaware then, but Liberals, Labour and assorted Lefties back home were busy denouncing the Tory Government over the invasion. That reporter was obviously one of the detractors who the troops came to believe were stabbing us in the back. As stated, many Lefties, some of whom were in the Labour Party, would have dearly loved to see the insidious tentacles of Communism spread into the Middle East. Fortunately Communist Russia had other things on its mind just then, as the Hungarian uprising had not long started and was seriously diverting its attention.

Even though on the first night word was passed that a ceasefire had been negotiated we remained in our positions for another two days, mortars mounted and ready for action. Anyway, the message hadn't got through to some, because there was still quite a bit of sniper fire going on. During a slack period I had a quick look around the streets in from the beach. The area was known as 'Shanty Town', with lots of small wooden huts, some of them on stilts because of the soft and frequently flooded ground. Everything was smashed to bits. I saw a tearful old woman sitting in what remained of her wrecked house. There wasn't a lot I could do except give her some water and a bar of chocolate. I went along to where the Marines were and had a chat with some of them. Everywhere was shell and bullet holes. The Commando lads must have had quite a battle when they came ashore. While I was there I spotted a familiar face: it belonged to a bloke whom I had known in the DLI called Hooper (I think that's what his name was). He was a tracked-vehicle driver in the anti-tank platoon. We talked for a while. He had been seconded to the Marines, as they were short of track drivers. He was a nice, unassuming little man, and there he was, a 'nobody' you could say, just doing his job and taking part in a historic event. He was undoubtedly one of many of our unsung heroes. When I returned to the platoon area the latest gen was that ceasefire talks were in progress. But talking isn't the same as ceasing, so just in case the war flared up again 1 Para was being withdrawn and sent back to Cyprus, where we would prepare for a possible parachute drop further down the Canal.

The British Paras also learned that the American President, Ike Eisenhower, had threatened to intervene in the dispute by using the power of the US 6th Fleet, which was then cruising in the Mediterranean. The Americans were desperate to avoid major conflict in the Middle East, which would not only disrupt vital oil supplies but possibly stir up a superpower confrontation of cataclysmic proportions with Russia.

Back in Cyprus, after a two-day journey on an aircraft carrier, we Paras immediately set to and began preparing for the possible drop further down the Suez Canal. We were on two hours stand-by to move. However, as the peace talks dragged interminably on and on, it became obvious to me and my comrades that we would not be going back on the offensive. The situation became more and more confused as everyone and his uncle shoved their noses in, including the UN. The British and French finally pulled out, leaving Nasser with a useless Canal, completely blocked with wrecked and abandoned ships. Later on it was the Royal Navy that did most of the clearing up, ironically. And while we had been popping over to visit friend Nasser, the 'heroes' of EOKA had also been busy. An Army ambulance had been shot at on its way through a village on the Kyrenian Mountains, and 1 and 2 Para were ordered to carry out a cordon and search in that village. The operation had to be kept secret, so we loaded up our trucks with mortars and equipment as if we were going on an exercise. Travelling up into the Kyrenian range in daylight we halted when we were in line with the target area, but on the opposite side of the mountains. There we left all surplus kit behind with a guard. Under cover of darkness we went on without lights over the narrow, winding roads. I was pleased that I couldn't see anything in the back of the truck, as those roads were bad enough in daytime, never mind at night. Once a cordon was in position, the next task was to round up all the men and hold them in a secure area in a fenced-off orchard and then begin the search in groups of four. I commanded one of the groups as Lance Corporal. I found some letters in one house signed by 'Dighenis', a name used by Grivas. They were literally all Greek to us, of course, so I handed them over to the Cypriot police. Several known terrorists hiding in an underground shelter were found by another group. These people were held in a separate compound for interrogation. Our platoon was resting near there after the search, and we watched the proceedings with interest. The EOKA men were handcuffed between the legs. It's very difficult to run or even walk in that position, believe me. To make matters worse, they had big square biscuit tins jammed on their heads, and every now and then a Cypriot policeman would come along and bang them with his truncheon. It was brutal, yes, and we never learned whether or not it had the desired result of softening up the terrorists. But I personally did not have much sympathy with any of them. Those people were either murderers themselves or were shielding others who were murderers. After a few more cordon and search ops, during one of which we handed over the reins to a Guards battalion, we returned to camp, spent a week packing up, and then 1 and 3 Para were flown back to the UK.

We arrived in Aldershot just in time to go on an extended Christmas leave. It had been, for me at least, a very eventful period. It was tense and, frankly, bloody hard work. But I had not let the side down and had really enjoyed it. These were exactly the sort of active operations for which I had joined the Paras.

Chapter 6

THE SAS: THE IRRESISTIBLE CALL OF BRITAIN'S FINEST

Back in Britain after the rigours of Suez and Cyprus I savoured a satisfying, relaxing leave and a wonderful chance to see my family again. One of my finest pleasures on leave was to have a long lie-in, which was especially acceptable in the winter months, but I also liked to wake up early and listen to the evocative sound of fog horns on the Tyne and the distinctive clomp of boots going down the street as hundreds of people set off for work at the crack of dawn. Drifting back to sleep I would not wake again until the gentle sounds of *Housewives' Choice* on the Light Programme of the BBC filtered through to me from downstairs.

Reading the newspapers I saw, like millions of others, that the political repercussions of the controversial Suez operation were still rumbling on unabated. Not only that, but a shortage of oil, caused mainly by tankers not being able to get through the Suez Canal, was starting to be felt. Like thousands of other British and Allied soldiers, sailors and airmen who had risked their lives in the massive operation I could not avoid feeling betrayed. As ordered, we had grabbed the objective, only to be let down by international interference and the dithering of faint-hearted politicians at home. There were many snide remarks made by some Liberal and Labour politicians to the effect that Suez was 'a complete fiasco'. It may not have been the wisest of political moves, but I can assure anyone who has any doubts that the military aspect of this operation was, in my humble opinion, anything but a fiasco. The troops and servicemen involved would wholeheartedly agree. There were some shortages of transport and equipment, but our forces overcame these in fine style. The RAF attacks were completely effective in grounding the Egyptian air force, and RAF Transport Command was 100 per cent effective with the aircraft they had available in the airlift of 3 Para group to the invasion DZ, where the paratroopers were brilliantly successful in their battle for El Gamal airfield. The Royal Marine Commandos landed with great *élan* on the beaches of Port Said, swept all opposition aside and gained their objectives swiftly, as per plan. The 2nd Para Battalion moved down the Canal road after landing in the harbour and completed their set tasks bang on time. As already described, 1 Para moved smartly into its allotted positions and was more than ready to support 3 Para or exploit elsewhere. The Royal Navy, as usual, showed every other navy in the world how this sort of operation should be done. No one could be faulted. However, many people saw only too clearly that no military force in the world can be effective if it does not have the backing of the politicians in control at home, and, as related, this was unceremoniously whipped away at the most crucial point. Afterwards it was not up to the military personnel involved to reason why – there was no point in any event, as we had had absolutely no input in the decision at the time. The important thing now, as always, in the aftermath of huge events beyond the control of stalwart soldiers like those involved was to rest, recuperate, shrug the shoulders and carry on. After leave I did just that and was promoted to a two-bar, fire-eating, full Corporal and sent to the School of Infantry Heavy Weapons Wing at Netheravon on Salisbury Plain to attend a mortar instructor's course.

On the course participants were split into syndicates and taken through teaching techniques, after which we then had to teach the lessons to others. The training progressed to mortar fire control, first in the classroom and then on the nearby ranges using live ammunition. After my extensive experience with mortars I enjoyed the course and did well, passing with a B plus, mainly due to the excellent instruction which the group received from our syndicate leader Staff Sergeant Dennis Rhodes.

At the end of the course we were all interviewed by the School's OC and given our grades. I was told I would have received an A grade, which would have qualified me as an instructor at the School, but my teaching technique was let down by having too low a voice, my typical lilting Geordie brogue being at times hard to understand by others. This decision was to have far-reaching consequences, as we shall soon see, for instead of occupying an unspectacular but vital post in mortar training I was to be propelled in an entirely different direction, joining the SAS Regiment and becoming, so I am told, one of the elite Special Force unit's better-known characters and a veteran of some of the regiment's fiercest actions. Meanwhile back in

Aldershot the Paras' training year was back in full stride. In the spring the battalion carried out an exercise in Cornwall, starting with a night parachute drop on Bodmin Moor. I had my softest landing ever, sinking up to my knees in an oozing black bog. From there the Paras had to capture a fictitious 'mad scientist' who was in possession of a jerrycan of radioactive 'heavy water' and take him and his water across country to rendezvous with a helicopter on a cliff near Newquay. On the way we were constantly being ambushed by 'enemy' forces. These encounters usually involved a lot of bangs, shouting and yelling, all taking place during the night. This endeared us to the local population no end. In fact they enjoyed it so much that they implored us *not* to come again. The reason, they said, was that they had laughed themselves sick at our antics at times, and they were scared in case they injured their stomachs or something! To be honest I was getting more than a little bored with this play-acting at being soldiers and was beginning to long for some real action once again.

Parachute training continued apace, however, including conversion to a new type of aircraft called the Beverley. This was a huge, four-propeller-engined job, with the wings over the top. The Beverley had an upstairs compartment with a boom sticking out at the back; on the underside of it was a hole for parachutists to jump out from. The downstairs part could be used either to house parachutists or for carrying and dropping heavy cargo. There were two side doors and two huge doors at the rear end with a vehicle ramp. Support Company spent a few days at RAF Watchfield near Swindon, a disused airfield where an Air Despatch Unit did their training. There they learned how to rig their platoon trucks onto heavy-drop platforms for dropping from the Beverley. The trucks, which could be fully loaded for dropping, were chained to the platforms, with two huge parachutes fastened on top. All potential snagging points were covered with the inimitable black masking tape, the stuff which veterans say held – and still holds – the British Army together. When the rigging was complete, the trucks were taken away to be loaded onto the aircraft. A couple of hours later saw us waiting by the DZ to witness the drop. Right on time the Beverley appeared overhead, height about 1,000 feet. Out popped a small drag chute from the rear end, pulling the platform from the aircraft. The load fell away and the main parachutes developed. It was amazing to watch – beautifully smooth as you like. Then disaster! The two chains holding one side of the platform came loose. The other side held, but the truck broke away and whistled into the deck. After standing mesmerised for a moment we ran over to inspect the wreck. It was our mortar truck. The vehicle had landed rear end down and had punched about a metre into the ground. Incredibly, the headlights were still intact, but all else was smashed and twisted. We had loaded up with dummy mortar bombs, which were scattered around. This caused quite a bit of a panic at first, because the airfield staff thought they were live and wouldn't go near them. At an inquiry later it was established that there had been a fault in the welding of the platform.

In the autumn there was a mass airborne exercise held in Denmark. The exercise was called Brown Jug and also involved many paras from the American airborne forces. We boarded our Beverleys at RAF Abingdon. Personnel were stationed up in the boom area, and our trucks full of kit were loaded on platforms downstairs. Flying time to the DZ in Denmark was five hours – at that time, we were told, the longest non-stop flight to a DZ anywhere. Once we were there the trucks went out first; then the men dropped through the hole. The air was absolutely full of parachutes. On the way down I could see hundreds of American chutes in the distance. Also there were hundreds of Danish civilians lining the DZ, watching. On the ground we discovered that our truck had landed across a hedge, but it was OK.

It was on this exercise that I found out about the hidden dangers of the plastic explosive (PE) No. 808, which was being widely used. Sometimes, in order to get a mortar pit dug quickly, we would use PE to loosen the soil. It worked a treat, but 808 came in sticks and had to be kneaded into a different size and then shaped for the job. It was the first time I and most of the others had handled the stuff, and we kneaded happily away, completing the task. Little did we know, however, that one of the components of 808 was arsenic, and after handling it for a while we developed raging headaches which lasted for hours. Some years later a safer type of PE was introduced.

Ten days after hitting the Danish DZ the Paras were back in Aldershot, bulling our boots in preparation for a major parade. The occasion was a special one – the Parachute Regiment was to receive the Freedom of Aldershot. On the day in question the whole brigade paraded in the local football stadium. After listening to a speech by the mayor we marched through Aldershot with fixed bayonets, band playing and drums beating. It was a spectacular and well-deserved day for me and my tough Para comrades. We marched six abreast through the streets with the band playing the regimental march-past, Wagner's 'The Ride of the Valkyries'. It was stirring stuff, and the locals lapped it up. In Nordic mythology the Valkyries are flying goddesses who carry the bodies of dead warriors from the battlefield to Valhalla. It was quite emotional, all those red berets and the streets thronged with cheering crowds. I felt really proud to be a Para.

Aldershot was a nice town. There were thousands of troops stationed nearby, but there was little trouble between units. The locals, at least the ones whom I met, were very friendly. It was an Army town through and through, and we all felt welcome and at ease there. However, I realised that I was beginning to get increasingly restless. I couldn't visualise myself staying in Aldershot much longer, welcome or not. No further promotion was in sight either. I had gained one of the highest grades ever in our platoon on a mortar course, and I was still only a corporal. Also, I had just been put on two stupid charges, so petty they were almost ridiculous. One was for sitting in the privates' part of the dining-hall against regulations and another for belching, inadvertently, on parade. When the Sergeant Major read out the charges (which were quickly dismissed) in the CO's office I was straining not to laugh, and the CO himself was furiously biting his lower lip in a bid to stave off laughter.

Other nit-picking by camp NCOs over very trivial offences against Army rules carried out while walking about town, including being (wrongly) accused of wearing military trousers off duty, finally galvanised me into action. Much as I loved the Paras it was high time to move on, I decided. Remembering my long-held wish to have a crack at joining the SAS – where action was virtually guaranteed – I marched straight to the camp orderly room and put in an immediate application to go on the first available SAS Selection Course. I discovered then that another bloke in the platoon, Paddy B. from Dublin (full name withheld), had also applied only the week before. Knowing that Selection consisted mainly of endurance marches and cross-country navigation while carrying heavy packs, we paired up and trained every chance we got, usually finishing up with a few turns round the assault course for good measure.

I still went out for a drink occasionally, though. One of our favourite pubs in Aldershot was The Globe, where we had many a good piss-up and sing-song. Long-term relations with women weren't a priority with me at the time, but I did have a few flings – three, to be exact – with WRAC girls. None lasted more than a week, but we all parted amicably, as they say in the best circles.

Paddy disappeared on his course first and then, just before Christmas leave 1957, the CO called me into his office and informed me that I was to go on the 28 December Selection. He seemed genuinely sorry to see me go and told me that I was a good NCO, which was decent of him. The CO's name was Major S.C.A.N. Bishop or 'Scan' for short. He was going bald, the reason for which, he told us, bizarrely, was eating too many bamboo shoots when he was a POW of the Japanese in the Second World War! Everyone liked Scan, and he was definitely on my list of top officers.

Meanwhile I had enjoyed my time with the Paras. They were mostly good lads, with only a few big-heads to spoil it – all mouth and trousers. I admired the National Servicemen in the regiment the most. They could have sat out their service somewhere and had as cushy a time as possible, but instead they chose to join a very active fighting unit and put themselves in harm's way. I'm convinced that this type of National Serviceman gained a lot more from his service than did the whingers, who not only moaned and groaned all the time but usually kept a record of exactly how much longer they had left to serve, even down to the minutes and seconds in some cases. It must have seemed like ten years to those people rather than two.

I remember with great pleasure the mortar platoon lads with whom I served. They were first-class comrades and friends. I can still recall some names: there was Joe Smith, a great comic and practical joker; Sergeants Taff Ball and Dick Aspey; Geordie Tate, who was nicknamed 'Scoff' because of his huge appetite; Johnny Walker from Yorkshire; and Corporal Freddy Blake. All good men and excellent soldiers. Although it had been well worth the effort to get into the Paras, with some superb training and active service experience thrown in, I did not fancy stagnating at Aldershot. I didn't have a clue what the future would hold, of course, but one thing I did know was that if I got into the SAS, I would be posted to where there was some lively action going on.

So, on 28 December 1957, after a short spell of Christmas leave, I collected a rail warrant to Brecon in South Wales. Derring Lines, Brecon, was where the SAS Selection Course was based at that time. I was pleased to discover then that another man from the battalion, Sergeant Arthur Watchus, was on the same course. Arthur had been in the Parachute Regiment in the war and had taken part in Operation Varsity. This major offensive drop was the last big airborne operation of the war, when British and American parachute and glider troops landed in large numbers ahead of the main Allied forces crossing the Rhine in March 1945. Arthur and I cadged a lift down to Aldershot station to start our journey to Brecon – and, I sincerely hoped, an exciting new chapter in my Army career. I was just a few weeks short of my twenty-ninth birthday.

My appetite for action was not to be disappointed, soon and in spectacular style . . . but first I had to pass SAS Selection, a task that the majority found beyond them and only the best could achieve.

Chapter 7

SELECTION: WINTER ON THE BRECON BEACONS

T he last leg of our journey was on a now-disused rail line from Newport to Brecon. Arthur and I were in a carriage with no corridor and no toilet, which meant, because the train was being pulled by a slow 'Ivor the Engine' type of locomotive, typical of this part of Wales, that we were both absolutely busting for the loo from halfway on the journey. Surely this wasn't an infernal opening twist of the selection process, we jokingly asked ourselves? To make matters worse there were two other blokes in our carriage who spent the whole time talking about how to get rid of wind. In the end one said, with obvious satisfaction, 'So, I drank four bottles of stout and whoosh, out it came.' I thought, 'Bloody hell, whoosh, it'll all come out of me in a minute!' Much worse was soon to follow, which physically and mentally broke the hearts of many of our fellow participants on this mission to join the most secretive and elite regiment of all. The rigours of Selection for the SAS are hard to put into words, but I will do my best.

We made it to Brecon just in time and learned on the grapevine that the Selection staff did not lay on transport to camp, so, together with some other SAS hopefuls already at the station, we piled into a taxi. At Derring Lines we found the office and reported in. The course was run by Captain J., with Sergeant Paddy Nugent as second-in-command, assisted by two other men. After being shown the billet we were issued with a bergen rucksack, sleeping bag, maps, a prismatic compass and a No. 4 rifle, without sling. No one mentioned meals, so we found the cookhouse ourselves. At a briefing, later, Sergeant Nugent told us that we would be expected to turn out at any time ordered, dressed correctly and carrying the necessary equipment. Absence from parade meant instant RTU (returned to unit). The first parade was to be the next morning at 0800 hr sharp, dress denims and boots. That first night, just before going to sleep, I vowed to myself, 'I've got to pass. I will pass this Selection and get into the SAS or bust.' Everyone felt the same way, I'm sure.

Next morning Sergeant Nugent double-marched us round to the camp assault course. It didn't look much: there appeared to be no high obstacles. 'Right,' said Paddy, giving us a big smile. 'I'll set you off one at a time. Go round the course as fast as you can, don't miss anything and don't stop until I tell you.' After four laps I realised the course was a lot harder than it looked. I concentrated on one obstacle at a time: up a muddy slope, over a wall, swing over a water-filled ditch, jump off a high ramp and so on, round and round. Prior fitness training was paying off, but it was still a hard slog. Several blokes were lagging already, and a couple had stopped altogether. I completed twelve laps before Paddy stopped me. The men who had lagged or stopped weren't immediately penalised; I think Sergeant Nugent just made mental notes and kept an eye on them. It was known that some blokes could start badly and then pick up and finish Selection well, so judgement was reserved until later. It was also well known that a man could pass all physical tests and then fail because of a poor mental attitude.

Map-reading tests came next. These were set in order to gauge ability. A certain standard was required before a man was allowed to go on his own up into the mountains, otherwise getting lost and dying of exposure could be the penalty. Anyone a bit dodgy on maps was given extra tuition.

Later on we were ordered to parade at 0600 hr next morning for our first test exercise. Dress was the same for all exercises – full kit, including rifle, map and compass, full water bottle on belt and rucksack to weigh at least 40lb. Food wasn't mentioned, so we organised that for ourselves, plus meal times and haversack rations. Next morning at 0600 hr, cold, wet and apprehensive, we were taken off by truck to a place called Cwm Gwdi (pronounced 'cum guddy'). These were rifle ranges on the lower slopes of Pen y Fan, the highest peak in the Brecon Beacons. From there we were set off in pairs to navigate cross-country to do reconnaissance on different 'targets'. No times were mentioned, only when the truck would return to camp. The round trip was only about 15 miles, but to make it more difficult we had to move unseen. Hedges and trees were scarce, and there were several roads to cross. Everyone made it back in time, though. The weather wasn't too bad that first day – just a steady Welsh drizzle. With only small breaks it rained, hailed and snowed for the rest of the course. Luckily there was a drying room near the billet to hang our wet kit in.

'Transport moves off at 0600 hr tomorrow morning,' said Paddy, after we'd tumbled from the truck. That night Arthur and I walked to Brecon and had a huge nosh in a café – egg, chips and steak, followed by two pints of draught Guinness in The Moon pub. Even though it was quite a long walk we did that every night when there was time. It certainly stoked up our boilers for the trials ahead.

After the first day all exercises were done individually. The truck would stop at intervals on the fringe of the exercise area, drop off one man who had been given instructions, and away he would go. Instructions were always verbal, and everything had to be memorised. Anyone captured on a real operation could compromise the whole job if the enemy found written orders or marked maps etc. Even a map folded to show a certain area could be a dead give-away. At that time of year the Welsh mountains are almost continuously veiled in mist and low cloud, with visibility very often down to a few yards. Within 10 minutes of starting on the second day I was completely soaked through with driving sleet, but I knew that if I kept moving I would be warm enough. Paddy had issued a dire warning before we left camp: 'Whatever you do, don't stop. Just keep putting one foot in front of the other. If you sit down to take five you could freeze to death.' To prove his point he told us how one bloke had actually died on a previous course. He had sat down, rucksack on and with his rifle across his knees, apparently to rest. He was found later, still in that position and frozen solid. Keep moving I did. Another thing is, of course, that if you are moving, however slowly, you are covering ground. Another warning from Paddy was 'If you see someone else in front, don't just follow along behind without checking. He could be going the wrong way.' I can't recall all our route on that second day, but the last leg entailed climbing over Pen y Fan. The weather had turned so bad, blizzards and deep snow, that from the second-last rendezvous (or RV) Captain J. had put us in pairs for safety. I was with Captain L.

On another day the exercise was cut short after we had reached the first RV. The weather was particularly nasty even for that area. The start was from the Brecon-to-Merthyr Tydfil road. From there we had to head west over Fan Fawr mountain, draw a sketch of the dam in the next valley and then go on over to the next valley to the first RV, a road track junction. The cloud was down to the road, visibility about five yards and the sleet was moving horizontally in the wind. I saw from the map that very steep, almost cliff-like ground was at the top of Fan Fawr, so I only climbed up so far and then round until I estimated that I was in line with the dam. I thought I had got it wrong at first, because it seemed a long way down, but then out of the mist, only a few yards away, loomed the dam tower. 'You jammy sod,' I said out loud to myself. I made my sketch, crossed the dam and plodded, stiff with the cold, up the other side. In the next valley I had to splash over a knee-deep stream to reach the RV. Captain J. was there with a Land Rover. I came to a halt, sloped arms, gave a smart salute, reported in and handed over my sketch. I was the first one in. Captain J. congratulated me on my display of drill but said that I should get my left elbow in a bit and lower my right hand a touch! He then ordered me into the Land Rover. The weather was so bad, he explained, that he was cutting the exercise short. He also said that if we could find our way this far in these conditions, then he was satisfied.

Each day the tests became longer and harder. One that I particularly recall became known afterwards as the 'Fan Dance'. For this one the course was split into three groups, each group starting, as individuals, from different points around Pen Y Fan, Cwm Gwdi range hut, The Storey Arms café on the Merthyr road and Torpantau railway station, which was (it's not there now) about 5 miles south-east of Pen y Fan. The task was to climb up to the top of the Fan, check in and then go down to one of the other start points to be checked in again. From there it was back up the Fan and down to another start point, then finally up the Fan again and down to the place we started from. To do this exercise in the required time it was necessary, because of the slow pace in climbing up, to have to run on the down bits and on the flat. Actually that was the case in most of the other tests as well. The 'Fan Dance', when all the twists and turns were added up, totalled about 25 muscle-aching miles. Going up the Fan for the third time I was down to a slow plod and wanted to rest. Then I remembered Paddy's advice: 'Just put one foot in front of the other.' Later he added, 'Switch off and think of sex.' Sex was far from my mind then. If Marilyn Monroe had suddenly appeared with her skirt up round her neck, I wouldn't have even glanced at her! (Well, maybe a quick peek.)

Halfway through Selection we found that our rucksacks didn't just seem to become heavier, they were deliberately made heavier by the addition of wall bricks that we had to carry. To make sure we didn't cheat our rucksacks were checked at various RVs. By that stage, also, several blokes had either jacked their hands in or been given the push. A couple of them, I noticed, had been on the booze every night until late. Too much drink, not enough sleep and early starts followed by marching over the Welsh mountains just don't mix, or only in story books and John Wayne films. This was for real.

The final exercise was called 'Long March', and not without reason: total distance, all within the Beacons area, was 40 miles plus, with numerous RVs en route. On that morning the weather had improved slightly. Instead of a howling blizzard or mist in which you could hardly see your feet there was a steady downpour of rain with blustery wind, and the mist had lifted sufficiently to see about a cricket-pitch-length ahead. It hadn't got much warmer, though. Any brass monkeys in the vicinity would definitely have been sexually retarded! Six of us successfully completed the 'Long March', and that was the same six (out of an original twelve) who passed Selection: myself, Arthur, Johnny Partridge (an airborne gunner), Guardsman Parry, Captain L. from the infantry, and a chap called Fitzgerald. As far as I was concerned, Arthur's and my regular ritual of steak, egg and chips followed by two pints of draught Guinness had been well worth the money.

After another week or so spent on extra training the successful six left Brecon for the Airborne Forces Depot at Aldershot, there to await transport to Malaya, where 22 SAS Regiment was based. At Aldershot I went to say a final goodbye to my mates in 1 Para. Then, after a couple of weeks' leave, it was off to the Far East. Air transport had just been introduced for troop movement then (1958), but the aircraft were slow and had to stop for refuelling three times before arriving at Singapore. On my trip it was Damascus, Karachi and Calcutta. Civilian clothing had to be worn for the flight because of restrictions on military personnel landing at certain airports. I had civvies, but some of the other blokes were issued with thick, hairy, dark-grey Borstal suits. Charming! Taking off from London Airport I gazed down at the little villages and green fields of England. This time I didn't wonder what lay ahead for me. I had a pretty good idea – and it was to be dramatic. I was now 19033387, Trooper F. Doran, a member of 22 SAS Regiment, selected and approved. It was the end of January 1958. A bit later in the ranks of the SAS than I had at first intended, but then I had been busy fighting other wars. The rank of trooper meant I was on the bottom rung again, but at least now there would be no bull and plenty of excitement.

Chapter 8

WHO DARES WINS:
MALAYA

The SAS were sent to Malaya as part of a British and Commonwealth force to help the Malays in their fight against CTs. Theirs was a dangerous and insidiously efficient organisation, whose aim was to overthrow the government and establish a Communist regime. The glittering prize for victory in the guerrilla campaign was control of the vast tin and rubber resources that made Malaya such a wealthy force in the region. If Singapore also fell to the insurgents, they would win domination of the Straits of Malacca to the south, so threatening the sea route to Hong Kong and Japan. Much was at stake in this ongoing and first full-scale SAS operation since the glory days of the Second World War, when victory was so brilliantly won behind the lines against the might of Nazi Germany, if at such cost in men tortured and executed. It was a sobering thought at the back of the minds of myself and all the men who were Malaya-bound. Would history repeat itself in the form of similar atrocities inflicted by a cruel and ruthless foe? Time would soon tell.

Meanwhile I was on my way to jungle conflict with the rest of the new intake of 22 SAS Regiment, making the best of things, as British soldiers have done from time immemorial. The aircraft, being a propeller job, was very noisy, and the seats were narrow and cramped. But it was much better than weeks on a troopship, and I soon settled down to kip. Damascus came and went, then Karachi, where we were marooned for four days because some bigwig commandeered our aircraft to fly back to the UK. I didn't mind, as we stayed in the Minwalla Hotel near the airport, which was very comfortable, with excellent food. A couple of us went outside the hotel for a walk, but it was so dirty, with hordes of kids pulling at us and shoving their hands in our pockets, that we didn't venture out again. After a brief stop at Calcutta we landed at Changi airport in Singapore, then went on by train to Kuala

Lumpur in Malaya, where 22 SAS was based. I fell in love with the Malay trains on the trip to 'KL'. They were very comfortable and always went at a gentle, civilised pace. There was a restaurant car, which was sit-in or take-away, and the beer, Anchor or Tiger, was ice-cool. On we travelled, clickety-click, clickety-clack, watching the jungle and the occasional little village slide by. The station at Singapore was very ornate but was more than matched by that of KL. If there's one thing we can be grateful to the old colonialists for, it's their architecture. Stations, parks and buildings of all types, from houses to shops and government edifices, are genteel and pleasant to look at, yet efficiently functional where necessary.

The men of 22 SAS were based in Wardiburn Camp just outside KL. All new men had to undergo a month's training before being finally officially accepted into the regiment, and so on arrival we were all put into the 'recruit training basha'. Basha, I soon discovered, was the Malay word for anything from a house to a poncho shelter! That first night I kept being woken up by a noise like someone stacking old-type metal milk crates which came from the basha behind. Next day I discovered it was the radio station. The duty operator had left the radio on full volume so that any incoming message would awaken him in case he fell asleep on watch. The weird noise was radio static.

There were ten new 'recruits' on parade next morning. The officer in charge of training gave the gen – there would be one week's fitness pre-training, followed by three weeks in the jungle. The issue of kit was next: olive-green clothing, including pairs of vile underpants called 'drawers cellular', dubbed by the troops as 'drawers Dracula', jungle boots with rubber soles and calf-length canvas uppers, green 44-pattern equipment, a prismatic compass, bergen rucksack and a large, heavy knife called a gollock. Gollocks – what a name! – were referred to by the Malay name 'parang'. There was a larger version of the gollock called a machete, but they were heavy and unwieldy, and because of their bluntness were known as 'tree beaters'. They didn't cut – they just bounced off wood. Personal weapons were the Belgian 7.62mm self-loading rifle (SLR) with a twenty-round magazine. Browning five-round pump-action shotguns were also used in the regiment, but we didn't see them until later.

After a week running, shooting and learning such things as how to make a hammock from several panels of a supply parachute, our intake finally packed our bergens with ten days' rations, collected the necessary maps and boarded transport for the jungle training operation in north Malaya. The jungle was referred to by the troops as the 'bungle' or 'ulu'. Bungle is self-explanatory, but ulu, which became synonymous with deep jungle, is Malay for headwaters and was used to differentiate between deep and 'fringe' jungle, where the logging and rubber industries were. There are few large, flat areas of jungle in Malaya, except in swampland. Most terrain is broken, with steep hills (dubbed bukits by the SAS, from the Malay word for hill), and many rocky, swiftly flowing rivers and streams – sungis. The training area was of the latter type. Deposited at the jungle edge near a little town named Grik, we were given our first task, a day's march into the training area to set up camp. During this march I discovered new aches, pains and more pores to sweat from than I ever thought possible. With the effects of very high humidity, especially carrying a heavy rucksack, which contained 60lb on that first day, a body is constantly soaked by sweat from the crotch up. Boots and legs are kept wet by wading through the inumerable streams and rivers – not to mention the teeming rain, of course. The Malay jungle certainly lived up to its name of rainforest. One lad, who was non-SAS, coming with us to man base signals, collapsed with heat exhaustion after a few hours' march. The immediate remedy, administered by one of the instructors, was to feed him with Oxo cubes, which are full of salt, washed down with plenty of water.

We were warned not to do any cutting unless it was absolutely necessary. Cutting leaves a trail that can be easily followed, is noisy enough to be heard for quite a long way and can also mask the sound of an enemy passing nearby. Silence was golden in the jungle. Communication was in whispers or sign language. In some jungle films you will see the hero, covered in muck, shirt open to show big hairy chest, grimacing fiercely and snarling as he lustily swings his machete, slicing at every little branch in sight. By the time he has travelled 50 yards, our hero will have felled enough timber to make paper for a year's publication of the *Daily Mail* and alerted all enemy within a mile. This perception is not real. It doesn't matter how careful you are, though, it is impossible to move in the jungle without leaving any signs at all. Most of our enemy, the CT, had lived for long periods in the jungle and were attuned to the slightest variation from the normal. Not only that, they often had jungle aborigines with them. These aborigines, whose lives depended on their ability to track animals for food, could follow at a run signs that were invisible to the untrained eye. It followed, therefore, that both we and our opponents, the CT, had to be as careful as possible. It was like a deadly game of chess played in semi-darkness.

During the march in the group had frequent stops, when the staff instructors would ask each soldier to point to where they thought they were on the map. This called for constant checking of maps and compasses, estimating speed of travel and taking mental note of the surrounding topography. Arriving at the base camp area we were allocated individual basha spots and 'stand-to' positions with all-round defence foremost in mind. 'Half an hour to make bashas,' was the brusque order. Out came the parangs, and two poles were fashioned for the hammocks, with two A-frames stuck in the ground for stability. The hammocks were fixed to the outside of the A-frames, with ridge poles attached to the tops of A-frames and ponchos over that for a roof, the whole contraption firmly tied down to nearby trees. We fresh SAS men soon learnt how to select the best wood for bashas. It had to be rigid but lightweight and small in circumference. I was very comfortable in my hammock inside my parachute sleeping bag. The night noises of the bungle kept me awake for a while that first night, but I soon became used to them. I did have one scare, though. Waking up, I looked at my watch, which was GS, waterproof and illuminated (as were all those with which we had been issued). It was midnight. Glancing to the side I froze. A few yards away were what appeared to be two cigarettes burning. Every couple of seconds they would move as if guided by hands. No one else in our party was in that direction. I stood up in my sleeping bag, groped for my rifle and shuffled forward, straining my eyes to see. The cigarettes seemed to overlap each other sometimes. Very peculiar this, I thought. Then, suddenly, one of the cigarettes whizzed past my nose, followed by the other one. Phew! I'd been watching the courting dance of a pair of fireflies!

The drill each morning was up before dawn and light a candle to show that you were awake. Then we used hexamine fires to make a brew while getting dressed. It was also a listening time. There wasn't much of a threat from CT in that area, but we took precautions anyway. I never bothered with breakfast, making do with a mug of hot sweet tea and snacking later. The main meal of the day, in the evening, was always curry and rice. The rations, usually issued in 24-hour packs, were quite good. Each pack contained tins of meat and veg, processed cheese, margarine, kippers or sardines, ghee (frying fat), and condensed milk and jam. There were also packets of tea, sugar, dried milk, nuts and raisins, hard tack biscuits, Oxo, oats, chocolate, long-grain rice, salt and pepper, matches and toilet paper. Most blokes would also buy extras such as curry powder, onions, garlic and a small type of dried fish similar to whitebait called ikan billis. In each 24-hour pack was a small tin opener – 'combat tin openers', we called them. I've still got one, and it works perfectly. Issued in addition to the rations were daily malaria and salt pills, and packets of solid fuel tablets, complete with stands. The fuel tablets had the advantage of being noiseless, giving off very little odour and burning even when wet. All that lot, as you can imagine, together with other items carried in the rucksack, added up to quite a weight. Very often, until some of the food had been used, I couldn't lift my rucksack and swing it onto my back in the normal way. I had to sit down, put my arms through the straps and then either get myself up somehow or ask someone to pull me up.

Navigation training and getting 'jungle fit' took up the first week. Maps were mostly drawn from aerial photographs taken by the RAF, and the newly fledged SAS found them quite good. Large rivers were shown accurately, and we could always get a fix on a prominent bend or where two rivers joined. This confluence was known in Malay as a kuala. Small streams were sometimes a problem to the SAS, as not all of them were visible through the tree canopy on photographs and might not even be marked on the map at all. Another problem was clouds. If there happened to be clouds when the RAF flew over the area to be photographed, then the cartographers could not put any detail in, and this appeared on the map as a white patch (or 'map cloud'), sometimes thousands of yards long and nearly as much wide. It was a case then of relying on the compass and picking a way through, just as the instructors persistently hammered away as the safest and most reliable navigation method. When this 'white patching' did happen patrol commanders would usually write as much detail in as possible on the map afterwards for future use.

The reason we did our training in deep jungle was because that was where most of the CT were. In the early days the CT had operated openly around towns and villages, ambushing roads, terrorising rubber estate workers and forcing the villagers to supply them with food and other goods. But by now the villages were closed off or the people relocated, and fringe areas of jungle were heavily patrolled, forcing the CT to move further and further into the jungle.

The 22 SAS Regiment, which had started life in the early 1950s as the 'Malayan Scouts', was given the task of pursuing the CT deep into the jungle. Three months was the norm for our patrols, with resupply by air every two weeks. Obviously this work called for a very fit and dedicated type of soldier who had to be highly skilled at living and moving in the jungle. The training was therefore specifically designed to that end. Day after day we slogged around, each day made deliberately harder by the staff. But everyone had to be very alert to their surroundings, not only navigation-wise but also in terms of being ready for possible ambushes and signs left by the CT. That could be anything from a snapped twig to a footprint. Plus, of course, you might meet them head on, and in that case it would be who was quickest on the draw. We always carried our rifles, with a bullet in the breech ready, in the crook of our arms, all set for a quick up, aim and fire. When you weren't having to move swiftly from A to B it was generally accepted that jungle patrolling should be a softly-softly job, slow and steady, soldiers even stopping and listening now and then. It was common sense, really, and that way a man would be better prepared, both physically and mentally, to respond to a sudden enemy contact – which was the way it usually happened.

Besides physical exertion there was a lot of nervous energy expended on patrol by everyone. With sweat stinging the eyes, bergen straps biting into our shoulders, arms aching with holding our rifles, and slipping and sliding in mud and leaf mould, it was a feat of concentration to stay alert moving slowly, never mind rushing. We soon discovered the worst going was in the rough, hilly country when moving up and down small stream courses. The ground there is even more broken, usually with steep rocky sides and with thick, slimy mud at the bottom. When crossing it was comparatively easy for the troops to go down a stream bank. It was simply a matter of sliding sitting down, feet first, to the bottom. However, it could be almost impossible to climb up the other side: there was simply no purchase. A fallen tree, if it spanned the stream, could be a fortuitous advantage, but definitely dicey owing to the many branches and creepers that could cause men to lose their footing and fall onto the rocks below, risking serious injury. I remember vividly that getting over, or under, a fallen tree that blocked the line of march could be a big drain on energy and a time-consuming business. Some of them were two or more yards thick and 60 or 70 yards long. 'Ball-aching' was the nicest phrase I heard from the blokes when carrying out these manoeuvres. It was at times such as this, even though we always carried out all-round observation as a matter of course, that we had to be especially vigilant, not only for enemy but also to make sure that we didn't leave anyone behind. Very often at the end of a day over such country we would find ourselves talking in high squeaky voices afterwards. It was not only 'aching' but totally energy-sapping.

Just to make it even more interesting God had decided to populate the jungle with many forms of flies, plus bugs, ants, hornets, scorpions, rats, leeches, mosquitos, lice and snakes – not forgetting the larger inhabitants, such as tigers, elephants, monkeys, bears and a host of other creatures. I have heard, read and seen a lot of silly dramatics about leeches. In many jungle films the hero, bare-chested of course, will be burning off leeches with a cigarette, all the while accompanied by music from a thirty-piece orchestra. In adventure books the hero or heroine will be covered from head to foot in black, slimy, blood-sucking monsters. Out will come the cigs again to do their duty. However, it seemed common sense to me and others at the time that we could just as easily burn ourselves as burn the leeches. In practice we non-smokers had to flick or pull them off, or sprinkle a bit of salt on them. Salt also helped to prevent any infection. One bloke I knew ignored the leeches altogether and let them gorge on his blood. When they were full they would just drop off. Leeches were nigh impossible to avoid. They perched on leaves and twigs, with their thin ends waving in the air waiting to attach themselves to a victim. Also, they could travel quite quickly over the leafy jungle floor. When the men were sitting to take five I have looked down and there would often be at least half a dozen of the blighters heading towards me with a hungry gleam in their eyes! Because of the high humidity clothing taken off at night did not dry very much, so we had to get used to putting it back on in the morning all soggy and cold. Not only that, but sometimes I would find several leeches had crawled up the legs of my trousers. One morning, a tiny green snake dropped out of the sleeve of my jacket! I got into the habit of shaking them first after that.

However, there were some very beautiful creatures in the jungle to distract the eye, such as huge multicoloured butterflies, which were best observed when they perched on a rock in a river while opening and closing their wings. There were also many spectacular birds that lived in the rainforest and whose movements in the high canopy sometimes caused hearts in the patrol to miss a beat, momentarily mistaking the noise for a more sinister human presence. But they kept mainly to the treetops and so were not often seen or heard. Sometimes, however, I could hear the big hornbills flying over, their wings making a distinctive rasping, swishy noise.

Some of the vegetation was also very annoying to the troops trying manfully to carve a path through the confusion of dense, green jungle. The men found trees with massive spikes on the bark that could impale an unwary hand. There was also a long trailing creeper with spikes on like fish hooks, called nanti sikit in Malay, which invariably caught in nostrils or ears and which had to be patiently worked loose. This temporary halt in the patrol was called the 'wait-a-minute'. Cursing vocabulary was fully exercised when caught in the nanti sikit! But there was friendly growth too. There were atap leaves, which could be used to make a shelter. In fact atap is Malay for roof. Some vines and most bamboo also held drinkable water. There was a type of passion fruit, and a tree with a top growth very like white cabbage. The latter could be boiled and eaten. Underneath the jungle canopy, out of the sun, it is relatively cool and dark, and only dappled sunlight gets through. At night, also, it is reasonably cool and pleasant, and the biting insects are not as troublesome. One biter, however, specialised in night attacks – the dreaded sand fly. Nothing seemed to deter the little terrors – mosquito nets and repellents had little effect. The only thing that I found worked was, bizarrely, to keep all my clothes on in my sleeping bag and wrap a towel round my head, leaving the tiniest of holes to breathe through. The dreaded mosquito was also everywhere, giving rise to the threat of malaria, an extremely debilitating illness which could weaken men so much that, untreated, they could be out of commission for days at a time, or worse.

There are many diseases that can be caught in Malaya, a lot of them common to other countries as well. Most can be prevented by pills or inoculations. As I've just mentioned, one of the more serious infections is malaria, passed to humans by the bite of a certain type of mosquito. We swallowed a daily pill called Paludrine to combat this. Another disease is leptospirosis, or 'lepto' as we called it. Lepto was caught mainly from water contaminated by rat's urine but could be prevented by taking such precautions as boiling water before drinking. A man could also be infected by contaminated water entering a cut or open sore, so it was relatively easy to contract.

Ten days into the training operation and my SAS comrades and I had to prepare a DZ for resupply by air. This meant having to cut down trees to make a space for parachute loads to drop into. An area of mostly smaller trees was selected so that parangs could do the job; otherwise explosives would have had to be used. During this task I accidently cut my pal Arthur's hand. We were both working on the same tree, and Arthur, who was left-handed, swung his right hand in front of my parang just as I was going in for the cut. Fortunately Arthur's hand was travelling in the same direction as my parang, and so the wound was not too serious. However, it was bad enough for him to be evacuated by helicopter the next day for hospital treatment. Meanwhile the air drop went ahead as planned. The pilot had a map reference to work on, but near the time of the drop a gas-filled orange balloon was let up on a line to guide him onto the exact location through the thick jungle canopy. On the first pass the patrol fired a green Very light to indicate that they were ready. During an air drop everyone on the ground had to be out watching. One reason was to spot loads that drifted off course and another was that if you were in your basha or elsewhere under cover, you wouldn't know if a load was coming down on top of you. Sometimes a chute got caught up in the branches. Shooting flares and burning the canopy usually worked, but if we had aborigines, who were extremely agile, with us, one of them would climb up and cut it down. The aborigines were allowed to keep some of the parachutes to make clothing from and considered this quite a perk.

Many years later, in the 1960s, a new system was developed in which the load was suspended on an extra-long line. This allowed the load to reach the jungle floor before the canopy could snag on any branches. Fresh food was always dropped in with the rations. A big steak sandwich was the joy of air-drop days. The RASC (Royal Army Service Corps) Air Despatch Company prided itself on dropping in anything requested, within reason. Fresh eggs were dropped in occasionally, usually unbroken. However, all extra items were ordered through the NAAFI and had to be paid for on return to camp.

The next phase of training involved the recruits being split into patrols and given certain areas to cover, making rendezvous with the staff en route. By now we were becoming much more attuned to the jungle noises that surrounded our patrol day and night. At first all was baffling confusion, but gradually we were able to distinguish the unusual from the normal background noises. There was a discernible pattern, and morning, afternoon and dusk were all distinctly different. Night sounds were different again, when each creature seemed to have its own time to sound off, with a lot of overlapping.

We SAS troopers had all been warned about animal traps, especially the diabolical pig spears, which were hidden, buried in the jungle to trap unwary animals who fell in and were impaled, but now these were often used by the guerrillas to kill or maim human prey. Several soldiers in the regiment had already been injured by pig spears, and two whom I knew well had sustained permanent disabilities. A typical pig-spear trap consisted of a length of bendy branch, one end fixed and the other – the business end – with several sharp bamboo spikes tied to it, held back under pressure. The trap was usually triggered by the victim being channelled along a deliberately narrowed path and onto a trip wire, or dislodging a holding branch concealed under the leaves. I found out later that the aborigines very rarely used pig spears, preferring to catch game alive to be killed when required. However, it was known that the CT often set traps of this sort to catch the unwary soldier. The CT also daubed their excrement onto the end of the spikes in order to increase the risk of infection. They were charming people.

To end the SAS training operation our patrol marched out, separately from the staff, to a road RV. Arriving early, we decided to walk on a few miles further down the road to where we knew there was an Australian Army camp. We had hoped to visit their canteen and have a beer or two, but the Aussies invited one and all into their cookhouse and treated us SAS men to a slap-up meal, followed by a mammoth booze-up. We were in seventh heaven after all our deprivations in the jungle. I hadn't seen any Australian soldiers since Korea, but they were just the same – really nice, friendly blokes, the salt of the earth. Back in camp, the battle-hardened CO, Lieutenant-Colonel Deane-Drummond, or 'DD' as he was referred to in the ranks, interviewed the men individually and told them how they had done. (As mentioned in the Prologue, DD was famous for his exploits during the Second World War.) The Lieutenant-Colonel was pleased with the standard of this latest intake to the SAS. All of the men passed except one, and even he was allowed to stay as a driver. I was officially an SAS soldier at last!

Chapter 9

ON THE TRAIL OF A PHANTOM JUNGLE FOE: WITH D SQUADRON SAS

The CT terrorists we were in pursuit of were a well-organised, elusive and resourceful enemy. They were on home ground, were utterly ruthless and knew the jungle intimately, so it was a distinct bonus if they could be lured into an ambush and eliminated. With great patience and skill this was possible and did happen, and valuable prisoners were taken for vital interrogation and information by the British. However, on most occasions the presence of regular SAS patrols like ours usually acted as a strong deterrent to CT action, spoiling and delaying their cunning plans and attempts to control and dominate the local populace. In many ways, as will be seen in this chapter, this tactic was even more disruptive to terrorist operations than outright face-to-face confrontation and violent skirmishing. One thing was certain: both sides had a common enemy, the jungle, an environment that was at times beautiful but always claustrophobic and deadly, and that demanded the utmost respect day by day.

Johnny Partridge and I were immediately posted to D Squadron, Johnny going to 17 Troop and me to 16 Troop. We joined the squadron on the west coast, where the main body had just carried out a parachute jump onto a beach. I was pleased to meet up there again with Paddy B. from 1 Para mortars, who was in 18 Troop. Neither of us had had to change our berets, only the badge, because the SAS then wore maroon berets which were the same as the Paras'. It wasn't until some months later that the SAS changed back to the now familiar and famous fawn or 'sandy' beret.

A couple of weeks later, after more intensive training and a practice helicopter jump, the squadron was on a secret operation deep into swampland on the east side of Malaya. The troops had to go the first twenty-eight days without resupply, so that meant carrying twenty-eight days' rations in with us – a hefty weight. A special lightweight twenty-eight-day ration was issued which consisted of, for one day, a normal-sized tin of corned beef, one small tin each of processed cheese and jam, packets of hard tack biscuits, soup, dried milk, rice, Oxo, matches and hexamine blocks for cooking. Thus the average starting weight, including rifle, ammunition and equipment, carried by each man was 120 to 130lb. The squadron boarded an open-top wagon train at KL for the first stage of the journey. Walking along the platform at the station we were all bent double with the weight of our bergens. Civilians there waiting for trains looked on in amazement, as they had seen nothing like this before. I was tense like everyone else but looking forward to action. Our train rattled on through the night as we huddled down and tried to kip. The train halted after about three hours, with thick jungle hemming the track in on both sides. The soldiers of 16 Troop quickly but quietly disembarked and moved silently into the trees. The train moved on to drop other troops further along the line. We walked away from the railway for a short distance before halting to await daylight. It was unrealistic to move in the bungle at night. It was not impossible, but impractical, because of noise, slowness of movement, the danger of being split up and, of course, not being able to see anything clearly at all. It was because of this fact that on active patrol we were assured of at least eight hours' kip every night, terrorists or no terrorists – unless we were rumbled. (As Malaya is near the Equator, days and nights are of almost equal length.)

The operational area was a seasonal swamp – that is, in the dry season, in which we were operating, the water was only about 6 inches deep, with plenty of exposed dry land to basha down on for camps. At other times the water could be 3 feet or so deep. Sleeping had to be in a hammock slung between two trees or, if time allowed, on a platform made with branches. Moving into the jungle for a further 5,000–6,000 yards we established a base camp from which to embark on light-order patrols. Each day several men were left in the base, including two aborigine porters whom we had with us. The latter were recruited from the jungle villages, known as kampongs. They were only small men, a mere 5 feet tall, and always scantily dressed. They wore just a pair of ragged shorts, or a sarong made from parachute material which covered their vital areas, and sometimes had a vest, but never any footwear. Their feet were broad, with widely splayed toes and skin like leather. Their main job was carrying the troop signaller's wireless set and batteries – huge, heavy items in those days – plus a hand-operated generator for emergency use.

The abos were really nice, trustworthy people, straightforward, gentle, always cheerful and very helpful in the jungle to us blundering Westerners. They were invariably polite. None of them would point with their finger. When they wanted to indicate someone or a direction of travel they would turn to face that way and throw out their lips in an exaggerated kiss. They were amazingly strong for their size and, like the Gurkhas (another formidable friend of the British), could carry hugely heavy loads, sometimes even carrying the leading scout's rucksack as well as their own. They would also do such chores as cleaning mess tins for payment in cigarettes. Their hunting and fishing skills came in very handy too, if ever we ran short of food.

Commanding 16 Troop at that time was Corporal Paul 'Archie' Archer. Archie had then been with 22 SAS for about four years and also had considerable jungle experience. The troop was soon organised into four-man patrols. I noted that 16 Troop was a mixed bag comprised of tall, short and medium-sized blokes with Newcastle Geordies, Taffs (Welshmen), Jocks from Scotland and irrepressible Scousers from all over Liverpool. In fact it was clear that the whole of 22 SAS had the same make-up at that time. Despite misconceptions held by the public it would have been hard to point to a typical SAS type. There were also, at that time, three National Servicemen in the troop. To be able to join the SAS a National Serviceman had to have at least 18 months out of his two years still to serve. That meant at most five months, in addition to other duties, to get fit for Selection. This was no mean feat, and so once again the SAS was guaranteed the best.

The men soon realised that existing maps of the operational area they were about to travel into were not of a very good standard and, because the terrain was flat and virtually featureless, they were to carry out most of their navigation by time, distance and compass. Parts of the maps were so bad, I discovered, that one day they followed a small stream which, according to the contours, flowed uphill! Swampland like this was vastly different from the hilly country we had seen, not only in topography but also the trees and the creatures within. Trees were generally not so tall, with thicker undergrowth to push through, and there were larger-rooted types. Some of the creatures were similar, but the mosquitos seemed to be bigger, and with longer and more vicious stings. The pig flies, which loved the backs of my legs, were angrier, and I saw two snakes which, I was told, lived only in the swamps. There was also more evidence of the type of creature that grubs around for food, such as pigs. These could make similar noises to approaching terrorists in the jungle and so could be alarming at times. Another noticeable difference was the humidity, which was much heavier, and we were now never dry, as we had to wade through water all day long. I also found that, like many others, I quickly became expert in devising an inexhaustible number of recipes to vary the troop's staple diet of corned beef, if with varying success.

Our patrol was commanded by Keith Norry, an experienced trooper and an ultra-reliable SAS man. (As described in Chapter 13, he was later tragically killed while taking part in high-altitude parachuting trials for the regiment in 1962.) He had great patience with the new recruits and furthered my jungle education in a thorough, logical and most pleasant manner. When I made silly mistakes he neither laughed nor made sarcastic remarks: he just pointed them out in his calm way. Keith had a dinky little aborigine parang which he wielded with seemingly effortless dexterity, casually but efficiently, snicking at any offending undergrowth. He was an extremely able soldier throughout the Malayan campaign, and his subsequent premature death was a sad loss to the SAS.

At the end of four weeks' hard slog on patrol the squadron had a resupply of food and ammo by truck at a logging road-head and moved on to another area. There followed twenty-eight more days squelching around in the swamp with not one sighting of any CT. Numerous SAS, including myself, saw lots of signs that indicated the possible presence of the CT, but no actual bodies were tracked down. In fact at this time contact with the enemy was quite rare, as they were a cunning adversary and adept at keeping out of the way as patrols approached. However, not seeing anything did not mean that the SAS squadron had wasted its time on this inaugural patrol for myself and the other troopers. On the contrary, it was discovered from captured CT that SAS patrols were causing a major nuisance, as the terrorists were forced to keep moving and, as a consequence, became largely ineffective as guerrillas. The long, gritty SAS campaign was bearing fruit, although there were many other factors involved, such as 'winning the hearts and minds' of the native populace and reaping the benefits of good intelligence from and cooperation with the Malays, factors that were crucial to our success.

Back in KL the squadron had a week's leave, which I spent either on my Dunlopillo sleeping mattress or downtown exploring and having a drink.

Nanto's Bar was the favourite RV, especially at the end of leave when money was scarce. Nanto gave generous credit, which he came to camp on payday to collect.

By the time I joined, some of the wilder elements of 22 SAS had either been tamed or had left. I heard tales of the early days, when these guys used to hit town after three months in the bungle, with a full beard and full wallet, full of frustration and a raging thirst. Then they proceeded to work it all off, finishing in bed in camp or with a woman somewhere a few days later, broke and knackered.

Within two weeks, after retraining and re-equipping, D Squadron was back in the jungle, this time on Operation Ginger, an ongoing op in the central highlands, an area of very broken and difficult terrain. The squadron moved to the area by road this time and then marched in to take over from A Squadron, which had been operating there for three months. After the base camp was established the men spent the first month on four-man patrolling. After the second fortnightly air drop half of 16 Troop, by then commanded by Corporal Arthur Weekes, was ordered to establish an ambush on an old CT camp about 5 miles away. On the morning our SAS squad was due to go I felt really ill and could hardly walk. However, off we went, with Taff Taylor the troop medic carrying both his bergen and mine too, until I had recovered sufficiently. Taff became a good friend of mine in the following hectic years but, sadly, he died in 1994.

Base camp was set up a short distance from the ambush location. The duty was set in pairs for four-hour stags, or watches, during which time all SAS soldiers involved had to lie perfectly still, watching and listening, rifles loaded and at the ready. Conversations were in whispers. If a man wanted to relieve himself, he would first indicate to the others what he intended, then slither slowly and silently to the rear. Washing and shaving in the jungle, especially on ambush duty, was sometimes banned. The CT, with their sharpened senses, could pick up the odour of soap from quite a distance. Also, soap suds in rivers could be seen a long way downstream before they dispersed. Lying in ambush I was again conscious that the jungle is never quiet, nor still. Among other sounds a troop of gibbons entertained us with their hooting most days. There was also the constant falling of leaves and debris from trees, and nearby a regiment of ants went about their business. Leeches gathered expectantly, and pig flies fed on the backs of my legs. Luckily we hadn't disturbed any red tree-ants when getting into position. They are vicious little buggers and have a pair of pliers for a mouth. We had to take all the bites and stings in silence, as a slap or curse could have alerted an approaching enemy and been fatal. I was on stag with Taff one day when we heard a noise like someone pushing through the bushes about 20 yards away. Our orders, if we heard any movement, were to get back to base and alert the rest of the patrol. This we did, quickly and quietly. Corporal Weekes sent out a cut-off group in the direction we had reported while Taff and I returned to the ambush in case whoever it was came back that way. No signs were found – only animal tracks. By this time I was fit again, but I never discovered what had ailed me. I was told that some SAS troops taken ill in the jungle were infected by new, unknown diseases, so we were pioneers in that regard. After two weeks the ambush was finally called off, and we returned to four-man patrols for the final two weeks of the op. During this phase we encountered lots of signs, such as footprints and cut foliage, but all these were quite old and hardly worthwhile following. Several skilled Iban trackers from Borneo had been attached to the squadron for the op, so if we had found any fresh tracks, they could have been called out to assist.

Our patrol had quite a frightening scare one day, however. We had just climbed down a small rockface in between two streams and were in a fairly exposed area when suddenly I had the eerie feeling of being watched. Taff, who was in front, stopped, held up his hand and pointed urgently to the left. At the same time I heard sounds of movement coming from the other side of the stream. They seemed to be slowly going away from us. We had a quick confab and decided to cross the stream further down and then circle back to see if we could pick up any tracks. It would have been foolish to have dashed straight towards the sounds, as we wouldn't have got there quickly enough to see anyone and if, as we agreed, it might be a ruse to lure us into an ambush, we would all have died instantly wading through the stream. After a stealthy approach, about 10 minutes later, we found a lot of disturbed undergrowth, some massive, round footprints – and a fresh, steaming pile of elephant dung! The elephant, known as gajah in Malay, must have been standing still and watching us as we climbed down the rockface. Then, deciding that we were not friendly, it had moved off.

Two days later, with the operation over, the SAS patrol returned to base camp, packed up and marched out to the road-head. We had left it too late to get out before dark, so we had to basha down for the night. Early on during the night, quite close by, a tiger let out a few terrifically loud and fierce roars.

The soldiers knew it was unlikely a tiger would attack humans that far into the jungle where their natural prey was plentiful, but the Iban trackers, who still harboured their native superstitions and finely tuned instincts, immediately lit a huge fire and kept it going all night. Next morning they refused to go on, saying that it was against the wishes of the spirits. However, there was a schedule to keep to and when we moved off the Ibans reluctantly followed us. I liked and admired the Ibans. They were of the same stamp as the Malayan aborigines, always cheerful and hard-working. They were great characters and could always be relied upon.

Arriving at the road transport RV we were met by the Regimental Quartermaster Sergeant (RQMS), who was immediately nearly sick at the smell of us. We had shaved a few times on patrol and had the odd piece of ripped clothing exchanged, but I don't think anyone had had an all-over wash for two months! Ten days' leave followed, which I spent in Singapore with Paddy B. We stayed at the Union Jack Club in the city. The accommodation was basic dormitory style, but OK. Exploring Singapore again was a great pleasure, and we had a walk round to see the famous Raffles Club, but we couldn't go in: it was officers only. Anyway, I was more than content to sit on the edge of the pavement eating a curry from a palm leaf or visit Bugi Street for a drink. Bugi Street was a favourite with troops. The bars, with lots of tables outside in the street as well, were always packed. The food was edible, but the main attraction was bottles of Tiger and Anchor beer. It didn't matter where you sat, you were always within listening distance of at least four juke boxes, all playing different tunes! Junk wristwatch sellers abounded. They had good brand names, but the works invariably ground to a halt after a week. We knew the watches were rubbish and the sellers knew we knew, but they still tried and had such good, amusing lines of patter, it was all part of Bugi Street fun. In Bugi Street you could not move much more than a table's length without being tapped up by a prostitute. Some of them were quite beautiful and, after a few days, I cracked. I was a strong, virile SAS man after all, you know. A week after our leave D Squadron was back in the bungle, this time in the Thailand border region. Apparently the CT, having been forced to move further and further north, were moving through that area to cross the border into Thailand.

On this op 16 Troop was commanded by Squadron Sergeant Major (SSM) 'Lofty' R. He was known as 'the Gloom' owing to his habit, when in the jungle, of sitting in his basha in the evenings and going into long periods of meditation, during which he would appear extremely melancholy. He was also very short-tempered, getting angry over seemingly trivial offences. However, out of his moods the patrol found Lofty quite amusing and also very generous. He had been awarded the Military Medal for his work with the SAS in the past, and everyone admired him for that. The country in the border area is very rugged, with no road-heads or railway then, so we were lifted in by helicopter. We were put down in a small clearing and the troop, laden like donkeys, was soon on the march. I was on first as lead scout for an hour, so my bergen was carried by a porter. About 15 minutes after starting I spotted fresh-looking footprints bisecting our line of march. I looked back at Lofty and gave him the sign – two fingers walking. Lofty came forward and had a look. After a short while, during which the Troop Sergeant also had a look, we went on. I don't know exactly why we didn't follow those tracks. Later the Troop Sergeant said they should have been investigated, but I think the Troop Leader may have been preoccupied with another more important objective that had to be achieved. This was not unusual, but it could be frustrating at times.

I basha'd down with Lofty on this op. Every night we pooled our shelter sheets to make a bigger and more comfortable basha. Most of the blokes paired in this way. It usually meant sharing food as well. I would boil the rice and Lofty would make the curry. He would throw everything in – porridge oats, raisins, biscuits and any other odd bits left over. It looked ghastly, but I would be so hungry it all went down.

Accompanying the troop was a Chinese bloke, an ex-CT known as an SEP (surrendered enemy personnel). He had agreed to help track down his former comrades. Pairing up with Corporal 'Sweeney' Logan, the Troop Signaller, he constructed their basha and did the cooking every night. Sweeney needed help, because each night when the rest of us were cooking he had to set up his wireless and aerials and get through to HQ in KL. Sweeney always had a good basha, because the SEP, after years of living in the jungle, could make a fine shelter, complete with a split bamboo floor, in a very short time. The SEP could also speak good English, and I spent many an hour talking with him and Sweeney.

It was extra hard going in this area, with lots of steep-sided ridges. We had climbed high into the hills bordering the two countries, and one relief we benefited from was the cooler air, especially at night. I noted that the trees were comparatively short, and there was a distinct feeling of height in the atmosphere. The air was more still and the jungle sounds seemed to be muted. After two weeks we withdrew half a mile or so from the border to take an air drop of supplies. No chopping was allowed because of the noise, so we took the drop through the trees, just putting a balloon up to mark our position. Fortunately none of the canopies snagged up. There was a bit of drama later when we were busy sorting out the bundles, though. Everyone was engrossed in the task when suddenly a huge black snake, easily 3 yards long and with its head held high, shot through the middle of us. We all froze, mesmerised, but in two seconds it was gone, vanishing into the bushes. Not long afterwards, with that memory still fresh, Lofty stood on a length of metal banding from around a ration box. The banding twanged up around his knees, causing Lofty to jump high in the air, his legs running. Everybody sniggered, but Lofty didn't think it was funny and was not in a very good mood afterwards. It was steak and egg banjos for tea! I had a letter from home and they had sent me a copy of the local paper, the *Newcastle Sunday Sun*, to read.

Next day, suitably fortified, we carried on patrolling. We became lost (or rather misplaced, as some prefer) a couple of times. On one occasion we got lost in a steep gulley, just as darkness overtook us, forcing us to spend the night there. We were stuck in this steep cleft, practically standing up on the bank for the rest of the night or perched on a little ledge, desperately trying to get some sleep, as it was far too dangerous to move in the dark. Another time involved a huge 'map cloud'. We were en route to the RV with the rest of the squadron and picked up some of our troop who had been left behind in KL. When we eventually arrived at the RV, late, the OC said to Lofty, 'You should have been here at twelve o'clock.' 'Why?' grunted the laconic Lofty, with a deadpan expression. 'What happened?'

The missing members of the troop were part of a larger group who were supposed to have followed the squadron in with a trial elephant resupply train. However, the trial was a huge flop and had been abandoned, as the bulky loads kept getting snagged up in the trees and the noise from the elephants tramping through the jungle was horrific. So our lads were waiting at the RV, minus elephants but full of stories to tell. Taff Taylor said he had been following behind the same gajah (elephant) for a week and knew every wrinkle on its backside. Gajahs didn't give a lot of notice before having a shit, either, so some nifty footwork was called for, and gajah farts are something else, believe me. It's not funny, you know, what our troop suffered for their country! Wild elephants were sometimes a help, however, as they made their own paths as they went which we could use afterwards – and often did.

One day, as our SAS troop was walking carefully up a shallow stream, I was second man in the patrol. We had just rounded a bend and there, only about 5 yards ahead, trying to hook something out of the water, was a fully grown tiger. We froze to the spot with fright, but the tiger looked up, calmly regarded our shaking group for a moment and then, with a giant leap up the bank, was gone. The same leap in our direction and it would have landed right on our heads – and I know who would have come off best. It was by no means my only close brush with death from the wild animals and reptiles of the jungle. I was lying on the ground in my basha one day when, turning over, I found myself staring into the eyes of a 'bamboo' snake, which were, I had been told, deadly poisonous. It was only about 18 inches away from my face, and I thought if I moved, it might strike, so I lay perfectly still and held its gaze. After a while, thankfully, it slid away. It may have been a trick of the light, but I swear it shrugged its shoulders first! Snakes underfoot were rare. I saw once, just in time, a long green snake hanging from a branch over the track we were patrolling on. Two more steps and it would have been inspecting my neck. Black honey bears, monkeys, porcupines and many more creatures, including small hairy pigs, used to come rummaging around our bashas at night looking for scraps. I heard a noise one night, and when I shone my torch two beady little eyes blinked back. It was a mongoose, and it was finishing off my curry.

Sometimes when we were on the trail Lofty, who was usually second man in the patrol, neglected to tell the lead scout when a change of direction was required. The troop was moving alongside a big river one day, and I was lead scout. On big bends the track usually split, one following the river and the other cutting off the bend. At the next bend I took the cut-off, but Lofty took the other without letting me know. Six or seven steps later I noticed a movement in the corner of my eye. Swinging round I brought my rifle up into the aim, safety catch off. I had no need to shout, because the man behind me should have been watching and looking where I was aiming. I had the light-coloured flesh of a neck in my sights and was just beginning to squeeze the trigger when at that exact second the figure moved a fraction further on and I saw Lofty's enamel drinking mug hanging on the back of his bergen. Somewhat shocked, I looked around and discovered I was alone.

The others had followed Lofty, probably thinking that he had told me to recce down the other track. It was an odd place to hang a mug, but it saved Lofty's life that day. We all had red cloth bands sewn around our jungle hats for identification, but Lofty's hat had become crumpled, so his red band was near enough invisible.

A week before the operation ended 16 Troop was ordered to form a base near a river to await 19 Troop, which was approaching from upstream. The soldiers of 19 Troop had located a 'lost' tribe of aborigines and were escorting them to a government-protected area. The reason for this was to prevent the CT getting at them and forcing them to provide food and shelter for the terrorists. Our troop was present in case any assistance was required. Richard Noone, an aborigine protection officer, was with 19 Troop organising the event. The Troop Sergeant of 19 was Harold 'Darky' Davidson. Dark-skinned, of Anglo-Burmese birth, Darky was the first man to contact the tribe, and the wags in the squadron said he was the first white man the tribe had ever seen. It was quite possible. Darky laughed more than anybody at that! He was a fine man and a brilliant soldier, and was to become a good friend of mine over the years. When he died some years ago it was a sad loss to the SAS community. In the afternoon of the first day we heard a handclap sounding loudly from somewhere behind the green veil of the jungle. It was the signal from 19 that they were close. We answered the clap and in they came. They did not stay long. The aborigines came through in single file, about fifty of them – men, women and children. I was amazed at the sight. They were some of the most beautiful people I have ever seen. None was over 5 feet tall. The men were handsome and muscular and the women graceful, shapely and really nice-looking. The children, some of them just babies, were all bright-eyed, with big smiles. They carried all their belongings with them. These people lived off the jungle all their lives, and they looked well on it. We greeted them and they all smiled and greeted us back. They were lovely people. I hope they were happy and well treated wherever they went.

The men of 16 Troop remained where they were at the base and prepared a landing zone (LZ) for a helicopter. A signal had been received saying that the CO of the SAS was coming in to visit. Lieutenant-Colonel Deane-Drummond flew in next day. He had only been with the men for 10 minutes when I was told he wanted to talk to me personally. 'Trooper Doran,' said DD when I reported. 'I have been looking at your records and discovered that you were a mortarman in the Parachute Regiment. Also that you gained a very high grade on a mortar instructor's course. Well, D Squadron is about to be sent on a top-level operation somewhere in the Middle East and will need trained mortarmen. I want you to train two crews before the squadron departs.' I was taken aback. 'Yes sir,' was all I managed to say in reply. I had imagined that I would have been jungle-bashing for another year or so at least. The CO had brought in a mortar training pamphlet for me to refresh my memory, but speed was of the essence.

There were several days left of the op, and we still had a lot of ground to cover. On we went, constantly soaked with sweat and, because we were now down among fairly big rivers, never dry from wading. We had an extra thought on our minds now as well. Where is the new operation going to be, and who is the enemy? Wading jungle rivers could be dicey. Rivers are clear spaces where soldiers can be seen and attacked. Also, most of the fordable rivers in Malaya were fast-flowing and usually covered with rounded, slippery stones. Sometimes, if the river was deep enough, it was possible to let the water take the weight of your bergen and walk lightly with the current, angling towards the other side and aiming for a low overhanging branch to pull yourself into the bank. I tried it once. I was going nicely straight for a branch when Lofty, who had already crossed, stepped into the water and held out his hand. 'That's jolly decent of him,' I thought momentarily, and reached out to grab him. Just then he pulled his hand away and I swept past, missing the branch and ending up 30 yards downstream tangled in nanti sikit, the vine with vicious hooks on in which troops got entangled that I mentioned earlier. That was Lofty's idea of a joke.

We met up with 18 Troop one morning and stayed talking for a while. I particularly remember that day, because one of 18 Troop, Corporal 'Duke' Swindells, a superb fighting soldier, made me a huge mug of hot chocolate. (Sadly Duke was to be killed in action in Oman just a few weeks later.) After leaving 18 Troop we had to do, on that same day, a 15,000yd march to a helicopter LZ from which we were to be lifted out next day. We followed a small river upstream. It was exceptionally hard going, with many large fallen trees to negotiate and steep, broken ground. Lofty tried to make us laugh again on the march, keeping us entertained with one of his favourite tricks. Whenever he encountered a low-hanging vine Lofty would lift it up until he was clear and then just let it swing down behind him without warning. Anyone following, unless they were watching or far enough behind, would get the vine right in the face!

I had a chat with Sweeney that night, and we both spoke with squeaky voices after our exertions. I was so knackered I turned in early, forgoing my usual hour or so of reading by candlelight. As I lay waiting for sleep to come I thought back over my time in Malaya. It was not a long time of service compared with some of the other lads in the regiment, but it was full of hardships and privations, all governed by the all-pervasive jungle. However, I had thoroughly enjoyed it and hoped to be doing at least one tour of two years' duration. Out of the eight months I had spent in Malaya seven of them were in the jungle. Not bad going, I thought. It had been very hard work on operations – physically and mentally. I had had to learn a completely new way of soldiering but was now satisfied that I had coped well.

Within two hours the troop had been helicopter-lifted out to a small airstrip near the town of Grik. We were sitting around waiting when 18 Troop came in to join us. As they passed by I saw Paddy B. 'Hiya Paddy,' I called out. Paddy looked at me blankly at first, then, coming closer, he exclaimed, 'Bloody hell, Geordie, I didn't recognise you!' It was no wonder. All of us had lost so much weight, and under our bristles our faces were gaunt and hollow-cheeked. They were all no better themselves, and, with their filthy, ripped and sweat-stained uniforms, were not a pretty sight. After a few days' leave, during which Paddy and I shifted copious amounts of T-bone steaks and beer, we started training for the future operation in the burning desert. It could not have been more of a contrast to fighting in the jungle.

I had been promoted to SAS Lance Corporal – all previous ranks were negated on joining the regiment. I had also been given ten days to train six men on the 3in mortar. Paddy had been allocated as my assistant. Johnny Partridge was also one of the six chosen for mortar training, having been a 4.2in mortarman in the RA. We also had a man from 16 Troop as our radio man but were a little wary of the latter, as he hadn't impressed us much in the jungle, where he always had a rusty rifle and seemed to be a general slack-arse. Anyway, ably assisted by Paddy I trained the crews as best I could in the time allowed, including live firing. The rest of the squadron had meanwhile been training on various other weapons – the No. 94 grenade launcher, which lobbed an aimed penetrating missile (useful against buildings and light armour), plus the 3.5in bazooka-type anti-tank rocket launcher, which the SAS found did not work half the time because of faulty ammunition. There was also sniper training, using the trusty old Lee Enfield No. 4 .303 bolt-action rifle, veteran of the Second World War and accurate up to 1,200 yards. To keep the ball rolling they managed to squeeze in a couple of parachute jumps, one on an airfield at Kuantan on the east coast and the other into the sea off Singapore, followed by an exercise on one of the small islands near there.

D squadron had a slap-up farewell party in the NAAFI before leaving KL. Two days later they boarded Hastings aircraft at RAF Changi, Singapore, bound for the Middle East. The local bartenders were apparently devastated – some of their best customers were in D Squadron! The troops touched down at Ceylon (now Sri Lanka) to refuel and then flew on to Masira, an island just off the coast of Oman. At Masira they changed aeroplanes and flew on in a Beverley to Muscat, the capital of Oman, landing there on 18 November 1958.

Just before we boarded the aircraft at Masira Major Watts, the OC told us where we were going. There would be plenty of action and fighting, he said, that was for sure.

I swear that not one of us had guessed our destination correctly. Little did we know that this next operation was to be *the* one that, many believe, ensured the survival of the entire SAS Regiment.

Chapter 10

HEROIC, HAIR-RAISING ACTION: 22 SAS REGIMENT IN OMAN

Our SAS force established a tented base camp at Beit el Falaj, not far from Muscat, near the sea, where our OC, Major Watts, got straight down to business and gave us the latest gen. A force of rebels, under the leadership of three men – Talib, Ghalib and Sulaiman, soon irreverently dubbed Freeman, Hardy and Willis by our men – had, in 1957, attempted to overthrow the Sultan of Oman. It had been a close-run thing, and the threat was still present from the rebel forces, so the Sultan had asked the British urgently for help. Ghalib ibn Ali and Sulaiman ibn Himyar were sheikhs in their own right. Talib ibn Ali was Ghalib's brother, and the treacherous Sulaiman was sheikh of the main Jebel tribe, the Bani Riyam. By the time the SAS arrived the rebels had been cleared from the low-lying desert areas by the Sultan's Armed Forces (SAF), assisted by some British units, and had retreated, some 600-strong, onto the Jebel el Akhdar, the famed Green Mountain stronghold. From there they were making raids out into the surrounding areas, laying mines on vehicle tracks to blow up following traffic and attacking SAF and British bases around the bottom of the Jebel. We were told that Saudi Arabia was the chief backer of the rebels, supplying them with weapons and cash. A lot of Omani men had gone to work in Saudi, so it was suspected that most of the rebels came from that group.

I listened intently to the initial briefing. 'The basic reason behind it all is oil,' said Major Watts. I knew that Oman was, and still is, rich in oilfields, which were just being developed at that time. Britain's economy ran on oil, so it was logical that any help the Sultan needed to stabilise his country, the SAS was prepared to give. The idea of employing SAS troops was to penetrate the rebel positions and kill the leaders, which, it was hoped, would cause their followers to give up. A somewhat sobering thought was that the last people to climb and conquer the Jebel el Akhdar were the Persians in

1265, and they had lost thousands of men doing it. After informing us that the operation was top secret and all letters would be censored, Major Watts finished by saying, 'We are an army on the cheap. We are going to have to do this job on a shoe-string, and some of us won't be going home.'

The background to the crisis was rooted, I believe, in the character of the Sultan of Oman himself. Although not a bad ruler he was very autocratic, making all the decisions personally. He was out of the country most of the time, so that little was done to modernise and improve the lives of his people. In 1958 Omanis were still living as they had done for centuries. There were no good roads, merely desert tracks. Houses were still being built with mud and straw. Donkeys and camels were the main forms of transport. Laws were strict and punishments very severe indeed. Thieves had their right hand chopped off, and adulterers were stoned to death. There was even an archaic law whereby anyone out at night had to carry a lantern or face a stiff penalty. Income tax was negligible, there being little money to tax, but taxes were levied on eggs, firewood, vegetables, donkeys, camels and just about everything else. Town and village headmen, called walis, were mostly corrupt and feathered their own nests. There were no schools, no hospitals, no telephones and no post. So this was the country that the SAS had been sent to save from the rebels – a country destined to become enormously rich from oil. The low-lying land in Oman is rock and pebble desert with a covering of dusty, dirty, 'get in every nook and cranny' sand, which quickly, when it rains, turns into glutinous mud. Watercourses, or wadis, were mostly dry and criss-crossed, making progress either on foot or by vehicle slow and laborious. In northern Oman where we were the landscape is dominated by the Jebel el Akhdar, a huge massif rising abruptly from the plain with hardly any foothills. It is a forbidding sight. The area of the mountain as far as our future activities was concerned was about 10 miles wide and 20 long, the highest points being 6,000–8,000 feet. The whole Jebel is well over 100 miles long by about 50 wide, and the highest peak, Jebel el Sham, is about 11,000 feet.

The Green Mountain is so called because there are many water catchment areas where a variety of crops can be grown, plus date and fig trees. Several villages existed on the mountain, and people also lived in the many caves to be found in the cliff sides of the huge wadis which split the Jebel from top to bottom. There were, then, ten or twelve donkey routes up the mountain, mainly in the big wadis. When we arrived in Oman the winter was just beginning. It wasn't so bad on the low ground where it rained a lot but was reasonably warm. However, up on the Jebel the weather was very severe. Temperatures frequently dropped below freezing, with rain and sleet blown horizontally by strong winds. Heavy rain often caused flash floods which moved everything in their path. People, animals, trees and boulders the size of garden sheds were all swept down the wadis by the irresistible force. To combat the cold we were issued with thick battledress trousers, Army boots and pullovers, woolly hats and camouflage smocks. On the sharp rocks the boots only lasted about ten days. The thick trousers and smocks were excellent camouflage but once wet took ages to dry out. We had our ponchos to make shelters with, and we were issued with gigantic airborne sleeping bags of Second World War vintage. The latter items weighed a ton: it was like carrying a roll of stair carpet around on our backs. Apart from all that I think we were set to enjoy ourselves!

The SAF, the military ally of the SAS, was commanded by a seconded British officer, Colonel Smiley. Most of his officers were also British. The SAF consisted of two regiments, comprising the Muscat and the Northern Frontier, with strengths of around 200 men each. As well as various small arms, their weapons included 3in mortars, some machine guns and a few artillery pieces. Desertions were common and so, unfortunately, was changing sides, which made security of information and intelligence sometimes difficult.

After a few days testing our weapons, preparing kit and going for a swim in the sea we SAS troops were ready for action. Incidentally, we were carrying the SLR, the same rifle we had used in Malaya. It took the troops a while longer to become physically acclimatised after coming so recently from a warm and humid country, where the visibility in the jungle was rarely more than 10 yards, to (at that time of year) a cold, desert land, where visibility was virtually unlimited. However, I was soon, as ever, in my element.

During those first days my friend Sweeney was sent to British Army HQ in Bahrain to act as our liaison officer for resupply and to pass signals to and fro. Because our op was top secret Sweeney had to wear a black Royal Signals beret to hide his connection with the SAS.

Both 16 and 17 Troops moved around to the north side of the mountain to probe for ways to get up, while 18 and 19, plus me and and my merry mortarmen Paddy, Jock, Mac, Johnny, Andy, Tich and Vic, were dispatched to Tanuf on the south side, where there was already a detachment of SAF based. It was a long, hard ride on open trucks to Tanuf, all on rough,

stony desert tracks. Halfway there, at Nizwa, where there is a huge fort, we
were met by a troop of Life Guards (LG) who were based nearby with their
armoured cars. From Nizwa there was a danger of snipers and mined roads,
so the LG, familiar with the area, provided our escort on to Tanuf. The LG
troop was with the SAS throughout the Oman campaign and, in my opinion,
performed first-class support with their armoured cars and in dismounted
action with their .30 Browning machine guns. They climbed the mountain
and were with us on the top carrying their own weapons. I cannot recall
meeting their officer, but the blokes were great, real good lads. I particularly
remember their Troop Sergeant, a Jock. He taught us some old Scottish
songs around our campfires on the Jebel, helped, I might add, by a vocal-
cord-loosening issue of medicinal rum. Next day at Tanuf we witnessed RAF
bombers blasting the top of the Jebel. I am not sure what effect it had on the
rebels' morale, but several natural water reservoirs were fractured, causing
them to dry up. That night 18 and 19 Troops SAS started probing patrols up
the mountain. We, the mortars, waited patiently. We knew our turn would
come soon. Paddy and I took a walk along to the local fort and made friends
with the tribesmen there. They all had a rifle of some sort, mostly ancient
Martini-Henrys which fired a round ball or crudely shaped bullets. Martini-
Henrys were known as 'woozers', because the bullets made a 'woozing' noise
in flight. Daggers called khanjars were worn at the waist and were also
fashionable with the tribesmen, being a sign of manhood and status.

We did not have long to wait for action, because the rebels came down
that night and attacked the SAF base. I was ordered to take the mortars there
and give support to the SAF. It was blind firing in the dark. We could see
the flash of rebel rifle fire on the slope above the camp, and so we plonked a
few rounds in their direction, but I don't know what effect we had. The SAF
had good mortar teams themselves, which I saw and admired then and on
other occasions. The SAF blokes whom we encountered were mostly friendly
but had, to us, some strange ways. Some of them were observed firing their
rifles over the top of their shelters without attempting to take aim. Their
philosophy was that 'If Allah wants the enemy to die, then Allah will guide
the bullet, inshallah [God willing].' Next morning, on the mountain above
Tanuf, our troops had a brief fire fight with a group of rebels, and 'Duke'
Swindells was seriously wounded. The OC ordered me and my mortar teams,
under the command of SSM Lofty, to escort Corporal 'Bill' Evans, the medic,
up to the troop position. It was quite wrong to send both mortar teams,

because if the troop had requested supporting fire, they wouldn't have got it. But that was what the hell we were there for, so up we went anyway. Halfway up we spotted some rebels about 50 yards ahead who looked as if they were manoeuvring to outflank the patrol on the top. They saw us at the same time, and before we could do anything they had disappeared behind some big rocks. There was no sign of them when we got there.

Halting just down from our troop position Bill Evans went forward to check what had happened and discovered that Duke had died. We remained there until dark and then, together with the patrol, started back down to base. Duke's body was carried in a folding stretcher which Bill Evans had brought with him. The mortar teams did a lot of the carrying, and it was bloody hard going. Even though we knew we couldn't hurt Duke any more than he had been, we were very gentle and did our best not to let him knock against rocks or anything. All the way down I kept remembering Duke's smiling face when he gave me that mug of hot chocolate in Malaya. He was a fantastic soldier.

For the next two days 18 and 19 Troops prepared to attack a cave full of rebels that had been observed on their patrols. I took one of our mortars round to the SAF position and carried out a few practice shoots. While this was going on one of our trucks, which was full of mortar ammunition, was blown up by a mine. The driver and his passenger, Bill Evans, were shaken up but not badly hurt. Bill was to be blown up twice more after that but amazingly each time escaped serious injury. The mortar ammo had been flung all over the place by the blast. I went to have a look and decided, because the bomb cases were still intact and there had been no fire, that the ammo was OK. When we inspected the bombs later we found that all the nose fuses and the charges on the tail units were undamaged. On the night of 30 November, after first putting the mortars in position, I climbed up the mountain with the troops who were already on their way to attack the cave. I had to get myself into an observation post (OP) from where I could direct the mortar fire. We had little walkie-talkie sets with a range, if you were lucky, of about 2,000 yards. Having reached a point overlooking the cave I joined several others there, while the troops went on to get in position for the attack. Included in our party was Sergeant 'Tanky' Smith, an immensely colourful character in the fighting SAS and later a much-loved SAS Association Secretary. He gave accurate and sustained covering fire with a .30 Browning MG (machine gun).

When it became light enough I had a look at the target. It was at an awkward angle but just possible to see. When Tanky manoeuvred into position with the MG the angle was so acute that it appeared he was about to roll over the cliff edge. Just then 18 Troop, which at that time was under the command of Captain de la Billière (DLB, whom I had met briefly in Korea (see Chapter 3)) were doing the actual attack, and 19 were in support further back. The boys of 18 Troop waited until rebels started to appear outside the cave before opening fire. I couldn't see the troop from my angle, but I heard the rattle of gunfire. The rebels were taken completely by surprise and had some casualties, but they soon recovered and returned the fire. Meanwhile Tanky was potting away again with the MG, and I had established communications with the mortars. Before long the signal to withdraw was given and after waiting a few minutes, I ranged in the mortars. I ordered white phosphorus (WP) smoke bombs to range as they could be more easily seen in that type of broken ground. As soon as we were on target I ordered a steady rate of high explosive (HE) fire.

As we withdrew from our position RAF Venoms swooped in and began strafing the cave area with rockets, the explosions adding to the thump of our mortar bombs. Back in our mortar position I found that my crews had fired off about 80 bombs each. Later, intelligence reports said that twenty rebels had been killed, including their chief mortar and machine gunners, plus some high-rankers. Our side had no casualties. My mortarmen performed very well; I was proud of them. Nobody knew exactly who bumped off who, of course, but I went with a patrol to the cave after the campaign was over and found a lot of mortar tail units and marked bits of shrapnel around the area where the rebels had been congregated. Meanwhile, on the north side of the Jebel, 16 and 17 Troops, operating from Awabi, had managed to find a way up the treacherous slopes of the mountain. They had already had a few skirmishes, culminating in a patrol of six men under Sergeant 'Herbie' Hawkins having a pitched battle with some forty rebels. Herbie was later awarded the Distinguished Conduct Medal for his part in the fight. On 3 December the SAS forces in the south were ordered to move to an area near Izki, a village on the road to Nizwa. From there 18 and 19 Troops were to patrol the Wadi Mutti. SSM Lofty was put in charge of twenty donkeys plus handlers to move stores from Tanuf. The donkeys, which had been brought from Somaliland, were unsuited to the work, the troopers noted, and proved quite useless. It took ten hours to move to Izki when the journey should have taken half that time.

The men of 18 and 19 Troops began patrolling on 4 December. Then, on the morning of the 5th, two patrols of 19 Troop found themselves pinned down by very heavy rifle and MG fire from a large force of enemy. Major Watts ordered the mortars to give fire support so that the patrols could withdraw as soon as possible. We had a fix on their location, but it was well out of range. A British officer from a nearby SAF unit had been on the OC's briefing and said that he knew of a good position to fire from and catch the enemy unawares. Lofty was put in charge and, after loading the mortars and ammo onto two trucks, off we went at high speed, with the SAF officer leading. Ten minutes later we stopped, but it looked a hell of a long way off to me. However, I laid the aiming posts out in line with the target, got the crews into action and ordered a WP ranging round on 2,000 yards. Thirty seconds later I saw a puff of smoke through my binos. It was at the bottom of the wadi, well short. We needed to be hitting the top at 2,000 so as to give a good overlap beyond the target. I told Lofty we had to move in closer. At the next position I ordered another WP at 2,000. It was still not close enough. I told Lofty that we must move further in again, but he said no, as we would then be in range of rebel snipers. He was quite right, of course; we would have been within range, and I appreciated his concern. But I thought of the patrols in dire need of our support. They were putting up with a damned sight more than a few snipers, I reasoned. I looked at my mortar crews, covered in dust and sweating. They had performed brilliantly, both in and out of action in record time on two occasions already. They knew we would have to move to shorten the range and waited for my order. The SSM stood watching me. I shouted to him, 'Bollocks to the snipers! We have to get within proper range of the target now, and fast.' I gave the order to load up again, and off we roared. I halted the trucks almost at the bottom of the wadi. The WP ranging shot landed just where I had wanted it to.

At this stage I knew there was a risk of hitting our own men, as I didn't know their exact location. However, they had seen my ranging shot, and gave a correction on the radio. I sent one more WP ranging shot to make sure before switching to HE. At this point Lofty came storming over and shouted again that we must move back to get out of the range of snipers. He and I then had a good ding-dong verbal battle, which ended with me yelling at him, 'We're in proper range of the target here, and this is where the fuck we are staying!'

I wasn't worried so much about snipers, anyway. If we were in range with our mortars, then I figured we must be in range of theirs, if they had any. However, no rebel mortar bombs came our way, and if there was any sniper fire, then I wasn't aware of it. I think, maybe, that Lofty was influenced by the SAF officer, because neither of them showed their faces from behind the trucks for the rest of the action. The mortar teams managed OK, but it would have been nice if our two chiefs had helped to carry the ammo!

Trooper Paddy Doherty, one of the patrol's radio men, was giving us corrections: 'Drop twenty yards', 'Right twenty yards', and so on. He said the rebels were so close that our bombs were almost dropping on our own heads. Small ranging corrections of the type Paddy was asking for were not marked on our mortar sights, so all we could do was put the indicator in between the marks suggested and hope for the best. We fired steadily on, carefully checking the sights between each round and not firing rapidly unless it was asked for. We were told later that our fire support had been very effective. At last the word came that the SAS patrols had managed to break out and were withdrawing safely. I checked our ammo stocks: each mortar had fired ninety HE and several WP. Quite a hot little action, and the mortar crews had handled their weapons excellently, calmly and efficiently. I was very proud of them. When we returned to base I mentioned nothing of my altercations with the SSM. The mortar crews had seen and heard everything, but I thought it best to keep quiet. On 8 December I was ordered to return to Beit el Falaj, taking with me one mortar and crew, comprising Andy, Jock and Vic, and from there travel round to Awabi on the north side and move up to join 16 and 17 Troops. Arriving at Awabi, complete with a 3-ton truck full of mortar ammo, we met up with an SAF party which escorted us a few miles along a wadi to the point where our ascent of the mountain was to start. We slept there that night ready to start at dawn the next morning. There was a long and hard 6,000ft climb ahead of us and, weighed down as we were by personal weapons, extra water bottles and seven days' rations in our bergens, we were going to need all the available daylight there was left to complete it.

A team of locals with donkeys had been recruited to carry the mortar and ammunition. Also, one of 17 Troop, Arthur Bigglestone, had come down the mountain to act as guide. I had a great admiration for Arthur, an SAS stalwart I was to get to know very well in future years. The route up consisted of an old donkey track. Looking ahead, sometimes we could not see any apparent way up the seemingly sheer cliffs in front, but then, miraculously, the track would continue in between huge rocks and up cracks in the cliff faces. We SAS soldiers gained an increasing admiration for the Jebel donkeys, who we thought were fantastic. Surefooted and fast, they nevertheless carried massive loads. One of them had a mortar barrel and bipod legs, plus other kit, which must have totalled well over 200lb. There was a strange incident concerning one of the donkeys on the way up. We had stopped to take a break, and I noticed that one of the handlers was getting agitated. He kept poking his donkey in the stomach, and it sounded like he was cursing. I could not see why, except that the animal's belly appeared to be bloated somewhat. Eventually, after a bit more poking and cursing, the handler lifted the donkey's tail up, shoved his stick into its arse and then, with more cursing, proceeded to waggle the stick furiously. A minute later the stick was withdrawn and the donkey let out a long and horribly rasping fart. That seemed to please the handler and, after he shouted something to his mates, we moved on. I thought, 'Kee-rist, I'm glad I've got Rennies for mine!' Talking about wind, as we climbed higher it became more and more difficult to fill our lungs with air. This made the climb that extra bit harder. It became a mechanical plod, left-right, left-right. In addition, of course, we had to stay alert for possible enemy ambushes. I kept a wary eye on the handlers too. I thought, 'What's to stop them giving us the mallet and taking our mortar and ammo to the rebs?'

After a ten-hour climb, during which we had stopped twice for a brew and a rest, we reached 16 and 17 Troops on the top. The area was called the Aquabat, as wild a piece of rocky mountain country as you will ever see – and it was bloody freezing cold. It was 12 December, with just a few more shopping days to Christmas! The troops had been getting sniped at and mortared just before we got there, so I was ordered straight into action with the mortar to give the rebels some harassing fire in return. It was at this point that we discovered the bracket for the mortar sights was missing. It had been removed to prevent damage and put in a box with other spares. The box should have been loaded onto one of the donkeys after we started walking. We knew it would arrive eventually, because another donkey train was coming up the next day bringing the rest of our ammunition. Meanwhile I would just have to cope without it. I estimated the range by the angle of the barrel from the vertical and deflections by turns of the traversing handle. I had practised this many times in the past. When the mortar was set up I ordered a WP ranging shot. Bods in the forward positions gave corrections over their radio, and very soon we had a good rate of HE going out. One of the blokes out front told me afterwards that it gave him a grand feeling to see HE crumping down on the rebels for a change. Our sight bracket came up next day, and this enabled me to go forward with my radio and direct the fire accurately. We had to conserve ammo, as each bomb weighed 10lb without packaging and had to be hauled up the Jebel somehow. Avoiding wasting our precious ammo called for accurate corrections and good handling of the mortar sights.

The RAF had already delivered several air drops, and a couple of days after I got there another one came in. Some of the canopies didn't develop fully, so the loads hit the ground too hard, bursting open and spilling the contents around. A few of the bundles contained mortar ammunition, both WP and HE. A number of WP cracked, immediately throwing out great clouds of dense white smoke. Actually there wasn't a great deal of danger, provided no one touched any white phosphorus, which could give severe burns. I decided to try to recover as much ammunition as possible. As I have mentioned already mortar ammo is so well packaged that I knew most of it would be intact. The mortar crew, 'Taff' Chidgey of 16 Troop and I began dragging the undamaged boxes out of range of the cracked WP, which were still belching out choking white smoke. The other troops looked on from a safe distance. I didn't blame them: they expected the HE to be exploding any minute and, almost certainly, they also thought that my helpers and I were being foolhardy in the extreme – which we weren't since it was a calculated risk. One of the watchers yelled out, 'What are you trying to do, win a medal?' 'No,' I shouted back. 'It's quite safe. Why don't you come and help?' But none of them did. One of the SAS chaps who was there wrote a book some years later in which he described the incident and said that I 'hid behind a rock, smoked a fag and waited for the HE bombs to stop exploding'. Well, no HE bombs exploded! If they had, I wouldn't be alive now. My helpers were brave because they didn't know there was only minimal danger; but bravery, as far as I personally was concerned, didn't come into it.

For two weeks after that we carried out daily harassing fire with the mortar. If we hadn't rescued those boxes, we would have run out of bombs and the situation could have had a very different outcome. During this time and in the following weeks, bouts of extremely severe weather and wind, rain and sleet battered all the SAS troops nearly every day. Endurance was tested; half our time was taken up by merely surviving. We had hexamines for cooking, but to conserve our stocks we built wood fires from the sparse scrubby trees which dotted the area. Parachute canopies made very good shelters, we quickly discovered – even though the material is porous to a certain extent, they kept most of the wet out. When suspended by the apex from a tree, the canopies resembled Red Indian tepees. All parachute canopies have holes in the top allowing air to go through, which has the effect of stopping the load or man from swinging too much. To complete the resemblance to Indian tepees the smoke from our fires billowed up through these holes. The mortar, which was left mounted ready for action, was our totem pole, and we did all our dancing around that . . .

After about a week the OC Troops, Captain W., decided to move forward a few miles to have a better base to patrol from. However, this meant having to move the heavy mortar plus the ammunition, of which there were quite extensive stocks. Fortunately a detachment of LG had just joined the SAS, bringing with them some Somali donkeys. There were initially high hopes, but the donkeys proved useless, and my crew had to hump the mortar plus its ammo along to the new location. One man from the other troops volunteered to help carry bombs, a certain Arthur Bigglestone. I left the radio man to guard the new site while the rest of my men went back for the remaining ammo. At all times we carried our personal weapons and two full water bottles, plus a survival ration in case of attack. We made six round trips of about two miles over very rough ground, carrying six bombs each time. The weight, with cases, was 70lb. Meanwhile the radio man had busied himself building a sangar for the mortar. Sangars are circular weapons pits made out of stone found lying nearby. They are constructed out of necessity when it is hard, or impossible, to dig down into surrounding rock or soil. We finished this one off and then made our own personal sangars. When that was done we had to go for water, which involved a long trip down into a nearby wadi in search of a water hole, and then we had to carry the full containers back up. By now I was getting used to breathing the thin mountain air, but it paid to move just a little bit slower than normal so as not to get too much out of breath. It was still pretty hard going. By early evening we had finished the move.

Captain W. came along then and told us there was a patrol of SAF, who had come up the day before, going out that night and that they might need mortar fire support. I climbed to the top of a small hill to view the proposed target. The SAF would be withdrawing through a certain area and, if followed, would fire a signal flare for mortar fire, relayed to the mortar position by an LG post on the hill. I ranged onto the target area with a couple of bombs, noting the range and line. Later on I arranged the night duty, with one man awake for an hour while the rest slept. I put myself on first stag, thinking that my second, sometime between 1 a.m. and 2 a.m., would be the most likely period when we would be needed. At about 11 p.m., I wakened my relief; I cannot remember who it was, but I made sure he was up and alert. The next thing I knew someone was shouting at us to wake up. The SAF patrol had passed through the target area just after midnight and, believing they were being followed, had given the signal for mortar fire. Unfortunately our man on stag had fallen asleep and missed seeing it. There was no time for questions then, as we had to get firing immediately. The next morning I held an urgent inquest. The bloke on stag after me said he had roused the next man; if that was true, then that man had gone back to sleep. It proved impossible to establish the truth, so I had to let it drop. Anyway, I was the man in charge, so I took full responsibility. A couple of days later we moved forward again.

Two more air drops came in, both successful. We carried out day and night harassing fire at every opportunity. Mortars are, in my opinion, the most effective weapon for harassing the enemy in close battlefield conditions. Bullets and most types of artillery shell have relatively flat trajectories and can be sheltered from more easily. A mortar bomb, however, will drop vertically and get down into areas where a flat trajectory weapon cannot reach. The only really safe place from mortar fire is under thick, overhead cover. Meanwhile word came that my other mortar, handled by Paddy B. and his crew, had done a good job in supporting an attack by 18 and 19 Troops on a rebel position at a place called Kamah.

On Christmas Eve Captain W. briefed the troops for an attack on an enemy feature consisting of two prominent hills, for which reason it was dubbed Sabrina, after a very well-endowed actress of that time. The mortar was to move to a site well within range of the objective and also to make certain of good communications with me in a forward OP. The OP would be on 'Rocky Outcrop', another prominent point, from which the troops would launch their attack. The vital mortar ammunition was to be carried by the SAF men. That night, after a last mug of tea laced well with Jamaica rum, I set off with the troops. For some strange reason the OC put me in front as lead scout. I didn't mind, but I thought that this was a strange move: supposing I was to be put out of action, who would take over mortar fire control? However, off we went. We had to approach the OP via a very rough wadi known as 'Walker's Wadi'. It was pitch-black and took a long time, but we got there before daylight.

However, a small but potentially disastrous incident happened just before we reached the OP. I was in the lead and had chosen to go to the left of two huge boulders just before emerging onto the OP itself. Unknown to me, or to the two or three SAS men following behind me (including the OC), some dickhead, followed blindly by the ones behind him, had decided to go around the other side of the boulders. These people got onto the OP a few seconds before I did. Then, as I rounded the boulders, with still about a yard to climb, I looked up. There, outlined against the sky, I saw three figures. They appeared to be talking quietly to each other. I immediately stopped and put my hand back to warn the man behind me. Crouching down, we observed the figures. One of the heads turned, and it looked to me like he was wearing a turban – rebels! That's fucked the contract, I thought. The OC was behind me, so I had to wait until he could get forward for a look. Meanwhile I eased my rifle up and released the safety catch ready. No way were we going to be able to pull back without being heard, so it looked like we'd have to start shooting. Just then one of the figures moved again, and I could see by his outline that he was one of our men. Stupid sods, I thought. They should either have kept in line behind or, if a change of direction was necessary, they should have passed the word to the front man, i.e. *me*. What I had thought was a turbanned head turned out to be a bloke who wore his woolly Army hat high on his head. But only I knew how close he came to not having a frigging head to wear anything on at all!

Next morning, Christmas Day, I established communications with the mortar crew, who were in position and awaiting orders. All that day, and again on the 26th and 27th, we lay quietly and observed the movements of rebels in and out of a cave on Sabrina. I ranged in the mortar and put down some harassing fire. Several of the bombs landed just outside the cave by pure luck, because the mortar is an area weapon, and at the range we were firing the 'beaten zone' (that is, the area where all the bombs will fall) was approximately 90 yards by 50, with a smaller zone inside where 50 per cent of the rounds would fall. So the accuracy odds were with us mortarmen.

On Christmas night the SAF men delivered some water to the SAS team. Then, on the night of the 27th, 16 Troop put in their attack, with 17 Troop held back to give cover. After a fierce battle lasting most of the night the assault was very successful. Later it was reported that nine rebels had been killed. One of the lads in 16 Troop told me that the rebels had put up a stiff resistance and had fought back well. I had to admire the rebels. They had been bombed and strafed by the RAF, outgunned by our troops and had no air drops of supplies. Yet they fought on regardless. I always admire bravery, wherever it occurs. And these men showed courage.

Just before we left Rocky Outcrop next morning Captain W. asked me if I could put a smokescreen down to cover 16 Troop's withdrawal, the lads of 17 Troop having already gone. I made a small adjustment to compensate for wind and ranged with one WP. It was just right, blotting out the enemy view from Sabrina. I ordered another six to feed it. 'OK, sir?' I asked. 'How's that?' 'Oh, yes, fine,' he replied. Then the whole troop gathered round to have their photograph taken. I was invited to sit in. I thought, what the hell, I'm the mortar NCO, but I am still in 16 Troop, so I sat on the end. By the time we had finished the smoke had blown away and we moved off, exposed. Luckily either the rebs weren't looking in our direction or they were busy doing something else. SAS 18 Troop came up that day to relieve 16 and 17, both returning to Beit el Falaj next day for a rest. My mortarmen and I stayed with 18 Troop, whose OC, DLB (de la Billière), carried on with patrols and observation. Meanwhile I carried on with our harassing fire. Then, on New Year's Eve 1958, just after 18 Troop had withdrawn from a spell on Rocky Outcrop, the rebels attacked it in force. We put a good mortar stonk right on them, just for auld lang syne, but they didn't stay around for the party.

Some time afterwards Lieutenant-Colonel Deane-Drummond, who had just flown in from Malaya, came up to visit the troops in Oman. He told each and every SAS soldier that he was very pleased with our work in curtailing the activities of the rebel forces and promised me promotion to sergeant for my 'sterling job' in charge of the mortars – a promise he was to keep back in the UK several months later.

Later that same day I was handed the opportunity to direct RAF Venom rocket attacks onto Sabrina's cave. This was because when the strike aircraft came over, the bloke who usually did the directing wasn't there, so I had a go instead. We had air marker panels in front of our position for ID (identification) and to point the way towards the target. As soon as I had communications with the pilot on the ground-to-air set he put one rocket down. I ranged him in from that, and his next shot went straight into the cave. I left him to it after that. Next day we put a mortar harassing stonk down on the same area, learning later that we had killed six rebs.

Back again at Rocky Outcrop I climbed up to direct mortar fire, if it was required, to cover the withdrawal of a patrol. Along with several LG men

I ranged fire onto the area chosen by DLB and waited. At about 2 a.m. the rebels mortared our position, some of the shots flying over the top and landing somewhere in the region of where I had sited our mortar. At exactly the same time I saw the signal requesting mortar fire from our side. I fired the signal to alert the mortar crew and opened up my radio set to give orders. There was no reply. I fired another signal flare – still nothing. I tried the radio. Silence. Shit – I wondered what was wrong this time. I remembered the enemy mortar bombs landing over in that direction. 'Christ! I hope they're OK,' I thought. The poor buggers might be lying dead or wounded. I considered walking back to find out, but that would have taken too long, a two-hour round trip at least over the treacherous mountain country in the dark. The only thing I could do was to keep trying with my signal pistol. After a few more shots it worked and, to my relief, the radio man answered. I immediately ordered the pre-arranged fire support.

I discovered later that at the precise moment of my first signal the mortar position had been splattered with the rebel bombs which had flown over Rocky Outcrop. No one was hit, but with their heads well down they had missed my first few signals. A few more bombs landed nearby after they had started firing the mortar, but doggedly they stayed with the job. They were good lads. Directly afterwards the SAS moved forward again to new positions, only to be suddenly drenched by terrific rainstorms. In half an hour what had been dry wadis became raging torrents. Ironically up to this point the men had been strictly rationing themselves with water, having just a little to spare for teeth-cleaning and none for washing. Then, just as suddenly, the weather cleared, and I had time for one of my deep, reflective thoughts. In the evening I was sitting having a mug of tea and was looking around. I realised that it really was some of the most beautiful country I had ever seen. There were wild, rugged mountains framed by vivid, multicoloured sunsets. It was, at that moment, so quiet and peaceful, as it would have been in normal times, except for the evocative sound of the constant wind. High above I glimpsed an eagle as it slowly circled, eyeing the ground for its prey.

Hammering away again with the mortar later, on 18 January, I heard voices approaching from behind. Figures then appeared, and it became clear that it was a group from A Squadron led by the Squadron OC, Major 'Johnny' Cooper, known to the men as JC. Though I did not yet know it, I was to take part several years later in another adventure with JC, this time in the Yemen (see Chapter 15). Meanwhile, DD, the SAS CO, was planning a final assault to finish off the rebels once and for all in Oman, and A Squadron had been ordered out from Malaya to join the SAS forces already engaged in the battle.

The plan was for a Troop of A Squadron to keep the enemy occupied on the Aquabat while the rest of us mounted the main assault up alongside Wadi Kamah on the other side of the Jebel. Meanwhile, our no. 18, with no. 4 troop of A Squadron, was to carry out an attack on Sabrina on the night of 23/24 January. The operation got under way, and, as A Squadron had their own mortar, they carried out the fire control for both their and our mortar teams. However, we were not needed, and I spent the whole night sitting in the rain on a rock in my sangar, which rapidly filled with water, waiting for orders that never came. Next day all of us, minus the A Squadron Troop, with whom we left our mortar, marched away down the mountain to Tanuf – a long, dusty journey that took eight hours.

At Tanuf we got the gen on the big assault. Six troops of SAS – the top brass weren't taking any chances – supported by a hundred or so donkeys with handlers, plus some SAF, were involved. We were to climb the Jebel on the following night, 26 January. It was absolutely crucial that the leading troops be on the top by first light next day in order to neutralise the defending forces, which could otherwise catch them cold on the mountain slopes in broad daylight, and then to receive a vital air drop of supplies. As a form of insurance false information was leaked to the donkey handlers, some of whom were suspected of being rebel spies. We stayed at Tanuf that night and prepared our kit. A new, lightweight sleeping bag was issued, one that could be rolled up and carried in our bergens. Next evening we bumped along in trucks for an hour or so to the start point, and there, as darkness fell, we lined up in the order of the climb. At exactly 2030 hr we began the ascent. At the same time, on the Aquabat, A Squadron Troop put in their diversionary attack. The donkeys followed, but late – apparently the handlers went on strike about something (which was suspicious) – so up and up we plodded. The pace was slow and steady, but we were carrying at least 60lb, plus a 3.5in rocket each (weight about 9lb), and the sweat poured off us. It was moonlight, but it was still a bit tricky underfoot because the ground was so broken and the moon cast such black shadows. Our night movement activities, when we first came to Oman, had not been so good – they were too noisy. Now all I could hear from those near me was laboured breathing and the soft scuffing of boots – there was no talking, jangling of kit or coughing. Not a sound. On we went, one foot in front of the other, each step lifting us and our loads a few more inches up the mountain. Unfortunately several exhausted men had to be left behind to catch up later. They were either unfit or trying to carry too much kit. At about 0500 hr it looked as if the lead troop wouldn't make it to the top on time, so the OC ordered them to drop their bergens and go as fast as possible to get there by first light. They reached the top with 15 minutes to spare before the air drop came in. As the Duke of Wellington once said, 'It was a damned close-run thing.'

Because of our successful diversionary tactics the only enemy encountered on the way were a .5in MG crew hiding in a cave who were caught unawares and killed. When the mortar crews reached this point we had to pause. There was a bit of a cliff to descend with the help of a rope, and this caused a logjam. While we were waiting some rebel snipers opened up from about 600–700 yards away. We tried a few shots back, but the range was too far for our rifles, which weren't much use over 400 yards. RAF Venoms were called in and fired off some rockets, which quietened them down. Just then the donkeys with the mortars on turned up, so we offloaded and put a quick stonk down on where we thought the snipers were. Our results were unknown, but we heard later that an A Squadron LMG man accounted for one sniper.

While this lightning victory was pressed rapidly to a conclusion tragedy struck three men in A Squadron: Troopers Hamer, Carter and Bembridge. A stray bullet hit a grenade in one of their bergens, causing it to explode and badly wound the trio. An RAF helicopter daringly flew in to evacuate them, a brave feat in the thin air at that altitude; the pilot, Flight Lieutenant Martin, was awarded the Distinguished Flying Cross for his action. Sadly, Carter and Bembridge died later.

Back at the scene of action even Jebel donkeys couldn't abseil, so from the cliff we carried the mortars, and near the bottom we came across the cave where the rebel .5in MG crew had been killed. Their bodies were still sprawled where they had fallen. It was another hour's march to the mortar position, where I left some of the lads to make sangars while the rest of us went back for the ammo. The route was fully exposed to where the rebel snipers had fired from earlier, but they must have been scared off, or killed, because nothing happened. The rest of the morning was taken up with building more sangars, ranging onto likely rebel approach routes, and defensive fire (DF) tasks. Also, another air drop came in, and we had to go out and collect our food, water and more mortar ammunition. I admired the

planning that had gone into the air resupply task. A lot of the stuff had had
to be brought long distances, some of it even from as far as the UK, but all
the drops were dead on time, with everything we needed.

A rebel .5in MG had been spotted earlier, firing at the supply aircraft as
they ran in for the drop. The MG was on the other side of Wadi Kamah,
which was out of range for our small arms, and, because it had clouded over,
Venoms could not be called in. The OC ordered me to take a mortar and have
a go at it, so off we trudged, carrying the heavy weapon and as much ammo
as we could. When I thought we might be in range we set up the mortar
and fired a WP on 2,000 yards. Thirty seconds later I watched for a puff of
smoke, but nothing happened. Then, just as I thought it must have been a
dud, a thin wisp of white came up from the wadi, well short. We packed up
and moved forward to try another shot, but it was short again. We moved
forward once more, right to the edge of the wadi cliffs, and tried another shot
on maximum range, 2,800 yards. Again, smoke came up exasperatingly from
the bottom of the wadi. We couldn't get any closer, so I called it off. Wadi
Kamah must be at least 2 miles wide at that point, with almost sheer cliffs on
both sides. By the time a patrol got round there the rebs had gone.

Meanwhile Radio Cairo had been reporting feverishly on the situation.
'Thousands of British Paratroopers have been killed while trying
unsuccessfully to storm the Jebel El Akhdar,' excited announcers said. The
SAS stayed on the top of the mountain for another week or so, during which
time A and D Squadrons sent out patrols to check several Jebel villages, plus
the many caves in the area. A few prisoners were taken, together with their
arms and some ammunition, but of 'Freeman, Hardy and Willis', the rebel
leaders, there was not a sign. They had vanished, leaving behind only a bit of
kit and some documents.

Colonel Smiley, OC SAF, accompanied by Saeed Tariq, the Wali of Nizwa,
arrived to interrogate the prisoners. Afterwards they were let go. They were
merely small fry, left behind to take the rap. I was told that Saeed Tariq was
reputed to be the Sultan's head jailer and torturer. He certainly looked the
part: big and portly, with a pointed beard and fierce eyes, which gave him a
satanic appearance. Tariq ran a hell of a jail down in Nizwa. Prisoners were
thrown into underground dungeons and given no food or water at all. Their
relatives were, however, allowed to pass food and water to them; otherwise
the prisoners would have died of thirst or starvation. All signs of rebel
resistance had faded, and we mortarmen, along with the squadrons, now

found ourselves redundant. On 5 February we withdrew down Wadi Kamah
to Nizwa. Although the force of gravity was on our side this time, it was still
a long, hard slog, and everyone worked up a considerable thirst. Near Nizwa
a beer canteen had been established to deal with such a contingency, and we
proceeded to take full advantage of it!

An RAF Beverley aircraft landed on a nearby desert strip. What's on it,
we wondered? Could it be goodies, or more beer? No such luck. Besides a
small quantity of stores the main cargo was bedside lockers. *Bedside lockers*,
for fuck's sake! A much more welcome, or useful, sight (apart from a few
dancing girls, that is) would have been a mobile kitchen complete with cooks
and a load of fresh rations: steak, egg and chips, followed by spotted dick
and custard. However, the bizarre workings of officialdom in this case were
certainly not sore comfort for our somewhat bleary SAS eyes.

A few days' rest was followed by patrols being sent back up the Jebel
to complete reconnaissance of routes and to look at the sites of our recent
actions. I went with a patrol that visited the cave attacked by DLB's troop.
Our mortars had covered our withdrawal, and I discovered there the evidence
mentioned earlier, such as mortar bomb fragments still with the HE markings
visible. There were also tail units, which are not normally fragmented but
sometimes drop straight down after the bomb has exploded underneath them.
By the end of February all patrolling was complete and both squadrons were
back at base at Beit el Falaj near Muscat.

Of the three men killed on operations, Carter and Bembridge were buried
near Beit el Falaj, and Duke Swindells was buried in a little cove on the coast
near Muscat. A party of D Squadron went to visit Duke's grave and laid a
concrete slab on top. The cove can only be reached easily by boat, which gives
the impression that it's on an island. Afterwards we stood in silence for a few
minutes and remembered the brave and calm Duke we had all known so well.

After two weeks of sea, sun, cans of lager and visiting the souk, a central
market area in Muscat, all of the SAS troopers were more than ready to go
home to the UK. On my last night in Oman I lay back on my camp bed, my
kit all packed ready to move next morning, and my mind wandered back
over the previous three months. It had been bloody hard work for all of the
squadrons, but, in my opinion at least, I was content that we had all done
a good job, especially considering the fact that we had had to acclimatise
ourselves to a completely different environment from Malaya where most of
us had just arrived from. We flew home from Bahrain in a Comet jet.

It was at Bahrain the following year, 1960, where the legend of 'Titus Gripus' started. Some imaginative troopers in A Squadron, suspected to be Sandy Powell assisted by his pal 'Flash' Cook, drew an enormous crab, later entitled Titus Gripus by Sandy, on the main runway for all to see. The mock-Latin sounding name was a pun on 'tight grip'. Flights had to be delayed until the offending crab was erased. But from then on the idea really caught on in SAS circles, and crabs started to appear all around the world for several years.

However, for now, it was still mid-March 1959, and I and the rest were arriving back in the UK to a rather chilly reception, weatherwise. We were duly sent straight home on three months' leave, merely with instructions to report to Merebrook Camp, Malvern, on 16 June. I later discovered that the spectacular success of the Oman mission had probably saved the future of the entire SAS Regiment, as there had been distinct rumours of a catastrophic disbandment by the powers that be in the period directly after Malaya. Such a tragedy for the SAS – and Britain – was now an unthinkable option, and the future of the world's finest Special Force was absolutely assured by the amazing Oman victory, which was widely admired both at home and all over the world by military experts and leading politicians. Surely whatever secret mission that the SAS Regiment had next in store for its tough troopers would not top the brilliant Oman operation, which many acknowledged had saved the bacon of a friendly foreign nation? However, rapidly changing world events – and the clever way in which the SAS evolved and reacted to them – were to prove that, where the SAS was concerned, there was always another major challenge and big surprise waiting just around the corner to test the mettle of every man in the regiment. In the meantime, for a short, exhilarating spell, I and the rest of my SAS Squadron would be introduced to some ground-breaking extra Special Forces training and complete an ultra-special high-level parachute jump course guaranteed to stir the blood.

Chapter 11

SPECIAL TRAINING, SPECIAL TROOPS: MALVERN

I thoroughly enjoyed my well-earned leave. I saw my family in Jarrow again after more than a year away on active service and then went to tour Ireland on my pushbike, harbouring a fanciful idea of tracking down any surviving Doran relatives in the ancestral village where my forebears were born. In one of those strange coincidences, on my first night in Dublin I was walking along O'Connell Street when I heard a shout, 'Hey, Geordie!' On looking round I saw my SAS mate Paddy B. just getting off a bus. We had a boozy reunion that night, fuelled by several pints of Guinness, before I headed off for Killarney.

It was my first time in Ireland, and I was pleasantly impressed, the countryside was so beautiful, peaceful and quiet. After staying at Newry I visited my forebears' birthplace, Mayo Bridge, in Northern Ireland, to see if any Dorans still lived there. There was no one around, so I went to the churchyard to look at the gravestones. I found one Doran there, but just then the church door opened and four men came out carrying a coffin, followed by a crowd of mourners, taking me completely by surprise. 'A funeral – so that's where they've all been,' I thought. I had picked the worst possible moment, and it certainly wasn't a time for explanations, so I jumped on my bike and headed for the Dublin road and the ferry back to the mainland.

I never did meet that long-lost relative, but my subsequent trip to Scotland was also a first, taking in Edinburgh, the Trossachs and Loch Lomond, before riding the 180 miles home to Jarrow via Glasgow. Further long-distance rides I made included a trip to the Lake District and then on to France, my bike accompanying me by air. In Paris, like millions of others, I just could not resist going up the Eiffel Tower but was unable to view one-eighth of my route from the top, even at that height. The total distance of my mammoth cycle jaunts was measured in many hundreds of muscle-testing miles, with an average 100 miles each day. This was a feat that most non-professional riders would find hard to emulate, but more revealingly, it also indicated the presence beneath the surface of a characteristic restlessness of spirit that active service in the SAS Regiment often instils in its members, requiring an almost obsessive physical outlet to satisfy it. At the time I was merely conscious of the need to travel, see new places and maintain my record of keeping supremely fit. Finally, on 16 June 1959, I said goodbye to my folks and headed south to Malvern to rejoin my comrades in the SAS.

Merebrook camp, about 3 miles from Malvern, had been a US military hospital in the Second World War. The SAS Regiment, now cut down to two squadrons, A and D, immediately began a typically tough training programme, much of which involved the troopers and officers re-acquainting themselves with the Welsh mountains that had broken so many of their hearts during Selection. As I was by now a highly qualified expert on mortars I was further employed training extra mortar teams, with live firing of the mortars taking place on Sennybridge ranges in Wales. On the way to Sennybridge we had to pass through Hereford, now the famous home of the SAS but then just another thriving market community filled with many shops, cafés and characterful pubs. Little did I realise then how much that city was to figure in my future.

Around this time the gongs were handed out for our action in Oman. A General Service Medal with bar inscribed 'Arabian Peninsula' was awarded to all who had taken part. Sergeant 'Herbie' Hawkins received the Distinguished Conduct Medal, and 'Scouse' Cunningham got the Military Medal. Both were well deserved. A plethora of awards for the officers included at least four Military Crosses and one Distinguished Service Order. This made me happy, because I had heard that unless it was for a specific personal act, such awards to officers were not just for them but also for their men. I have not the shadow of a doubt that those awards were earned by the recipients, and I am also quite sure that the officers concerned thought of them as medals for all of us and not just for them.

It was soon back to intensive and ground-breaking training. In August we did an exercise in Germany, starting with a night jump near the River Weser. I was number one in our stick, and as I stood in the door waiting for the green light I could see down below the Weser winding and glinting in the moonlight. I never dreamt all those years before, when I had last seen the river while serving in the KOYLI shortly after the war, that the next time

I saw it would be from the door of an aircraft 1,000 feet up and with a parachute on my back! I was part of Squadron HQ, consisting of the OC Major Johnny Watts, 'Dad' Morgan the Signaller, me and our new SSM. The SSM had been in the Independent Parachute Squadron attached to 22 SAS in Malaya and on the strength of that was now serving in the SAS. As part of the Guards Parachute Company of Pathfinders in the Second World War he had dropped into the ferocious battle of Arnhem, when British and American airborne forces had attempted to capture three sets of key bridges in Holland so that armoured forces could outflank the Germans and drive on into Germany and shorten the war. I admired him for that, but he had an air about him that I didn't like. He wasn't my favourite SSM, and I definitely was not his favourite NCO, so we got on like a house on fire – me inside and him outside striking the matches! After the exercise, which was a success, we reorganised at an RA camp at Lippstadt. From there we motored south to the Bavarian Alps in the US zone to visit their Special Forces at Bad Tolz. We carried out exercises both with the Special Forces and a German mountain unit, the 'Gebergsjäger'. We made great friends with both the Special Forces and the Germans, so much so that we were invited back the next year for ski training with the Gebergsjäger.

Back in Malvern I bought my first car, a 1939 Morris Eight, for £125. It was a comfortable vehicle with real leather seats. I was in great demand as chauffeur, as not many of my SAS comrades had cars at that time, and because I had 'wheels' I was also quite well in with the ladies. The Winter Gardens dance on Saturday nights was the best chance to chat up a girl, and the favourite SAS pub in Malvern was The Red Lion. There was a big room upstairs where the troopers used to give it stick, drinking and singing. Next door The Unicorn pub took the overspill from The Red Lion. The landlady there became famous for throwing a glass of water or squirting soda over anyone she heard swearing. Many an SAS man had his carefully coiffured hairdo ruined in there of an evening, I recall!

The next big exercise, which lasted two months, took place in Libya, just after I received a long-overdue promotion to sergeant. The SAS landed at an airfield near Tripoli, the capital, and from there we moved to Tarhuna, an old pre-war Italian barracks way out in the desert. All senior NCOs were accommodated in one basement. It was cool down there but very cramped, and RQMS 'Black Jake' Mathews snored like a camel blowing through its lips and kept us awake all night! One reason for going to Libya was to learn desert navigation using sun compasses, which worked by the sun's rays striking a pointer and casting a shadow on a gauge, the direction of travel worked out by complicated calculation. This is all old hat now, of course, with the advent of satellite global positioning systems (GPS), but apart from the prismatic compass that's all we had then. At the same time we practised living in the desert and camouflaging our vehicles, like the LRDG and SAS of wartime fame. So we thrashed all around Libya, navigating and rediscovering the well-tried skills. We soon found out that service-issue clothing and camouflage netting for deserts was mostly unsuitable. They were all the wrong colour. They were sand-ish, yes, but deserts are not always sand. They are sometimes grey pebbles, and where they are sand there are always some black shadows and scattered, dark-green shrubbery. The desert Arabs thought we had one peculiar vice, though, and that was getting washed with water from a well. They looked very put out when they saw this. Well water was strictly for drinking only, as far as they were concerned. After we had finished at Tarhuna we moved to a camp near Tripoli to await a flight home.

On the way to Tripoli I rode in the front of a truck and there was a load of SAS blokes and kit in the back. When our group arrived at our destination, I was told by my perennial 'friend', the SSM, that he was putting me on a charge for allowing the men to drink beer in the back of the truck. I was flabbergasted, as I had no way of knowing what the men were getting up to in the back and would have reacted promptly if I had. I think the SSM was gunning for me anyway, and the OC dismissed the charge out of hand.

After Christmas and back in the UK I attended a Motor Transport Officer's (MTO) course at Bordon in Hampshire. There I was taught all about the insides of an engine, how to drive properly and teach others, plus the paperwork that went with it all. My little Ford van went like a bomb afterwards. However, Bordon, or boredom as I called it, was a grim hole, and I couldn't wait to get away from there. When naughty soldiers die, they don't go to hell – they go to Bordon, believe me.

Returning to Malvern I was just in time to go with the squadron to Mittenwald in Bavaria for ski training with the German mountain troops. Most of the British troops were billeted in the main camp at Mittenwald, but I went with a small group to stay in a farmhouse near the alpine village of Oberjoch. Our instructors were first class and very friendly, and they taught us everything. From early on we called ourselves the 'wet-arsed British' because during turning-on-the-spot lessons, when you have to lift one ski in front, we all managed to fall backwards about ten times! After we had learnt to maintain a more or less upright position on the skis we graduated to the nursery slopes, where we provided plenty of entertainment for the watching Germans, starting off wrong and being dragged up the slope face down by the lift bar, for instance. After a few days I was hurtling down the hard piste, going well. I thought, 'Geordie, you've cracked it – all you have to do now is slide to a graceful halt at the bottom.' I could see a crowd of people at the end, obviously waiting to see what would happen. I'll show the bastards, I vowed. Just then I saw a woman ahead langlaufing (walking on skis) slowly across the piste. I could see we would crash if one of us didn't alter course, so I shouted and whistled, but she seemed oblivious. Just my luck, a deaf skier! I tried a turn, but if anything it brought us more in line, and by then it was too late to try anything else. I went right over her skis, between her toes and the curly bits at the front. Two seconds later I lost control, fell on my side and spun horizontally about four times. When I looked back, there she was, still serenely going along. I reckon she was sent deliberately to get me; or maybe she just got her kicks that way.

Oberjoch was – and still is – a beautiful, scenic little village, with a fairytale quaintness about it. The SAS congregated at a pub called the Kematstreid, which, I discovered on a recent trip, is still there. Our new OC Squadron came to stay – Major John Slim, son of Field Marshal Slim of Burma fame. Next day we had a flying visit from some bigwig who arrived in a helicopter. As I was senior NCO I thought I had better do LZ duty and guide the pilot down the last bit. I stood there facing the chopper with my arms outstretched as per the drill and, because the snow was fairly soft, I had my skis on. The helicopter slowly descended. Unfortunately I had forgotten about the downdraught and was blown back on my skis, ending up about 20 yards away, still upright, with my arms still outstretched and with a face full of snow! Before leaving the farmhouse we had a great farewell party, at which I took a group photograph, which I still have.

Our SAS Squadron flew back to the UK in a German military aircraft. (It was believed to be the first time since the Second World War that such an aircraft had been seen over Britain.) Back in Malvern the planned move to a new base at Hereford – destined to become the world-famous home of the SAS – was already under way, to be completed just before Easter 1960. A glittering new era was about to dawn for the regiment, and I was fiercely determined to play my part in it.

Chapter 12

DAREDEVIL HIGH FREE FALL:
FROM HEREFORD TO FOREIGN
MISSIONS

enerations of SAS soldiers have over the years developed a special
soft spot for Hereford. It has housed various shadowy bases that
have been the launch pad for countless clandestine SAS missions the
world over. Consequently we SAS now universally regard the area as our
favourite second home. The city is a beautiful rural community with a fine
cathedral and has many superb, characterful pubs and hostelries, and the
people are exceedingly friendly and accommodating. But that, veterans say,
is not the whole secret of the city's allure. There is also an indefinable mix of
atmosphere, history and character exuding from every brick and stone in the
place that cannot be entirely pinned down by logic. Many would also say that
it is not entirely surprising that Special Forces soldiers of this calibre, ready
to travel anywhere in the world at a moment's notice, risking their lives in
dangerous hot spots, need and appreciate a familiar place to return to, a safe
anchor to normality after so many extraordinarily abnormal sights, threats
and sounds. I know that is exactly how I have always regarded the city.

The history of Hereford goes back a long, long way indeed. A town has
stood here on the banks of the River Wye for many centuries; its name,
Hereford, is an Anglo-Saxon word meaning 'army ford', where the river could
be waded at this important crossing-point. A wooden bridge was built over
the ford in the twelfth century but was washed away by floods to be replaced
in 1490 by an old stone bridge, which is still there. Just upstream, built in
1965 to take the extra traffic, is a modern, single-span bridge. Sometimes
Hereford has attracted criticism for being too quiet and too much of a rural
backwater, but these are two of the attributes that many SAS soldiers like me
admire most about it.

Returning to my narrative, Bradbury Lines was our new home, a wooden-hutted camp built during the Second World War. It was obvious that the unit we took over from couldn't have had a very good reputation, because some of the pubs and cafés in town were out of bounds to them. We set out to put that straight right away. The locals were a bit apprehensive of us at first, as the SAS was relatively unknown then, but a rumour had spread that we were a 'tough guy' regiment, and they didn't know what to expect. However, we must have made a good initial impression, because 22 SAS rapidly built up good relations with the people of Hereford that have existed ever since. I personally liked the city immediately and can truthfully say it is one of the few places I have never become fed up with. One thing that many SAS soldiers noticed about the city straight away was the abundance of pretty girls, which was certainly no drawback! Little did I realise it then, but it was there I was to meet my future wife, Ann, have children and grandchildren, and settle for most of my life.

I met my first girlfriend within a week of arriving. Over Easter that year, 1960, most of the regiment disappeared on leave while others were taking part in the Devizes-to-Westminster canoe race. Someone reliable was needed to look after the camp – so they put me on guard! The guardroom phone rang and a female voice said, 'I'd like to apologise for last night.' It was an operator speaking from RAF Credenhill, a base situated near Hereford. Apparently she had been rude to the previous night's guard commander and thought I was he. 'I wasn't on last night,' I replied. 'But if you like you can apologise to me in person and I'll pass it on. I can pick you up tomorrow night.' She accepted, and we went out with each other for a year or so. She was a very nice girl, but I spent so much time away on training and so on – plus she was posted elsewhere – that we just drifted apart, as happened to so many SAS Hereford romances.

In May, D Squadron was sent to Kenya for training. I was one of the advance party sorting out the vehicles and making sure the camp was properly set up. In fact I was on quite a few advance parties throughout my SAS career, which led me to believe they either send the best men out first or, which is more likely, I was among those considered expendable! The camp was about 100 miles north of Nairobi, near the little village of Nanyuki, and was smack on the Equator. Nanyuki, which is more than 6,000 feet above sea level, is on a giant plateau with Mount Kenya looming not far away in the background. 'Tree Tops', a safari hotel, then owned by

Hollywood heart-throb actor William Holden, was situated in the forest near Nanyuki. The squadron spent many weeks in the forests on the slopes of Mount Kenya and the Aberdare Mountains. We soon noted that the jungle was very different from that found in Malaya. It was not as humid or dense, and the trees, quite different in type, were not so tall, with less undergrowth. In the clearings were patches of a very vicious stinging nettle. We caught glimpses of many different creatures, including buffalo, rhino and a tiny deer-like animal called a dik dik. There was also a bird, which we never actually saw, but whose call – a warbling, whistling sound – was very distinctive, and it became adopted as the D Squadron rallying call, especially on night jumps when we had to rendezvous at the edge of the DZ after parachuting in.

A trial resupply air drop with no parachutes from low-flying light aircraft resulted in a culinary disaster, everything being mashed together, including curry powder, sugar and jam! There followed an exercise with the Kenyan Special Forces acting as the enemy. This went well, except on one occasion when my patrol attacked our opposition's jungle camp. The Kenyan lads got mad and drew their pangas (parangs), looking as if they intended to do some dissection on us. I managed to calm them down, but my diplomatic skills were tested to the limit. In spite of that, I liked the Kenyans. Most of the ones I saw were of the Kikuyu tribe, and they always seemed cheerful, pleasant to talk to and straightforward in their manner. A battalion of the King's African Rifles (KAR) was stationed nearby, and whenever I had to visit them in connection with motor vehicles – one of my jobs was Squadron MTO – I always found them very helpful and friendly. I visited Nanyuki several times; it reminded me of a Wild West town, with covered boardwalks and hitching rails for horses. There wasn't much there, just a small café and shops selling clothing and trinkets. The squadron next set off north, to the semi-desert region of the Northern Frontier. We travelled via Isiolo and Marsabit, some of us staying near Marsabit while the others went on almost to the Ethiopian border and over the Chalbi Desert to Lake Rudolph. At Marsabit our new CO, Lieutenant-Colonel Wilson, who had taken over from Deane-Drummond, came to visit. He had been in Kenya serving with the Royal Northumberland Fusiliers during the Mau Mau troubles, when terrorists had murdered many white settlers and farmers and their families in the hope of driving them out of the country and taking their land. He was very familiar with the area, and on the way back to Nanyuki he showed us where there were some hot springs to bathe in, a very welcome facility in the fierce heat. Finally the troops did a parachute jump

'Don't mess with me, boy!' A menacing-looking Geordie emerges from the Malayan jungle in the early 1960s with self-loading semi-automatic rifle at the ready. A moment's hesitation in the jungle often meant the difference between life and death – and the SAS invariably shot first.

A photo taken to celebrate the 1937 Coronation of King George VI shows Geordie already displaying courage and determination at the age of 8.

A proud-looking Geordie, aged 17, the day after he joined the Army for general primary training before being posted to the Light Infantry, November 1946.

Successful candidates for the tough P Company course for entry into the Parachute Regiment, May 1956. Geordie is front row, extreme left; Instructor Mike Reilly is centre front.

Two Durham Light Infantry pals on leave at Port Fuad, Egypt, 1954. Geordie is on the left.

Camel-riding in the Canal Zone in the mid-1950s. This early practice was to come in handy for Geordie later in his SAS career during a dangerous, clandestine mission in the Yemen.

Geordie and mortar platoon comrade Peter Welsh in their sandbagged bunker in Korea, 1953. Attacks in the British sector came suddenly, and often with overwhelming force and violence.

Armed to the teeth and ready for action! Geordie (top centre) and Para comrades on active anti-terrorist EOKA operations in Northern Cyprus, 1956.

The 1 Para mortar platoon, which included Geordie, is readied for battle at Port Said soon after arrival during the Suez Crisis, November 1956.

A brief time of relaxation in the war zone – beers all round at a Christmas party at Fanara in the Canal Zone, 1954. Geordie is second right.

D Squadron SAS members training on the then new 81mm mortar, which replaced the old 3in weapon, at Sennybridge, near Brecon, South Wales, in the mid-1960s. Geordie's comrade Derek G. is pictured loading the weapon alongside Dusty G. in beret at the rear; another comrade is on the right. Geordie had just been given special training on this weapon and was instructing the other squadron members in its use. The weapon is now in standard use in the SAS.

Native Iban scouts don SAS and other headgear for a light-hearted picture taken by Geordie in Malaya, 1958. These tough, resourceful men were the backbone of the SAS and British forces' tracking effort and vital scouting missions in the unforgiving jungle.

Native tribesmen loyal to the British SAS bring in supplies to the troops by bamboo raft and river in Malaya, February 1962.

A fierce Kelabit tribesman – friendly to the SAS, but hostile to Britain's enemies – stands next to a muscular and very fit-looking Geordie in North Borneo in March 1963.

Live firing training in Britain after the regiment returned to the UK in 1959. SAS machine gunners, in the shape of Geordie's D Squadron comrades, let rip on practice grounds in Sennybridge, South Wales. They are using US Browning medium machine guns, similar to those used in the Second World War, light to carry but with a high rate of fire – an ideal tool for the job.

SAS comrades gather round in Malaya just prior to operations in Oman, autumn 1958, as mortar ace Geordie Doran explains the best way to get the most out of the key close-range weapon. In the sort of terrain that the SAS often operates in mortars are very often used as the regiment's 'artillery' – and to deadly effect.

D Squadron SAS comrades training for Oman with 3.5in rocket launchers, supervised by George Medal winner Mick Reeves. This legendary SAS soldier, whom Geordie knew well, later daringly climbed out of an aircraft in the UK to release a fellow trooper's static line that was hooked on the plane's tail, leaving him trapped helpless, before releasing his parachute and operating his own, resulting in both men landing safely.

Distinguished Conduct Medal winner Sergeant Herbie Hawkins supervises Geordie's D Squadron comrades in the use of Energa anti-tank grenades fired from 7.62mm rifles. As a result of his Oman heroics courageous Herbie had a hill named after him called 'Herbie's Hump'. Sergeant Hawkins was out on a small patrol when his men were attacked by an overwhelming enemy force. He coolly told his men to switch their rifles to automatic fire, and they beat off the terrorist force, inflicting heavy casualties.

SAS on exercise in a Land Rover in Wales 1959 – Geordie is at the left rear, with Titch Moore and Scouse Cunningham, who previously won the Military Medal in the Oman, in front driving.

The free-fall high-altitude SAS parachute course at RAF Abingdon, June 1961. Geordie is kneeling, front left.

Geordie in 'position anglaise' after exiting at high altitude from a de Havilland Rapide at Chalon-sur-Saône, training para airfield in France, 1961. This position was later superseded by the 'frog stance', which has since become the classic free-fall position used internationally by military forces. In this, the knees, arms and elbows are slightly bent to give greater stability while the parachutist is plummeting towards the ground.

Sergeant Rozeniuk, American Special Forces, on attachment to 22 SAS, scales the dizzy heights of a giant, sheer rock face in the Lake District in August 1960.

SAS comrades Alex and Nat with a young Arab Oman army boy signaller and his young sister. Geordie's two comrades were awaiting sea transport to Aden after a special training operation in Oman in 1961.

The RAF mounts a pinpoint raid on the summit of the Jebel el Akhdar in Oman in November 1958, just after D Squadron SAS arrived in the area for the historic operation. Geordie has snapped the action while visiting the water well on the right of the picture.

These fierce and proud warriors of the Sultan of Oman's Armed Forces fought alongside the SAS in Oman in 1958 and were rated highly by the British forces for their resourcefulness and detailed local knowledge. Here they bring a 3in mortar into action, as Geordie, who was standing nearby, took this action photo.

SAS troops plaster the enemy positions with mortar bombs during the brilliantly successful assault on the Jebel el Akhdar. The hardness of the ground can clearly be seen by the limited amount of digging-in that was possible. To overcome this the SAS built sangars out of stones to give troops protection from incoming fire.

This superb photo, taken by a comrade of Geordie's, is one of the best-ever records of the SAS in action. Here Geordie and crew range a 3in mortar onto enemy targets and enemy approach routes during the legendary assault on the Jebel el Akhdar at the climax of the attack by A and D Squadrons 22 SAS, January 1959. Geordie, standing, is the NCO in charge operating the sights of the weapon, with comrade Paddy seated and another SAS colleague, who has just fired the mortar, obscured.

D Squadron SAS training on mortars at Ibri, Oman, 1961.

Geordie's SAS mortar team inspect the effects of a mine laid by terrorists set off by a supply truck, at Oman, during active operations, November 1958. The explosion blew out the rear of the truck, leaving the cab relatively undamaged and the driver and medic inside unharmed. It was a lucky escape, because the cargo was 3in mortar ammunition, which was flung out and later recovered. But the amount of damage is indicative of the power and effectiveness of these anti-vehicle weapons. Photo taken by Geordie.

Geordie and para comrades of the SAS give a display jump at Hereford racecourse in 1961 on return from active duty. Geordie is on the far left.

A superb group photo of 22 SAS at Fort Bragg, the headquarters of American Special Forces, 1962. Geordie is fifth from the left, standing in the second row. American and British Special Forces have often cooperated in peacetime training missions and have also closely cooperated in countless operational missions in action, right up to the present day.

Geordie riding a camel just after crossing the border into the Yemen on his historic 1963 clandestine mission, in which he was told he had a possible survival chance of just fifty-fifty.

The Yemen secret mission June/July 1963. Geordie is watching over the camel supply train en route to the Kowlan Mountains to join royalist forces. Note the heavily armed native guards. The weapon Geordie is holding is a Swedish Carl Gustav 9mm sub-machine gun, his personal choice of weapon on the mission.

The height of the Suez Crisis and installations around Port Said harbour are burning after the British attack on 6 November 1956. The 1st Battalion the Parachute Regiment mortar platoon is approaching the battle zone in a tank landing craft to reinforce the Royal Marine Commandos, who had landed the day before, and the 3rd Battalion Paras, who had parachuted into El Gamal airfield. Geordie took this fine action shot of the famous, but ill-fated, campaign.

just before leaving Kenya. The DZ, near Nanyuki, was called 'Bastard's Field' and was owned by a bloke, coincidentally, named Bastard – I joke not. It was 7,000 feet above sea level, and the thin air meant very fast descents indeed. Fast descents mean hard and sometimes painful landings. For the SAS that field certainly lived up to its name.

After leave, the regiment laid on a parachuting and SAS equipment display at Hereford racecourse. The main event was a free-fall parachuting competition between an SAS team and a team from the US Special Forces. The latter won, as, in my estimation, they had had more practice. Quite a lot of the civilians there that day still didn't know what the letters SAS stood for. A number of the girls were told it was 'Sex And Sex'. After experiencing the real thing at first hand, some of them would have been inclined to believe that version in future – we were red-blooded soldiers, after all! During the remainder of 1960 D Squadron trained at Otterburn in Northumberland, where I took my mortarmen on live firing. An exercise in Denmark then followed, and in between times we carried out numerous practice parachute jumps. On one of these jumps, a night descent onto Sennybridge DZ in Wales, I landed next to 'Dad' Morgan, the experienced Squadron HQ Signaller. 'How did it go, Dad?' I asked, as we rolled our chutes up. 'Oh, just normal,' he answered. 'What do you mean, normal?' I said. 'It was a night jump.' 'All my jumps are night ones,' explained Dad. 'I always keep my eyes closed until I hit the deck!'

For the Denmark exercise we were first flown to the German island of Sylt in the North Sea, because a battalion of Paras was already there and it was designed to be a joint affair. Sylt, which is connected to the mainland by a causeway, was sparsely populated then, with long, almost empty beaches. We had to work a bit of sweat off, so back in camp we had a game of mass football with the Paras. There were 100 blokes on each side, and we played with four balls, no rules and no referees. Nobody knows to this day who won the game, but there was a substantial amount of blood left on the pitch at the end! On the day before we left Sylt the SAS did a public relations march through Westerland, the main town. With the Paras already departed we had no rivals for our special parade and so marched six abreast, dressed in camouflage uniform, proudly wearing our SAS berets, bergens and rubber-soled boots, and carrying our SMGs slung in the ready position. We were led by Trooper Jock Martin playing a stirring tune on his bagpipes. Miraculously, as we did not usually have time for 'bull' of this kind, all of us were in step, so that apart from the pipes all that could be heard was the clump-clump-clump of boots. German civilians lining the route stood watching in silence. It was actually quite moving, and I for one felt very proud to be a British SAS soldier.

We parachuted into Denmark the following night. The object of the exercise was to provide an 'enemy' for the Danish troops, who wanted to be ready for the real threat, which at that time was invasion by Soviet forces. Denmark is mostly flat, with few obvious features such as hills and rivers, which makes it fairly difficult to navigate over at night. The maps were good, though, so careful route-planning and frequent use of the compass paid off. To add realism the Danish population had been warned to keep a look-out for us. This was an added incentive for us to use good tactical movement to avoid capture. My patrol had one scare. Just before daylight one morning we saw a torch about 50 yards away shining in our direction. Whoever had hold of it was weaving the beam from side to side as if searching. Down we went, lying perfectly still. Nearer came the light, but just when I thought we would be discovered it turned aside, and we saw a stooping man go past with a bucket in his other hand. He was collecting mushrooms and was so intent on his task he didn't see us! After the exercise we stayed in a Danish Army camp near Viborg.

Back in the UK the SAS Regiment prepared for its annual FFR (fit for role) inspection, which was due in early December. However, on the Sunday before the FFR was due the troops received an urgent call from the Hereford police and civil authority to provide assistance in a local flood relief operation about to get under way. The River Wye, as a result of heavy rain in Wales, had overflowed catastrophically onto surrounding farmland, posing a serious threat to the city and villages downstream. Parties of SAS, including my squadron, were immediately sent out to rescue farm animals that had become isolated on small patches of high ground. It was difficult and dangerous work, and many stranded civilians were rescued using assault craft which had been pressed into service. These craft were flat-bottomed and powered by outboard engines or paddles, and so were ideal for the job. I was in a group sent to Hampton Bishop, a village a few miles downstream; numerous people there were helped out of their devastated homes. Conditions were truly appalling. Many tales were told afterwards of that day. One boat pulled up by a garden gate which showed just above the water. Shouts brought no response, so one SAS bloke jumped out to go and knock on the door, but once through the gate he sank from sight: the path to the door was sunken, with steps at either end. Our group stayed for a while in a nearby police station that night, drying what clothes we could on the radiators. Later the river rose once more, and we couldn't get back through Hereford. Next day we SAS swung into action again, ferrying stranded people to work in the city by truck. After a few days the water level dropped, and at last we were stood down to endure the pleasures of our annual inspection, which went off, as usual, without a hitch. But the good folk of Hereford were furious! City folk considered it a disgrace that the SAS who had come to their aid in their hour of need did not get a few days off after their sterling work in the floods. A big headline in one local newspaper said it all: 'FLOOD, TOIL, THEN SPIT AND POLISH.'

D Squadron's next trip abroad, comprising specialised desert training in Oman, was scheduled from January to May 1961. Just before Christmas the advance party, including myself, was flown to Aden to issue vehicles and go by sea with them to Muscat. Arriving at Aden we met with some reluctance from the Royal Army Ordnance Corps (RAOC), who were definitely not keen on working during the holiday to issue vehicles. However, the machinery eventually creaked into action, the trucks were loaded onto the appropriate ship and off the squadron sailed on the Arabian Sea. At Muscat we were put ashore by landing craft onto the same beach from which we had swum before the Jebel campaign two years previously. Nothing had changed. It was still a grot hole, and the same dogs were hanging about waiting for scraps. The rest of the squadron arrived at Muscat by air a few days later. From there we drove to the base camp near Ibri, a village about 150 miles westwards. It was rocky desert tracks all the way, and, because we had to skirt around the Jebel via Izki and Nizwa, the journey was more like 200 miles, taking two days and nights to complete. A previous unit had left the tented camp at Ibri more or less intact, so it didn't take us long to get things organised. Our A Squadron SAS, including Sandy Powell (the originator of 'Titus Gripus' the crab), had trained in the area in early 1960, and a reminder of the SAS's visit was still there in the form of a giant crab painted on a rock on a nearby hill. Daily training consisted of fitness marches and live firing of weapons. The crab on the hill became a favourite target for 3.5in rocket launchers and my mortar teams, who eventually obliterated all signs of it. (Sorry about that, Sandy!) As a demonstration of what mortar fire could do to people, I positioned a group of twenty figure-11 range targets, roughly the size of a crouching man, in a 50-yard-wide area. After putting five rounds' rapid HE down on them we went to inspect. Every target was torn to shreds by shrapnel.

Someone (I don't know who) had written a report on the Jebel campaign of 1958/9, stating in it that 'mortar fire had little or no effect on people or sangars' in that ferocious battle. I do not agree. It is true that a well-built sangar would certainly give good protection from mortar fire, except from a direct hit, but anyone caught out in the open would not have much chance of avoiding death or injury. The danger area of a 3in mortar HE bomb then was 100 yards all round, and it was especially lethal on hard, level ground, with the shrapnel travelling between knee and head height. It is a well-known fact that the mortar is one of the most versatile and feared weapons in close battle conditions, right up to the present day in operations in Iraq. It is my belief, and that of many other people, that the weight and accuracy of the mortar fire on the Jebel had a significant bearing on the successful outcome of this key operation.

Desert driving in Oman was similar to that in Libya, except that the sun compass was hardly necessary until the Jebel el Akhdar had disappeared into the distance. Once that point was reached it was possible to get a fix and revert to the old, trusty wartime SAS/LRDG method of navigation. As a driving exercise, and to do more live firing, we motored down to a place called the Fahud Basin, about 75 miles south-west of Ibri. The Basin is extremely hot and dry, a place where you could drink water non-stop and still be thirsty. A couple of the squadron blokes got lost for a few days there and only survived by drinking water from their vehicle radiator strained through a sock. It's amazing what soldiers will resort to when their needs are dire! There were several 'capped-off' oil exploration bore holes in the area, we noted. When the oil company people had left they abandoned all manner of equipment, including some trucks of the same type we were using. Our vehicle mechanics consequently soon had a fine stock of spare parts. After a week in Fahud some of the squadron drove on to south Oman while I moved back to Ibri with the remainder, driving at night and steering by the stars. Whenever we could we would go to Ibri for a bath in the falaj. The falaj, which is an underground stream originating on the Jebel, was partially exposed at Ibri; the locals used it for washing clothes, watering animals and drawing water for cooking from a well. The Arabs never ceased to be amazed at us foreigners getting stripped off and lying in the water. It was pure heaven. I always kept my underpants on, as there were loads of tiny little fish that would bite at any exposed equipment – definitely not to be encouraged! A couple of times I caught some of the village women, whose jug-filling area was nearby, having a sly peek over the falaj wall at the abluting SAS men. I didn't fancy getting stoned to death, so I moved on sharpish!

While at Ibri several of our trucks were damaged by mines, as there was some kind of dissident organisation still operating in Oman and obviously still bearing a grudge. No one seemed to know who they were or what they wanted but, clearly, British troops were one of their targets. We tried night ambush patrols to catch the mine-layers at it, but the area was too large and we didn't have night-viewing equipment then, so we were at a distinct disadvantage. The mines were all small-scale. They would blow the wheel off a truck maybe, without injuring anyone – no more than that. But they were a nuisance, and drivers had to travel by different roundabout routes each time. This had its humorous side, however, when one night I was on guard and the duty driver had just set off for Ibri. Minutes later we heard a loud bang, and I sent a couple of blokes out to investigate. Back they came with the driver, whom they had met staggering back towards camp. His clothing was in tatters and his face was black, just like in a comedy film. 'I hit a mine,' he croaked in a tiny voice. He looked so pathetic we all creased up laughing! The driver was OK, but we were still left short of a truck.

Ibri was then a typical Arab village, all mud-walled buildings and palm trees waving in the breeze. There was hell to pay if we damaged any of those buildings: the owners had to be reimbursed with Maria Theresa dollars – very expensive. (Maria Theresa dollars were the currency used in Muscat and Oman at that time.) As related, I was D Squadron MTO then, and a driver walked into my tent one day, covered in dust and looking very worried. 'What's up?' I asked. 'I hit a wall,' he replied. 'Did you make a hole?' 'Er, yes.' 'What size?' 'About the same size as my truck.' 'Shit, did anybody see you?' 'No.' 'Good, get your truck cleaned up and we'll say nowt.' 'Can't,' muttered the driver. 'The bloody truck's still jammed in the hole!' After a lot of humble pie and much haggling it cost 400 dollars to get out of that one – a small fortune in that part of the world.

Meanwhile some of the squadron were out on camel patrol trials. Lawrence of Arabia did it, so why not us, we mused? My part in the trials was to air-drop a resupply of camel food in to our men. The food looked like long green grass, and we had to drop it in bundles through a hole in the floor of a Twin Pioneer aircraft. On the day another bloke and I were flown around for ages trying to find the patrols. The aircraft, being light, was buffeted about a lot, and I was feeling very sick. Eventually the pilot spotted a line of camels and gave the order to drop. Unfortunately the pilot had mistaken some genuine Arabs on camels for our patrols. We immediately landed nearby and ran to scoop up the grass before the rapidly converging Arabs could get their greedy hands on it. They didn't look at all pleased when we flew off again, but by the time the patrols were located I had brought my hoop up. Spew everywhere. I wiped the floor with the last bundle of grass before I threw it out. I hope the camels enjoyed it.

I had another trip in a Twin Pioneer a few days later, on that occasion flying to Bahrain to collect vehicle spares. On the way we flew over the Jebel el Akhdar mountain area. It was a fantastic sight from the air; it seemed incredible that we had operated on active service among those massive cliffs and peaks not that long before.

I spent a few days in Bahrain before flying back in a Beverley, which, being a short-take-off-and-landing aircraft, was able to land on the small strip near Ibri. Talking about Beverleys, another one came in a few days later and couldn't take off again. It was a catastrophic power failure. However, one of our SAS mechanics, a chap called Charlie Surridge, managed to get it started. It was quite a feat. Charlie could be fussy sometimes, but he was a red-hot mechanic. He wired half-a-dozen Land Rover batteries up together for the job and, amazingly, the Beverley engines roared into life.

The feast of Ramadan was on when our SAS squadron was operating in Oman. Ramadan is when Muslims, which is most of the Arab population, are not supposed to eat or drink during daylight hours. We had half-a-dozen locals working daily in camp, and sometimes they couldn't be found anywhere. Then one day, as I was walking past the cook tent, I noticed a slight movement behind one of the tent walls, which had been folded back. I went to investigate, and there in the space behind the wall sat six Arabs, all getting stuck into lots of grub and guzzling drink. They gazed at me, food poised by their lips. I think they expected a right bollocking for being caught breaking the fast, but I just walked away. It wasn't my job to monitor their religion, but – wonder of wonders – all of a sudden we could now find our six Arab workers again any time.

A US Special Forces soldier on detachment to the SAS came out to join D Squadron in Oman. Dick Meadows, a Master Sergeant, was – according to all of his new-found SAS comrades, including me – a great bloke. He was very professional and easy to get on with. Dick was to gain fame in later years as an outstanding Special Forces soldier. One of his exploits was to help organise a mission to rescue an American POW held in terrible conditions in Son Tay, North Vietnam. It was a very daring and risky operation, but it all went for nothing in the end, because unfortunately, owing to a lack of sufficient aerial surveillance of the target, the raid went ahead without the knowledge that the POW had been moved to another camp some days before.

At the end of April 1961 the squadron left for the UK. The rear party, including me, dismantled the camp, loaded everything on the trucks and headed north on the 200-mile journey to Dubai, where a ship for Aden was waiting. On the way our SAS contingent stayed a night at Buraimi Oasis. The fort there looked just like the one in the Foreign Legion film *Beau Geste*. That evening, as if in farewell, I saw the most fantastic sunset ever in my life. Half the sky was a blaze of colour, fiery red dominating, with various shades of pink, blue, green, yellow, grey and half a dozen more. It was overwhelming. I stood and marvelled at it until darkness came. They say it is caused by the dust in the desert air refracting the sunlight. Whatever it is, it was *perfect*.

Arriving at Dubai we drove past the Sultan's palace. There was a high, turreted wall around it, but we could see the minarets and towers above. Dubai was at that time merely a huddle of typical Arab buildings arranged down either side of the harbour. The main form of transport was camels and donkeys, supplemented by a few rattling old trucks and the odd long-wheelbase Land Rover. We stayed in a nearby SAF barracks for one night. They had a signals set-up there, and I was amazed to discover that most of the operators were very young boys. These lads could send and receive morse at terrific speeds: it was a sight to behold. The trucks were loaded quickly, despite a huge windstorm blowing at the time, and four days later we had docked at Aden. After handing everything in we had a few days off. Aden was then garrisoned by the British Army as a Protectorate; everything was available, from tea to sex. I met a WAAF in town whom I had known in Hereford. We had a night out together, and I walked her back to her camp near Steamer Point, where we just sat and talked innocently for a while. I hadn't seen a female face all the time I had been in Oman. Every woman there was completely covered, except for their eyes, and they rarely spoke.

Next day we SAS troopers emplaned at RAF Khormaksar, bound for the UK. This was where my career was definitely going to go up in the world, courtesy of one of the first ever free-fall courses in the SAS.

At this stage in the development of the SAS Regiment each of the four troops in a squadron was being schooled in a series of specialisations. These included free-fall (FF) parachuting, boat and mountain skills, and Land Rover mobility. It was volunteers only for FF, but I and several others had already volunteered, as we were keen to experience this exciting new challenge. Consequently, shortly after returning to base at Hereford, we found ourselves on the way to RAF Abingdon for intensive training. FF was in its infancy then in the SAS: in fact the course was only the second one to be run for SAS personnel. I made many nerve-tingling jumps, ranging in height from 2,000 feet to a mind-numbing 21,000 feet, and vividly recall the sheer devil-may-care approach, which meant that we fledgling SAS sky-divers had no fancy clothing for FF in those days – just a camouflage overall. This was complemented by jacket and trousers sewn together, a motorbike helmet with goggles, and that was about it.

The first week of the course was spent hanging face down on the end of a wire, practising aerial techniques and manoeuvres. After that we made three or four ordinary parachute jumps to get the adrenalin moving before attempting our first 3-second-delay FF from 2,200 feet. This took place on 23 May 1961. I still have the details of all my FF jumps recorded in my log book, including the opening height, when we pulled our ripcords. This was usually 2,000 feet, so the higher we jumped, the longer the delay. In those early days it was a highly skilled – and dangerous – art. We completed twenty FF jumps in all, progressing to 20-second delays, jumping at night and with equipment strapped on our front. For the night jumps we had a little torch fixed to our harness which shone on the altimeter or watch, whichever we were using. Besides falling in the flat, stable position we practised turns and tracking, which involved moving across the sky at great speed. The latter was necessary if you had been dropped off target and had to make up ground quickly. The terminal velocity (TV) is the fastest speed anyone will fall in any given position, up to about 125mph in the flat, stable position. For tracking you have to arrange the body in a head-down, bent-at-the-waist attitude, with arms to the side and hands cupped. This increases speed and air pressure, thus moving the body forward to an astounding velocity of more than 200mph!

I had a big scare one day just after I had opened my canopy. I was floating down nicely when I heard a whooshing noise coming from above. A second later a body went hurtling down past me in the flat, stable position. The other man was desperately close – only about 10 yards away – and I felt the air move violently. Until then I hadn't fully realised quite how fast 125mph was. His canopy opened just below me, and it was a very close thing, but we both got down safely. On the final night of the course we had a farewell party with our instructors. I would like once more to praise the RAF men. They were professional all the way, and damned good blokes with it.

There was a period of relative peace in the world at this time, at least as far as British forces were concerned. EOKA was still performing its acts of terrorism in Cyprus, but the top brass didn't seem to think there was a job there for the SAS. There was trouble in central Africa, Vietnam was just starting for the Americans and the massive Eastern Bloc Red Army was poised on its border ready for the invasion of the West. The Berlin Wall was also about to go up to stop East Europeans escaping to the West. So, that summer of 1961, the regiment held another open day on Hereford racecourse. The main event was an FF competition between the RAF, US Special Forces and the SAS, but to warm the crowd up the SAS made a series of static line jumps from Twin Pioneers. I was number one on the first jump and was designated the 'drifter', that is, I was required just to float down without compensating for the wind. This way, the true effect of any wind could be assessed before the others jumped, the correct amount of compensation taking place for safety and accuracy. I landed right in the middle of a patch of high nettles. I didn't fancy a face full of stings, so instead of rolling I did an illegal stand-up landing. How many sacrifices did they want in one day?! All was well, but the American team won the competition.

Following that event D Squadron saddled up and headed north for two weeks' climbing training in the dizzy heights of the Lake District. We set up our tents near a pub in the Langdale Pikes, the nearest suitable climb being vertical pitches on Bowfell Buttress and Middle Fell. Early next morning, in murky, drizzly, misty weather, we found ourselves being led to the cliffs (it felt like to our doom) by the seasoned veterans of the regiment's elite Mountain Troop. Their climbing kit consisted simply of a piece of rope tied around the waist upon which was fixed one karabiner, a metal oval-shaped ring with a snap or screwed-shut gate opening, plus a well-used climbing rope. That was it. No special boots or clothing and no safety helmets. SAS berets were the only head protection – fine against rain, but not a lot of use against falling rocks.

I vividly recall the experience. We were given a demonstration on rock climbing first. The Mountain Troop lads were very good, and watching them move easily and safely around the rock face gave me great confidence. After that we split into groups to be taken through the techniques step by step. One thing was really emphasised by the instructors: 'Always have at least three extremities on the rock face at any one time. This can be two feet and one hand, or two hands and one foot, but nothing less.' The first climb I did I tried to get my teeth on the rock as well – it was stimulating, to say the least! However, in a very short time we progressed from low, semi-vertical rocks to high, very vertical cliffs. On each climb our instructor led, followed by a line of roped-together, trembling-legged pupils. At intervals the leader would drive a piton (a metal spike with an eye on one end) into a crack in the rock face and fix a karabiner onto it. The purpose of this was to pass through the rope to which we were attached, so that if anyone fell, the piton would hopefully take most of the strain and, again hopefully, save all the other bods from being dragged off with him. When we reached the pitons we had to remember to loosen off our waistline karabiner underneath and refasten it afterwards. I parted company with the cliff face once at about 80 feet up while trying to negotiate a corner. Fortunately the leader had just reached the top and had fastened the rope onto a rock, so I was held steady. They told us not to look down, but of course that's exactly what I did. A wild thought went through my head: would it help if I held my feet and knees together Para-wise when I hit the ground? After swinging out and back in again I made a frantic grab for the rock face and managed to finish the climb minus only a few fingernails.

Abseiling was next, involving going down a cliff face at speed on a rope. Lowering myself backwards over the precipice at the start of my first abseil was the time when I wished I had been a good boy and said my prayers more often. The faces of the blokes waiting to follow me looked exactly as I felt, if not worse, grey and green about the gills. However, once you got confidence in the technique it became almost enjoyable. An exercise right at the end of the training finished with a night abseil, which is as difficult an abseil as anyone could hope to complete. It was pitch-black, and just as I thought I would never reach the bottom I suddenly felt my whole body touch the ground and lie flat instead of standing on my feet. A torch cracked on and shone directly into my startled face. 'What the hell are you lying down there for, Geordie?' asked one of the instructors as a suppressed smile played around his face.

There was another US Special Forces man with us on this trip, Top Sergeant Rozeniuk. 'Rosie', as he was known, was a tough and likeable character. He had been a refugee in Eastern Europe at the end of the Second World War, but eventually, after many privations and difficulties, he made his way to the USA. Rosie loved his drink, companionship and carousing, and we heard later, sadly, that one night, long after he had returned to the Special Forces, while in full flow, he had suddenly fallen backwards off his bar stool, stone dead. It was probably exactly the way he would have wanted it, though.

Saying goodbye to Cumbria we had a farewell booze-up at the pub on the last night and motored back to Hereford the next day, nursing our sizeable hangovers. At that time a group of us used to go FF parachuting at weekends using privately owned aircraft based at former RAF airfields. These included Halfpenny Green near Wolverhampton and Staverton near Gloucester. The aircraft we used were single-engine Piper Caribbeans; with the co-pilot's seat removed they could carry three parachutists at a time. We paid for these jumps ourselves. It cost around £5 each up to 3,000–7,000 feet. We practised spotting, or guiding the pilot to the spot on the ground 'release point' over which we jumped. The release point was determined by throwing out a streamer at opening height over the landing target, to see where it landed, and from that we gauged the wind strength and direction. The parachutes, bought privately, were ex-US Air Force survival parachutes, and I think they were only supposed to be used once. The panels were alternate red and white so they could be seen easily by a search party. They were modified to make them steerable, with two spaced, vertical panels cut from the rear that could be controlled by the jumper using pull cords to turn the canopy, and a horizontal slot that provided forward thrust to counteract wind or go with it to gain ground.

Sergeant Pete Sherman, the SAS Regiment's REME armourer, who was a very experienced free-faller, usually came with us on these weekends. Pete was in 22 SAS in Malaya but fell out with his squadron OC – the same one I was to fall out with later – and was RTU'd to REME. While awaiting his RTU Pete was on the training staff that supervised my jungle selection. In my opinion he was an extremely good soldier. Pete taught the new recruits most of what we needed to know about living and working in the jungle. He also saved my life on one occasion. One weekend at Staverton, just before our final jump, Pete was doing a safety check on my parachute. Everything had been OK on the last descent, during which I had performed some violent back flips and other manoeuvres.

But now Pete suddenly noticed that several straps were almost loose on my harness. If we had not bothered with checks each time I would not have noticed the loose straps and would almost certainly have fallen out of the harness on the very next jump. Now, whenever I remember that moment, I break out in a cold sweat. There we were going up and down like yo-yos in once-only parachutes – no wonder something came loose.

To further our skills and gain more experience several of our SAS group booked to go on an advanced FF course at Chalon-sur-Saône in France. It was of three weeks' duration, from 27 July to 17 August, and the trainee had to pay towards the cost. The other members were Sandy 'Crab' Powell, Pete B., Captain D. (all of 2 Troop A Squadron) and the CO, Lieutenant-Colonel Dare Wilson. The school, about 200 miles south-east of Paris, was managed by the daring but eccentric Monsieur Bernard, whose favourite trick when jumping was to land just outside the packing-shed door. This way, he maintained, he did not have far to carry his parachute for repacking! It was a brilliant course. We got in eighteen jumps each, the highest being 11,800 feet. M. Bernard was a good teacher and critic and got the best out of us. He didn't like the flat, stable position of parachuting, basically a delta shape, which we had been taught to adopt at Abingdon. 'Position anglaise,' he called it. 'No good.' He taught us, appropriately we thought, the 'frog' position, where the arms are held as if surrendering and the legs are bent at the knee. The frog, we found, was a very comfortable and easy-to-maintain position.

The aircraft used at Chalon were de Havilland Rapides, which could carry up to eight parachutists at a time, had two engines for quick climbs and high wings with a big door underneath for easy exits. For the first few jumps we had to stand on a bar outside the door and hold onto a wing strut waiting for the 'go'. On all subsequent jumps we dived head-first out of the door. I liked that best, because I didn't have time to look at the ground. We used French parachutes and repacked our own after use. The French chutes worked differently from ours, which had a nice smooth opening: with the French there was a hell of a sudden jerk at the end. On the first jump I doubled up and smashed my nose on the altimeter, which was fixed on top of the reserve parachute. Ripe British swearwords filled the air! Also, French altimeters were marked in metres, so we had to remember to pull at 600 metres, roughly equal to 2,000 feet.

Sleeping accommodation was in the airfield, but for meals we had to walk a mile or so to a hotel. Every night after dinner anyone who had dropped their ripcord that day had to stand up and be jeered at. Also, if it couldn't be found, they had to buy a new one. I spent 5 minutes each morning improving my grip.

A familiar face turned up at the school one day – Mike Reilly. Mike, by then a civilian, had been my instructor on P course when I joined the Paras (see Chapter 5). He had brought his own parachute with him, all patched up with black masking tape – something that, as I have mentioned earlier, will be familiar to all who have served in the British Army from the early 1950s to the present day. I have seen it used as black patches on camouflage nets, as a cover for shiny tin water bottles, for tying prisoners' hands together, holding two weapon magazines together to facilitate a quick change, mending holes in tents and ponchos, securing soft material to rucksack straps to stop chafing, wrapping around baggy trousers to prevent them from swishing when you're trying to move silently at night, stopping bleeding – the list is endless. When good soldiers die and go to heaven they will be issued with black masking tape to hold their wings on! And there was Mike, laughing and joking and testing his limits with a taped-up parachute. It was typical of a bloke like Mike, though – rough and ready, always with a big grin on his face, always friendly, a really nice man. We all liked him. Sadly, Mike died just a few months later in a parachuting accident. He was working as a stuntman in an American film about the US Army Air Force in the Second World War and had to bail out of a 'shot-down' bomber over the sea. However, something went badly wrong after he had jumped, and he was dead when he was picked up by the rescue boat.

D Squadron was off to North Wales for more climbing experience when I got back to Hereford. I had really enjoyed it in the Lake District last time and was raring to go for more of the same. The soldiers pitched their tents in a valley by Lake Ogwen in Snowdonia. The nearest village was a little place called Bethesda, and we spent the time climbing and carrying out night exercises. On one of these we SAS men went out in four-man patrols and just plodded around the hills. We had to make radio contact with base now and then, but that was all. Some of the older hands thought it would have been much more instructive and interesting to have had to find different locations and perhaps describe targets. After a few hours I decided to halt my patrol and have a brew. It was very cold and threatening rain, so the squad rigged a poncho shelter and we crawled into our sleeping bags to keep warm. The tea was brewing and the signaller was just getting through when the OC's face suddenly peered under the shelter. 'What are you doing?' he asked. I explained, but he suspected we were settling in for the night. This was not the case, but the damage was done. My obstinate streak was about to land me in trouble – and not for the first time. Next morning we had a debrief and I plunged myself further into the OC's bad books by denouncing the exercise as a waste of time. On return to Hereford the OC promptly had me transferred to A Squadron. I must say I was pleased to get away from him. He had an irritating habit of looking down his nose at me in an arrogant and haughty manner. I was just one of a long line of people who fell foul of him, but I was only sorry to be leaving my comrades in D Squadron.

I reported to Captain D., OC 2 Troop A Squadron, as one of their two sergeants, the other being Arthur Watchus. A Squadron was scheduled to go to Corsica that November for training with a French *parachutiste de choc* (PDC) battalion. In preparation for that we spent a lot of the next couple of months up in the Welsh hills on fitness and navigation training. Among other things we did were sketch-map exercises, showing only the river lines and heights. This was more like it, I thought: it was the kind of training I liked, that stretched you and made you think. Most of the time we were on the Cambrian Mountains, and the weather was typical of that area – non-stop rain. It was very testing, but it kept us hard and fit. The rolling, gentle-looking Welsh hills are extremely tiring to walk over, especially when you're laden with a heavy rucksack and rifle. The tufty grass and patches of black bog make for slow, laborious progress. The tops of the hills are mostly rounded, and it is heartbreaking when climbing up to keep seeing false crests ahead, only to have to plod on and ever onwards. It is very beautiful country, though. I was surprised at how many different colours there were on apparently green hills – every shade of green, brown, grey and yellow, all of which would suddenly change when a rare burst of sunlight swept across. One of our marches took us over the top of Plynlimon, where the Rivers Wye and Severn have their source. I thought about all the many towns and cities that the two waterways go through or pass by before they reach the sea. Apart from when they flooded, millions of people mostly took for granted the mighty rivers flowing along near them, and it all depended on the rain, which at that moment was beating down directly on my head – some drops over there for the Wye and some drops over there for the Severn.

There was no let-up in our FF, and one weekend towards the end of September I took part in a competition at Perth airfield in Scotland. It was a basic jump, pull and land on the target cross, but I thoroughly enjoyed it. We did three practice and three competition jumps. I didn't do very well on the first two, but on the final jump I paired with Budd, a member of the SAS Regimental FF team, and followed him out of the aircraft. As my canopy opened I heard Budd yell, 'This way!' I looked and saw him heading for the cross. I thought, 'He's a bit close, but if I wait until he lands I'll be way off', so I followed Budd as he landed on the centre cross and just missed his head to hit the same place. That was the first time I had worked with Budd, but I got to know him quite well later, and we became good friends.

Returning to Hereford the squadron and I were ordered to go to Corsica for yet more training. We were flown to Ajaccio airport on the west coast of the island and from there travelled north via the coast road to Calvi, where we were billeted in the PDC camp just outside town. There was a Foreign Legion outfit based nearby, but we SAS saw little of them.

Next morning, after a talk by the French OC, we were invited to tackle their assault course. The camp was built around an old castle with a dry moat, and the assault course was incorporated to a large extent within the castle walls. First we had to shin 5 yards up a drainpipe to a small ledge. Then, holding on to that ledge with our feet on another, we had to traverse along the wall to a corner. There were two windows en route. Female typists working inside took not the slightest notice of the grim faces passing by outside – they were obviously used to it. The next move, as the ledges ended at the corner, was to feel round for hand- and footholds. Steel spikes had been driven into the wall, but the SAS – unfamiliar with the imaginative course – couldn't see them. On and on we went, up, down and across. At one point we had to jump from the end of one wall onto the end of another that was about 2 yards lower and the same distance away. Crossing the moat on two parallel wires followed, and then the finish, a jump down into the moat of at least 4 yards. It was knackering, but we did it. Later we were invited to go round again, this time in the dark. How could we refuse? It was OK until the bit where we had to jump from one wall down onto another. We all did it, but it was quite dicey: the lower wall was almost invisible and a very small target. Afterwards the French officer told us that the wall jump should have been missed out at night. I wonder why he didn't tell us before? He then showed us a whole room covered with a model countryside, including an electric rail system. The PDC used it for sabotage training. After an hour playing with it we literally had to be dragged out.

The PDC had an enviable parachuting system. Next to the camp they had their own airfield, complete with Nordatlas transport aircraft, all under their own control. Within an hour of thinking about it they could be up in the air and jumping, the DZ being right next door. We, on the other hand, had to give the RAF plenty of notice of jumping, sometimes months ahead, and then it was a long journey to an airfield.

I visited Calvi several times. It is a typical north Mediterranean coastal town, with its cafés, bars, blue sea and little beach framed by scrub and conifer-covered mountain scenery, complete with tiny villages hanging by their fingertips to the sides. The weather at the time was quite mild in the low areas but cold in the mountains, with snow deep enough to ski on, much to the delight of our Mountain Troop. Our training dress then, in the early 1960s, consisted of a thin, windproof camouflage jacket with hood, olive-green trousers, rubber-soled boots and ankle puttees. I liked thin clothing for marching in: it was cool and dried out quickly. We were still using the heavy bergen-type rucksack. They weighed a ton when dry and empty and two tons when wet and full.

The PDC had organised several exercises. On one we played enemy saboteurs and had to guard installations. My patrol had to guard a rail junction, and I picked an OP on a small rise nearby. One exercise rule, which was emphasised, was that everyone must wear military uniform at all times. Along the line came a gang of men in civvies tapping the rail and checking things. I was suspicious but let them go by. Afterwards the PDC claimed they had blown the line. I informed the exercise umpire, who vetoed the claim. It was stupid. Why cheat? It is like cheating at patience: the only one you cheat is yourself. Some might say, 'Oh, but it's only an exercise,' but in my opinion the soldier who does this is doomed. Training is more important than war.

On another exercise we were escaped POWs being hunted by the PDC. Before the exercise we were stripped and searched and given old French uniforms to wear with 'PG' (*prisonnier de guerre*) on the back, plus an empty bottle for water and two matches. We were dropped off in pairs along a road in mid-Corsica, from where we had to find our way to an RV on the north coast, a distance of more than 50 miles. There were no specific rules. My partner was another sergeant, 'Big Frank' Williams. Frank had somehow acquired a compass after the search, so we had an advantage. After being dropped off the truck at night we immediately turned our jackets inside out to hide the PG, made for the nearest north–south road and, without success, tried to thumb a lift. We had walked about 20 miles when a police car pulled up and a fat gendarme jumped out, waving his hands and shouting. However, we had already disappeared into the scrub. A mile or so on we spotted a house and, after checking for telephone wires, we approached. There was one old bod there on his own, so we asked him for a drink. He either liked the look of us or was scared – Big Frank was a huge man, well over 6 feet tall – because he gave us wine and made some sardine sandwiches. Half an hour later, with 20-odd miles still to go to the RV, which we had to reach by morning, we carried on north, cross-country this time. We had to make for a nudist camp by a beach with an *épicerie* (grocery store) at the entrance. It was closed for the winter. Making the RV with a couple of hours to spare, we took great pleasure in handing in our unused bottle and matches. All our blokes evaded capture and reached the RV on time.

There were several more exercises, plus a day out on their demolition range where we played around with PE. Just before leaving Calvi six of our free-fallers and six PDC did a farewell jump together. At 9,000 feet we lined up in the aircraft ready to go, with the British in front. The French despatcher glanced out of the door, then nodded for us to go. I was last out, and as I fell I looked up. No French had followed. Then, about 5 seconds later, I saw six figures emerge, very fast. Looking down I observed that the ground target cross was a long way off. I tracked for as long as possible before pulling the ripcord, but I could see that no Brit was going to make it to the cross or get anywhere near it. Meanwhile the French were floating down in a tight little group, straight for the target. The bastards had cheated again! I suppose it was their way of evening the score after their humiliation on the POW exercise. It was obvious that their despatcher had lobbed us out early, then held his men back a few seconds to exit over the correct release point. When we got back to the parachute store the French were in full snigger. Pathetic. It's obvious they still haven't forgiven us for Trafalgar and Waterloo. Their hospitality, however, was excellent, with good accommodation and food – pity the military side didn't match up.

On arrival back in Hereford the troops were just in time to go on Christmas leave. It was 23 December 1961. In the past few months we had crammed in a tremendous variety of activities and valuable training. Now we were to return to our old stomping ground, the Malayan jungle, but, as we were soon to discover, many new dangers lay just ahead . . .

Chapter 13

HIGH-ALTITUDE PARACHUTING: JUNGLE MISSIONS WITH THE SAS

Knowing that we were to go out to Malaya for jungle training in mid-January 1962 the SAS A Squadron troops, including myself, did not waste the intervening time. After leave we went out into the local woods and swotted up on jungle tactics. There were a number of veterans like myself who were already well experienced in the bush, but for many men who had recently joined the squadron it would be their first time in the jungle – and it is a daunting place for the novice.

The main operation, of six weeks' duration, was to take place near the border with Thailand where, it was suspected, there still lurked a number of CT and possibly one or two small aboriginal tribes that had yet to be contacted by the British. The squadron had a week's warm-up 'bash' in the local jungle near Grik first to get tuned in. Captain 'Charlie' Beckwith, an American Special Forces officer who had been with the squadron in Corsica, also joined up with our boys from the SAS in Malaya. He was a brave and resourceful officer who was to gain fame in early 1980 when he led part of 'Delta Force', one of the crack groups of the American Special Forces, in a well-documented but ill-fated attempt to rescue American hostages trapped in Iran. A lot went wrong on that operation, and there appeared to be some in-fighting among the top brass, but having observed Charlie at close hand during his time with the SAS I believe he would have performed his job well. He was a bit flamboyant, but a hard worker and a gentleman.

Just before the main jungle op started the SAS were joined by some of 2 Troop, who had stayed behind to take part in high-altitude parachuting trials on Salisbury Plain. They had been jumping from 34,000 feet with breathing equipment, and all seemed to be going well. Unfortunately, however, one experienced man, Corporal Keith Norry, of 16 Troop, D Squadron, was killed. For some unknown reason he had failed to open his parachute and had plummeted to his death. Although there was an investigation, and many theories of explanation that were discussed privately in SAS circles, the actual reason at the root of the tragedy never became clear. When checked out by the RAF everything appeared normal and as it should be. Keith's parachute and breathing equipment were in order. It was completely baffling. I had known Keith since joining the regiment, and he had been very helpful to me as a recruit and was a good friend. Sadly these accidents sometimes happen – and often to the best.

After that tragedy the top brass decided that some kind of a memorial should be built to commemorate the dead of 22 SAS, including all attached personnel. This would cover the period since the Second World War and would continue into the future. Eventually a three-faced clock tower was erected in Bradbury Lines, the original barracks of the SAS at Hereford. This was renamed Stirling Lines – and, more recently, the clock was moved to the latest SAS base, at Credenhill just outside the city. The clock tower has the names of the dead, their date of death and where they died inscribed on brass plaques on its sides. On the front of the tower, below the clock, is fixed a large SAS badge. Below that, inscribed on another plaque, is an extract from *The Golden Road to Samarkand*, a poem by James Elroy Flecker (1884–1915), which contains a famous and often-quoted stanza:

> We are the pilgrims, master; we shall go
> Always a little further; it may be
> Beyond that last blue mountain barred with snow,
> Across that angry or that glimmering sea.

Meanwhile, returning to Malaya, at the start of the operation each troop entered the jungle from different points. The men of 2 Troop, me included, went by helicopter to the east, where we went in through a village. As our first resupply air drop would not be for two weeks, off we tramped, each carrying at least 90lb of food, equipment and ammo. We had several aborigine porters for the radio and other equipment. The bungle, as we still called it, hadn't changed a jot. Dark and gloomy under the tall canopy, it was still slippery, wet, muddy and itchy below, and infested with leeches, bugs and mosquitoes. It was hot, humid and very difficult to walk through – and I loved it! My appreciation was because it was natural and unspoiled. Man had taken no part in its making. The animals within it roamed free. It was like a giant safari park, but without the gates or wardens. The price we paid to be in there was sweat – and lots of it. All went reasonably well for several days, but then our officer kept taking us off on odd tangents. It is just about impossible to go in a straight line in the jungle, but if you are heading for a point which is to the north, like we should have been doing, then the general direction should be north. Ours was much too far west.

I couldn't seem to exert any correcting influence on the officer and was getting thoroughly brassed off. So one day, when we were plodding up a bloody great big hill and going in completely the wrong direction, I decided I had had enough. 'Fuck you!' I yelled. 'I'm off. I'll see you at the RV.' Whereupon I turned to the right and struck out on my own – north. Two minutes later I realised that I had done the wrong thing. However, I said aloud to myself, 'Sod it, I'm going on, even if it means getting chucked out of the SAS. I can't soldier with people like that.' Looking back on it now, maybe I was too critical, I don't know; but at the time it was very important to me that we operated properly, and I was, perhaps, harsh on people who I thought didn't measure up. So on I went. I spent my first night alone on a tiny ledge by a stream, with barely enough room to make a shelter and cook a meal. Later, listening to the night noises of birds and animals, I felt very small and a bit scared. No one knew where I was, and I doubt whether anyone cared. Next day I hit a big river flowing north. I knew this would lead me to the resupply RV, where another river came in to join it from the east. Trudging along by the river I came across a small sitting shelter made from atap, a jungle plant. It faced the river and was probably a fishing point made by aborigines. I sat there for a while and made a brew of tea. As I was looking at the far bank a big tiger poked its head out of the undergrowth, had a look up and down the river and then faded away again, just as suddenly. As I moved on I heard, somewhere downstream, a troop of monkeys hooting like mad.

I needed to be on the other side of the river to make sure of finding the RV, so at the next shallow-looking part that had accessible banks I waded in. The current was quite strong, and I found the easiest way to maintain balance was by facing upstream. However, it was deeper than I had imagined, easily reaching my chest. As I leaned forward against the pressure, the water was brimming just below my mouth. Also, the bottom of the river was covered in round, slippery rocks, so that I had to inch my way carefully along, making sure one foot was planted firmly before bringing the other one to it. My rucksack floated, which helped a bit with balance, but was being buffeted by the current. All the while I had to hold my rifle above my head to keep it dry. I prayed to St Christopher to get me safely across. The river was only about 20 yards wide at that point, but it took me 15 minutes to get over. St Chris must have heard, I thought, as I clambered thankfully up the other bank and searched for a level spot to make a brew and dry off. Just before dark I had reached the RV and made myself a posh basha with a pole hammock. All I had to do then was wait for the troop to catch me up. In the morning I looked around and found evidence of past occupation, including bits of Para cord and old tins. Then I remembered that our officer had said he had been in this area with his previous unit on training.

While waiting for the storm to catch up with me I had a nice, peaceful day resting and reading my book, but then next day, around noon, I heard sounds of someone approaching. There was a handclap, and Corporal Bob S. appeared with the troop officer behind him. Surprisingly the officer didn't say anything about my having gone off alone. He merely asked me how long I had been at the RV and said that the troop were still some distance away. Bob and he had come along to find me. I packed up and followed them, crossing the river again and rejoining the troop about 3 miles upstream. They had been thinking about making rafts to get to the RV but as time was short had abandoned the idea. We had a change of diet that night. The aborigine porters had caught some fish, which we cooked, in green bamboo, over a fire. It was delicious, but very bony. Next day we returned to the RV and cut a DZ for the air drop. Some of us had asked for extra bread on this resupply. Soldiers in the jungle often miss bread and especially big steak sandwiches, with slices oozing with butter and jam to follow. But usually, in the real world, we got Spam or corned beef instead! It was while we were waiting for the drone of aircraft coming over that I discovered that our troop officer had forgotten to order the extra bread. Tonight, I vowed, I'm going to make a mud effigy of our beloved officer and stick big thorns in it. However, even though I was to have more rows with him in the future, I found it hard to dislike him. I realised that he was quite a good bloke really, and that I had been a harsh judge. The troop split into searching patrols until the next air drop.

One day my patrol found an empty aborigine camp. The camp, which consisted of a circular barricade of atap with a central fireplace, appeared to have been lived in until quite recently. There were one or two abandoned items, cooking pots and so on, which seemed to suggest a hurried departure. About a week previously we had heard loud explosions coming from the direction of one of our troops operating in another area. Maybe these aborigines had been scared away by that. Later we were told that the other troop had blown an emergency helicopter LZ clearing to evacuate a sick man. This was Charlie Beckwith, who had collapsed with fatigue after contracting a jungle disease, leptospirosis (see Chapter 8). Unfortunately, because of the noise, the disturbance had spoiled one of our objectives of meeting up with an aborigine tribe to gather information about terrorist activity and movements.

The next air drop was delayed for two days owing to bad weather. To supplement what rations we had left we ate rambutan fruit and the top growth of certain trees. The porters caught and cooked an iguana, but that didn't go far among all of us. The resupply finally arrived, but a longer delay would have meant getting seriously organised for survival. One of the lads in the troop was John 'Lofty' Wiseman, who later became well known after he had left the Army through his famed publication of *The SAS Survival Handbook*. But that was many years ahead. The final phase of the op was to march to a jungle fort RV called Fort Brooke, join up with the rest of the squadron and from there be airlifted out to Grik.

The initial security clearing for the site of Fort Brooke had been carried out by an SAS patrol under the command of Major 'Johnny' Cooper, who was one of the Original SAS recruited by David Stirling in the Second World War. He had built the Fort Brooke site in 1953 when his patrol was in the jungle for an incredible 122 days. (Johnny Cooper gives an excellent description of this event in his 1991 book, *One of the Originals*.) Meanwhile wildlife of the big-toothed kind was ambushing us SAS troopers as we made our way to Fort Brooke. We found ourselves just feet away from a tiger which was crouched down stalking a porcupine. He took not the slightest notice of us passing by. Another time we were sitting taking five when a black honey bear came crashing down out of a nearby tree and ran off like the clappers. Another day we came across a clearing by a big river where elephants had recently destroyed some aborigine huts. They had made a hell of a mess, and there was debris strewn all around. We had a look in case there were any injured people, but they must have made good their escape.

After a debrief at Fort Brooke we all had to shave off our six-week beards before being flown out to Grik. Beards are essential in the hot steamy jungle – they are good camouflage and stop your neck getting sore from sweating.

From Grik we moved down to the Australian Air Force base at Butterworth near Penang on the west coast. We had a long-awaited day off to sample the fleshpots of Penang. Penang is an island, which at that time was reached by ferry. It still had the appearance of an old colonial town, typical of the Eastern British Empire. First things first: I had a giant curry in an Indian restaurant on the main street, from where it was just a short walk to the Boston Bar across the road. Inside I ordered a beer and eyed up the talent. A very beautiful Malayan girl was sitting with some of the squadron blokes. I squeezed in next to her and asked her if she would like a drink – after all, I had been in the bungle for two lonely months! I shall draw a discreet veil over the rest of the night; suffice it to say that we both had big smiles on our faces as we showered together next morning. Later on I learned that I had inadvertently pinched the girl of a mate of mine, John 'Taff' Prescott. In spite of that we have remained friends ever since, but he never lets me forget that I stole his classy Malayan girl. It couldn't have been my looks, so maybe she thought I was a better financial prospect.

At this time some A Squadron members of the regimental FF team had brought parachutes to Malaya, hoping for a chance to get in a few practice jumps. An aircraft, a single-engine Beaver, was available at RAAF (Royal Australian Air Force) Butterworth, and the weather was fine, so away we went. I gladly volunteered, replacing Keith Norry in the team after his fatal accident. In the next couple of days we completed four jumps each, all from 7,000 feet. We practised the international competition sequence, which starts with a back loop, followed by turning full circles to the left and right, then another back loop before finally we pulled the cord at the correct height and aimed for the DZ target cross. Dropping near some paddy fields just outside the RAAF base we all managed, barring one bloke, to descend onto a dry patch. Not so the other man. To help the rice grow the planters spread a liberal amount of manure, animal and human, onto the paddy. This may be good for the rice, but it did little to enhance the appearance, or smell, of the unfortunate man who landed right in it! This was my final trip to Penang, but on the train journey to Singapore for our flight back to the UK the troopers had a few hours' break at KL, and I snatched some nostalgic visits to old haunts, including Nanto's Bar.

Arriving back in Hereford on a Thursday the squadron spent Friday on admin and looked forward to a weekend off. No way! On the Saturday, at 0300 hr, I was awakened by the Orderly Sergeant shouting 'Grabstakes!' This was a codeword meaning that all personnel had to report to the guardroom asap, dressed and equipped for operations. There we were briefed by the OC and then issued with rations and weapons. I always kept my rucksack and belt kit packed as much as possible, ready for a quick departure, so I was down at the guardroom in about 10 minutes flat. By 0400 hr the squadron was present and ready, weapons issued, but only with blank ammo and no rations: it was a practice op for A Squadron, after all. We were given various tasks to perform and spent the rest of the morning bombing around the local countryside, at one point reaching the top of Dinedor Hill, about 2 miles from camp. From Dinedor Hill we finished the exercise by running back to camp along a road known locally as the 'straight mile'.

However, I had a big shock in store. By this time we were getting a bit hot and steamed up, so most of us had removed our berets and tucked them away. But just before reaching camp we got properly dressed and reported back in good order. As we waited the SSM (the gloomy one referred to previously) came out of the guardroom and said someone had phoned in complaining about us going along without our berets on. The blokes started honking, and I said, 'The bastard wants to try running with a full bergen and rifle and see how *he* likes it.' With that the SSM went back into the guardroom, and a moment later the OC came out. 'Right, Sergeant Doran,' he said. 'Go and pack your kit: you are for RTU.' I was stunned. RTU – the most humiliating punishment in the SAS – just for that! I could not believe it. Later on, however, back in the bunk while filling my suitcase I thought, 'Ah, yes, that solo effort in Malaya – I'm being gunned for. But if that was true, why didn't they just say, instead of beating about the bush?' Anyway, after packing I lay on my bed waiting. I didn't fancy going back to the Paras – that was a closed chapter. I wondered what it was like in the Foreign Legion. I mused, in the words of the song, that I would 'fight the savage foe' in some far-flung corner of the French Empire. Just as I was warming up to that idea there was a knock on the door and I was informed that the OC wanted to see me.

Waiting for me by the HQ hut the OC said, 'You are not being RTU'd now. The CO says you are to stay.' 'Good,' I thought, with relief. The CO, Lieutenant-Colonel Wilson, had saved my bacon. He was to me at that moment, as always, a shining beacon of common sense. 'By the way,' said the OC, a few minutes later, as we strolled by the side of the barrack square. 'Why don't you ever say good morning or afternoon to me when we meet?' I stopped and looked at him. 'Because I don't like you, you bastard,' was what I would have liked to have replied, but I thought, 'Hold on, Geordie, this situation calls for a bit of diplomacy.' So I replied that I had meant no disrespect; it was just that I had became used to saluting officers without speaking, which was normal practice in my former units. That wasn't strictly true, of course, but it allowed me to break off contact with the 'enemy' and beat a tactical retreat! In recent years I have met my former OC at reunions many times. We have shaken hands and had genial conversations. I hold no grudge, and I hope he doesn't. The reason for relating this episode at all is merely to illustrate the ups and downs of my SAS life and my thoughts at the time.

Following that bit of a do I went downtown to catch up on my social life. The City Arms in Broad Street (now Barclays Bank) was the in-place then. Large numbers of SAS gathered there nightly to exercise their elbows and, hopefully, strike up a relationship with a member of the fair sex. I went with a girl I met there for about a year. I had also noticed another girl who went there quite often. She had a nice, smiling face and lovely legs. All her other bits were nice too! Trouble was, she was always with some other bloke. We did clash eyes occasionally, however, and I found out her name was Ann. I had no idea then that she was eventually to become my wife and we would still be happily married as I write this, many years later.

Netheravon on Salisbury Plain was the next port of call, where my SAS comrades and I carried out yet more FF parachuting. In between I taught the troop how to handle the 3in mortar, including live firing on the nearby ranges. On the final FF jump, in April 1962, there was a strong wind, and on landing I was dragged along the ground, tearing ligaments and breaking a bone in my right shoulder. My arm was in a sling for a few weeks, but by May I was back in action and just in time to go on another Denmark exercise.

Once again, the SAS played the 'enemy' for the Danish Home Guard. Khrushchev, the Soviet leader, was busy shooting his mouth off again, and the threat of invasion by his Eastern Bloc armies was still a grim reality. Sometimes the exercises descended into pure farce, almost inevitably where I was concerned. Afterwards my patrol rendezvoused with the rest of the troop on the coast where we waited to be picked up by boat. Now Denmark is home to a species of huge black mosquito which does its best to eat humans alive. They were out in force that night, and as we were cursing and swatting the Home Guard attacked. We slaughtered them with blank ammo, but instead of being good boys and lying down dead they came at us, waving their rifles and looking very aggressive. I thought, 'Christ, they want a real war!' One charged at me, so I punched him between the eyes. He had glasses on, and I felt metal, glass and bone crunch under my fist. We did a runner then and hid until they had gone. Later we were picked up and sailed into Copenhagen, where a boozy night followed. After leave it was back to training and preparing for our next trip abroad in July, which involved both A and D Squadrons training with the US Airborne and Special Forces at Fort Bragg, North Carolina.

In late July we left for the USA, travelling in a mix of aircraft. When the SAS arrived the Special Forces had lined the road into camp to greet them, and afterwards we were given a welcoming speech from Brigadier Yarborough, US Special Forces. I was impressed. Gigantic is the only way to describe Fort Bragg. There were two huge airfields and numerous helicopter areas, each one of which held more machines than our RAF and Army Air Corps put together. Also there were two full airborne divisions, the 101st and 82nd, plus the Special Forces. Twelve PX canteens, equivalent to our NAAFI, were spread around the camp. Settling in well we spent the first week having lectures and demos on Special Forces techniques.

One day we went for a keep-fit march, complete with bergens and rifles and wearing our beige berets. This caused quite a stir among the passing airborne soldiers in camp. The look in their eyes said, 'Who are these guys?' We parachuted at night into our first exercise, in which our squadron's main task was to attack a railway bridge over a big river. The exercise was held in the Blue Ridge Mountains, West Virginia, and our 'enemy' was the 101st Airborne, the famed 'Screaming Eagles' of D-Day renown. The aircraft we flew in were very noisy. Most of us landed in the trees at the side of the DZ, and I found myself bouncing gently right on the top of a conifer. It was too dark to see the ground, so I dropped my helmet to see how long it would take to fall. After a few seconds I heard a dull thud, and I found I was about 10 yards up. My bergen, with rifle attached, was hanging below on a line, so I lowered that as best I could, undid my harness and clambered down. I slid the last 10 feet or so and landed astride a barbed wire fence. It was my lucky night . . .

Hiding in the forest next day I was introduced to corn on the cob. We sneaked out to a nearby field, nicked some cobs and boiled them in our mess tins. They were delicious! We had been issued with US Army rations, which were fabulous. They had everything – there was even tinned bread. One US 24-hour ration alone lasted me 48 hours.

That night I took one man with me to recce the railway. As we were following the line a set of headlights approached on a nearby track. We dodged behind a pile of sleepers. The vehicle, a car, stopped a few yards away; the driver got out and looked all around. He then went over to another pile of sleepers, reached behind and lifted out a huge liquor jar, the sort they put 'moonshine' in. Then, jumping back into his car, he drove off. I don't think West Virginia was a dry state, but illegal stills were operated to avoid revenue payments. (I saw some later on other exercises.) We went over to see if the bloke had left any money, but no luck.

Then, a week or so later, after sneaking around the forest and being chased by the Screaming Eagles, we finished up at a town called Dawson, where a huge barbecue was laid on. The State Governor was there in person to greet us. We then trained in camp for a while, during which time I visited Fayetteville, the nearest town, and spent some evenings in the main PX canteen in camp. They liked their beer cold there – so cold it was like an ice lolly in a glass!

The next big exercise involving me and the SAS took place in the Smoky Mountains, near the border with Tennessee. The 'enemy' this time was the 82nd Airborne AA (All American). Only one SAS man parachuted in: Lieutenant-Colonel John Woodhouse, who had recently taken over as CO. He had been in 22 SAS on and off since helping with its formation in the early 1950s. The CO landed in a tree, unfortunately, broke his ankle and had to be lowered down by ropes. The Smoky Mountain country, which is part of the Appalachian range stretching to the north-east of the USA, is vast and beautiful. In that area a lot of battles had been fought between the British Army and the 'Colonialists' during the American War of Independence. Now history was repeating itself as the SAS were ambushing the USA and being in turn chased by the All Americans for a couple of weeks before returning to Fort Bragg, where we were split up for troop activities. These included for some of us amphibious and jungle training in Florida and Panama, while the FF men carried out their jumps at Fort Bragg.

I was included in a small group introduced to HALO (high-altitude low-opening) parachuting. Our first descent was from 14,000 feet using breathing apparatus. There was a barometrically operated opening device called a 'mouse' fixed to the harnesses, which worked at 4,000 feet. If for some reason that did not work, then the parachutist still had plenty of time to pull the cord manually. Instead of a normal ripcord handle there was a green knob which was easier to grip with gloves on. The parachute canopies had an oval-shaped hole cut in the back called a 'Tojo' slot for drive and steering, but they did not prove very effective. Within Bragg there were five huge DZs, all with different names and shapes. We were shown aerial photographs of the DZ in current use so that we could recognise it after jumping. It was a good job too, for on our first jump I could see all five DZs and was able to pick which one to aim for. Unfortunately we had been dropped wide, and some of us landed among trees at the side.

The Russians must have decided that I was having too much fun, because the 'Cuban missile crisis' started the very next day. The world was on the brink of nuclear war until Khrushchev called back his missile ships bound for Cuba. Immediately all aircraft were commandeered by the 82nd and 101st Divisions and flown to Florida for a possible invasion of Cuba. But by and by, when it appeared that Comrade Khrushchev had backed down, our HALO was resumed. Time was getting short now, however, and we managed only three more descents, two from 21,000 feet and one from 20,000 feet.

On the final jump I had a bit of bother. My breathing equipment had seemed to be working OK at first, but halfway down the mask suddenly clamped itself to my face, and I couldn't breathe at all. Frantically ripping the mask off, which caused me to tumble – a highly dangerous and uncontrollable situation – I was just in time to stabilise myself before the 'mouse' opened the canopy. I think the oxygen bottle must have been set on low pressure, and so when I fell into denser atmosphere outside, air pressure clamped the mask to my face. It was pretty hair-raising. Anyway, I still managed to land within 5 yards of the target cross on the DZ – which only goes to prove that if you have a thick head, you don't need so much air in there!

A few days later, just before the SAS were due to leave, a farewell parade was held on the main barrack square. As part of the finale two groups of free-fallers, one Brit and one US Special Forces, were to jump and land, it was hoped, in front of the podium where an American general was to give a farewell speech.

Our SAS men did a practice jump in the morning from a helicopter at 10,000 feet. All went according to plan, but for some reason small fixed-wing aircraft were used for the event in the afternoon, the Brits in one, Special Forces in the other. My spotter was a Special Forces man, a bloke called 'Stinky' Sherrat. Out we went at 11,000 feet, and straight away I could see that we were miles from the square. I went into a track immediately. We had smoke canisters on our heels, and when I looked around I saw the other SAS men also going like the clappers, trying to get into a good opening position. Being the first man out I had the furthest to go and didn't make the DZ. I and another lad landed among some accommodation blocks near the square, just managing to drop onto the only piece of grass in the vicinity and narrowly missing some outbuildings. The general, accompanied by his entourage, came to see if we were OK. 'Thank goodness you're all right, Geordie,' he said. It had been another close call. Our spotter, the man in charge of seeing that parachutists leave the aircraft in time to drop accurately on the DZ, came to see us later and wrote an apology in our log books. I did not realise it then, but that was to be my last FF jump.

The drink flowed freely at a farewell party that night, after which our SAS lads threw out a challenge to our American Para comrades to compete in the infamous, rollicking and hilarious 'Dance of the Flaming Arseholes'. This is a well-known test of character and nerve among SAS circles. The dance was a test to see who could endure the most pain, the winner being the last one still performing. Each competitor had to strip naked and hold an equal length of paper between their thighs, right up to the crotch. Both ends of each man's paper would then be simultaneously set alight. As the paper burnt the dancers would have to perform a wriggling movement like a belly dancer. Meanwhile the audience would chant the 'Hyzickazoomba' song, as follows: 'Hyzickazoomba zoomba zoomba, hyzickazoomba zoomba zay.' I won't repeat the rest (it's much too filthy). All the while the papers would be burning and dancers dropping out one by one, as their nether regions were singed red-hot. Our reigning champ was Jackie B., who once let the flames singe the hairs on his arse, they got that close. A couple of brave Yanks put up a decent show on this night, but they were no match for Jackie, who emerged victorious.

Two days later the SAS took off from Fort Bragg in Bristol Britannia aeroplanes and landed in the UK on 19 October 1962. We later heard that the Special Forces men had talked of 'the party' for many years afterwards, and the night has now gone down in SAS folklore. The American Airborne Forces had truly lived up to their motto, which was emblazoned in big letters over their camp gates: STRAC, meaning 'Skilled, Tough and Ready Around the Clock.' To some wags in the SAS this was interpreted as 'Shit, The Russians Are Coming!' However, for many years afterwards in the SAS to be 'strac' meant you were ready.

Back in Hereford we had to carry out familiarisation training jumps from a new type of aircraft called the Argosy. One fine night a planeload of SAS were approaching Watchfield, a disused airfield near Swindon used as a DZ. We were all standing up ready to jump when there was some kind of hitch on the ground. We had no alternative but to sit down again and wait while the aircraft flew in big circles. Round and round we flew, the lights of Swindon coming and going below. I started feeling sick, and so out came my sick bag, ready. I noticed that several men had already filled theirs. An agonising half an hour later we were out, finally. I have never been so happy to jump from an aeroplane. However, if I had known what was waiting for me on the ground, I wouldn't have been so chuffed. I landed heavily on the side of a hole and snapped a bone in my ankle. The pain was terrific. I felt for my foot in the dark and discovered it was bent over at right angles. Without hesitation – as a sort of natural reflex, I suppose – I grabbed hold of it and straightened it out. Seconds later another bod thudded in nearby, and I heard a yell of pain. I found out afterwards that he had suffered exactly the same injury as myself. The DZ safety team had heard the other bloke's cry and came rushing to investigate. The medic gave us both a jab of morphine and carted us off to hospital. Coming out of dock with a plastered foot I discovered to my joy that I could still safely drive my newly acquired Morgan sportscar.

Fresh girlfriends came and went, but the night I had my plaster removed I got talking to the girl with the nice, smiling face, Ann (later to be my wife), with whom I had clashed eyes in the City Arms. On Christmas Eve 1962 I met Ann there, and she asked me if I would do her a favour and play Father Christmas at a family party. One child of Santa-believing age would be there, Ann's 4-year-old niece Susanne, and they wanted a voice she wouldn't recognise. I readily agreed and sped off in my Morgan to Credenhill, where the party was being held. I dressed as Santa, roared 'Ho-ho-ho', gave out presents and made a little 4-year-old girl happy. But the punchline came many years later when Ann told me that after I had removed my disguise her mother had exclaimed, 'He's the ugliest man I have ever seen in my whole life! Just the sight of him makes me feel ill.' I took the knock-back philosophically, saying, 'Now there's gratitude for you!' Well, you cannot be as strong as an elephant, brave as a lion, swift as a gazelle, good-looking *and* please the future mother-in-law. After the family party, well and truly sozzled, I went outside to pee and fell backwards into a ditch. Ann hid my car keys, so I slept there that night – in their house, that is, not the ditch. A few days after Christmas Ann invited me up to their house on Dinedor Hill just outside Hereford so I could meet her folks properly. I don't know whether Ann's mother ever changed her mind about my looks, but I think she grew to accept me, because I used to saw wood and prune roses for her. What a creep!

However, the Christmas spirit had hardly departed when storm clouds were again appearing on the horizon in the Far East, where a revolt in the British protectorate of the Sultanate of Brunei was causing great concern. Orders came for A Squadron, including me and the ever-present veterans of the SAS, to be put on standby to go and carry out its familiar anti-terrorist role, this time operating in the jungles of Borneo, where the Communist-supported trouble was threatening to spread. Lieutenant-Colonel John Woodhouse had volunteered the regiment as available, and the men were, as always, ready to move out and fight, if necessary, at a moment's notice. We were told that just before Christmas there had been a revolt in Brunei, followed by an attempted coup. Royal Marine Commandos and Gurkhas were rushed there from Malaya initially to deal with the situation. The SAS, as ever, would not now be far behind; A Squadron comprised the chosen few. Our standby orders were top secret, and one dark morning, unseen, the squadron slipped out of Hereford to begin the long journey to the Far East . . .

Chapter 14

THE SAS 'HEARTS AND MINDS' CAMPAIGN: BORNEO ON THE BRINK

Borneo was ripe for revolution at this crucial time in its history, fermenting into a lethal cocktail of opposing territories. These comprised Sarawak, a former British territory, and Sabah, a former British protectorate, both of which, together with Brunei, were in the north of the island, while the southern half, called Kalimantan, belonged to Indonesia. The British strongly suspected that Indonesia was behind the rebellion that was about to sweep the island, and it was certainly proved to be providing the weapons and training involved. However, to complicate matters further, Chinese Communists were also heavily involved via the Clandestine Communist Organisation (CCO), a subversive movement which was pursuing its aims of obtaining territorial gains and influence by force and blatant coercion of the local populace. Fortunately the British Government, secret services and military top brass foresaw the storm clouds inspired by the Indonesians brewing on the horizon and began a rapid military build-up in the area.

This is where the SAS now came into the picture. I was one of around fifty Special Forces soldiers rushed out to plug the breach in Borneo's wavering defences; we were to strive hard to get the local populace on the side of Britain by living and working among the natives. However, our stringent attempts to maintain absolute secrecy were unintentionally blown by others on the way. At Heathrow Airport we caused some heads to turn. We were in civilian clothes and carrying rucksacks, fifty or so fit-looking young men all travelling together. 'Who are you lot, then?' someone asked. 'The Hiker's Club of Great Britain,' came the instant reply from one of the squadron blokes. Just after taking off I watched the snow-covered English countryside below fade away into the distance. We were leaving behind a Britain shivering in the coldest, snowiest winter we had had for decades, and

I felt I was lucky to be flying off to a nice, warm climate, a feeling tempered somewhat by the knowledge that we were possibly heading for a highly dangerous jungle war. However, on arrival at Singapore our cover was well and truly blown. We had just trooped into the arrivals hall with civilian and other military passengers all around us when some bloke from the Military Movements Section appeared by one of the exits and shouted at the top of his voice, 'SAS this way!' Then, to make sure everyone had heard, he yelled it again, louder!

Later, after we had been settled into a transit camp, we were told that the General Officer Commanding Malayan and Borneo areas had decided that we were not 'brown enough' and needed a period of acclimatisation before going on to Borneo. This scintillating gem of a decision brought forth howls of derisive laughter from the squadron. Acclimatisation would no doubt have been necessary for a unit that had spent the last five or ten years in Europe, but our SAS men had been training extremely hard in many different countries, including the jungles of Malaya, for the past three years or so. We were fit and ready for action. But orders were orders, and the squadron was moved to a training area in Malaya, where we proceeded to get browned off. However, Sergeant 'Archie' Archer and I were given another, more pressing task, comprising the squadron advance party to Labuan island, which lies off North Borneo. There was an airfield on Labuan, but for some reason we were sent by sea on an RASC vehicle transport craft.

All the way over the South China Sea we met with huge waves. Each wave lifted our flat-bottomed craft up and then slapped us down into the following trough with a resounding thud. This went on for hour after hour. I wasn't seasick, but I had a cannonball in my guts for the three days it took to get to Labuan. I fervently promised God that I would be a good lad if only he didn't send me to sea again! At Labuan we contacted the local RAOC depot about kit and waited for the squadron to arrive. God must have been checking, because I went on another sea journey within a week. The rest of the squadron arrived, and we sailed by ferry to Brunei. Also on board was an Indian 'char wallah' from our SAS Malaya days. He was known as Macgregor, or Mac, and stayed with the SAS in Borneo for three years, giving sterling support. Mac didn't get any medals, but we all thought that he deserved one for his splendid service.

Squadron HQ was set up in a building known as the 'haunted house', not far from Brunei town. It had for many years been reputedly haunted, long before we got there. Whose ghost it was I have no idea. The OC was Major 'Dolly' Edwards, a soldier whom the men respected greatly. A week later I was informed that I would be going to Bario, near the border with Kalimantan, to relieve Staff Sergeant Roy Ball, who was already operating there with Stan Jenks, a troop signaller.

There was a grass strip at Bario, so I was flown in, accompanied by a man called Tom Harrison. Tom, a government officer and former SOE (Special Operations Executive) agent who had worked with the Kelabit tribe of Bario in the Second World War, was visiting friends. Weight was critical because of the extra passenger, so I had to leave a lot of my kit behind, including my camera. Luckily Stan had one there already. The country in that area is very broken, with many steep-sided hills and ravines. Flying below the clouds that encircled the hilltops I caught glimpses of huge hornbills skimming over the jungle canopy. Suddenly the valley of Bario opened out in front of us. The pilot took one precautionary circuit of the strip before making a neat, near-perfect landing. When I first saw the Bario valley from the air it immediately reminded me of the film *Lost Horizon*, in which a group of people have survived an aeroplane crash in a remote Himalayan region. After trekking through a mountain pass they find themselves in a lush, green valley where the people are happy and never grow old. The name of the valley is 'Shangri-La'. Shangri-La at Bario it most certainly was. It was indeed lush and green, and the people were very happy and friendly.

First Roy introduced me to Mr Lian Bala, who looked after the airstrip, and then to Mr Toynbee, a Canadian, who was head teacher at the local school. Meanwhile Tom Harrison had gone to the village longhouse to speak with the headman. Our accommodation was in the government resthouse, then unused, a wooden building on a small hill overlooking the airstrip. There was just one room for sleeping and one for cooking. Stan was there waiting. He was a nice, quiet man, though not afraid to speak his mind, and had been with the troop for about two years. I immediately got on well with Stan, and we have remained friends ever since. Roy showed me his map of the area which he had been patiently and accurately making. Maps of Borneo at that time were either non-existent or virtually blank pieces of paper. At first we made our own as we went along. The aircraft had to leave then, so Roy left us to get on with it.

Our main task at Bario was to win the hearts and minds of the locals and assure the people that we were there to protect them from any incursions by the Indonesians. Next day I met Mr Toynbee's assistant, a young Kelabit man called Roland Agan. Roland came to see us nearly every day after that, sometimes bringing eggs, small tomatoes and potatoes to supplement our Army rations. Also, if the tribal hunters had brought in a pig or two, Roland would bring us a dish of beautifully cooked pork. We gave our tins of Army ration condensed sweetened milk to Roland for the longhouse babies in return. Most days Stan and I would take a walk around the airstrip and along to the school, saying hello on the way to Mr Lian Bala, the airstrip man, and another official, Mr Mawan Bala, from the Department of Agriculture, who lived nearby. I liked to chat with Mr Toynbee and the Kelabit children. The Kelabit tongue is very similar to Malay, so between our Malay and their English, which they were taught at school, we managed to communicate quite well. Children who lived in outlying villages and had a long way to walk to school through the jungle slept in a dormitory, only going home at weekends. They were all lovely kids, and we enjoyed having a kick around with them on their football field. One of their favourite sports after a heavy shower of rain was to run and dive into a shallow pool on the field to see who could slide the furthest. I didn't try that, or Stan!

My para-injured ankle was healing nicely by this time, so I went for a walk cum jog around the valley now and then. The route I followed took me right by the tribal longhouse where the Bario families lived. I never attempted to go in there, though, as people like that don't like to be pushed. I waited until we were invited by the headman. It was a traditionally built longhouse, built up on stilts, with an atap roof and rough-hewn timber framework and floor. To enter, we all had to climb a single log ladder with cross pieces fastened on it. Inside the longhouse was divided into open-fronted family cubicles; there were about fifteen families living there then. Cooking was done mostly on a communal basis and consisted of chicken, pig and sometimes even monkey. I never saw fish there, as the nearest big river was too far away. Going to the toilet was performed outside mainly, but there was the odd hole in the floor here and there as well for emergencies! Also down those holes would go fag ends, swill and other waste, all of which was eagerly devoured by the domestic pigs penned under the longhouse floor.

The headman, Jawi, who had been awarded the British Empire Medal for his services against the Japanese in the Second World War, was a grizzled old warrior in his fifties. He had a great sense of humour, and I loved talking with him. Jawi smoked roll-ups, and as we sat talking he would flick his fag end straight through one of the holes in the floor about 2 yards away, never missing and laughing like hell as he did so. After the initial invitation to the longhouse we were free to go in at any time, but we always stood at the bottom of the ladder and requested permission to enter first.

Tom Harrison had warned us to leave the Kelabit women strictly alone, which we would have done anyway. It wasn't that we didn't fancy them: they were very nice-looking ladies. But in situations like that it is too easy to antagonise the menfolk, and part of our task was to win over the hearts and minds of all the locals. We may have succeeded in winning over the hearts of some of the girls, but no way would that have won over the minds of the men. Kelabit men, small of stature but all handsome, muscular and manly, were renowned as fierce warriors, with a particular reputation as headhunters. Headhunting was officially banned after the Second World War, and if the Kelabits still had any recently chopped-off heads tucked away, then they kept them well hidden, because I didn't see any. A mixture of Eastern and Western style clothing was worn, and both sexes went in a lot for bead ornaments which they made themselves. The men didn't go in for body tattooing like some other tribes, such as the Muruts or Punans, but they did have a tradition of wearing huge, heavy earrings – so heavy that their ear lobes became stretched as far as 6 inches. When they go hunting the earrings are removed and, as a precaution against getting them snagged on branches, the lobes are tied above their heads. Very odd, but practical! As with all the other tribes of the interior of Borneo, the Kelabits lived off the land, growing their own crops of rice, tapioca, tomatoes, and other fruit and vegetables. Hunters went into the jungle and caught pigs, iguana, monkeys, snakes and many other edible creatures. In fact there wasn't much that was inedible in their eyes, including most insects. It was a fine sight to see a hunting party return to the kampong (village), their spears and blowpipes over their shoulders and live pigs in woven baskets slung on their backs. I didn't see any large animals around Bario, but Stan and I encountered a huge black snake one day on the track by the school. It was at least 6 feet long and poised there waiting for us. We always carried our rifles and, as there were children nearby, I decided to frighten the snake by firing a shot near its body – but with that it came straight for us! I fired another shot, and it must have decided that enough was enough, because it streaked away into the long grass. I was pleased that it got away and that I didn't have to kill it. I am no 'big game hunter', and people who kill things just for sport make me sick.

We didn't have any alcohol at Bario, not even medicinal rum, but we did manage to get drunk a few times. For instance one day I received a note from Mr Lian Bala, the airstrip man, asking if we would like to go to his house for 'some rice wine drinking'. Lian welcomed us in by handing each of us a cup and pointing to a massive jar that stood in a corner of his living-room. The technique was to press the cup into the mixture – rice grains were still in there – and attempt to get liquid only. I failed and had to drink with my teeth clenched to stop the grains going down. A dozen or so people were there, but only the men were drinking. The women seemed content to sit and watch while having a good giggle. The Kelabit men had a set routine to make sure everyone drank their share. They would utter a short chant ending in 'Ugh!' On the 'Ugh' whoever's turn it was had to take a good gulp of wine. After five or six 'Ughs' Stan and I were well and truly pissed, literally under the table and talking a load of gibberish. I vaguely recall hearing the women giggling. Now I know why. When it was time to go we both climbed out of the window and shinned down the wall outside, much to the amusement of everyone there. We had hangovers equal to at least ten 'Ughs' the next morning.

Stan made contact with HQ twice daily on his military set. He was a good signaller, never failing to get through. I wasn't a signaller myself, but I knew enough to appreciate the tremendous difficulties under which our regimental signallers very often had to operate. There was a daily battle with aerials, atmospherics and cantankerous sets, and sometimes they would still be struggling to get through hours after everyone else had their heads down to kip. These days signals are bounced off satellites and everything is hi-tech, which is exactly how it should be – why struggle if you don't have to? But we didn't have a clue what the rest of the squadron was doing at that time. We learned later that patrols were doing more or less the same as we were, plus some were mobile, moving along the border and filling in their blank maps as they went. In case of an emergency withdrawal Stan and I had made special plans and cached some food about half a mile away in the jungle. An empty hard tack biscuit tin made an ideal container, and we filled it with tinned stuff plus matches and hexamine tablets. I had found some cement powder in another room, so at the cache location we mixed it with sand and water from a nearby stream and buried the tin in a concrete casing. Two months later we showed our relief force where it was, and it was still OK. I have often wondered if it's still there now.

We had been ordered not to leave Bario, but we were getting fed up with just hanging around, so I decided to pay an overnight visit to the nearest Kelabit kampong about 5 miles away through the jungle towards the Kalimantan border. The break for temporary freedom came one afternoon after Stan made his call to HQ early. We shouldered our bergens and set off. It felt great, striding along a jungle track again with our rifles under our arms, ready. We had told Roland what we were doing and he promised to look after the building. At the kampong we were made very welcome. All the villagers knew who we were, of course: many of them visited Bario, and the children went to the school. They had a big longhouse and lived in the same way as the Bario people. That night, before dossing down on the longhouse floor, we had a drink and a talk with the headman and were treated to a splendid meal of meat and rice. An early start next morning found us back in time for Stan's first call. We went back a couple of times to that kampong and became good friends with the folk there. You couldn't possibly be anything else but friends with the Kelabits – they are truly delightful people. About a week before we were due to leave Bario the headman made Stan and me his honorary sons and planted two orange trees near the school in our honour. We were also presented with some bead ornaments, a headband, a necklace and a pencil cover, all made of hundreds of tiny, different-coloured beads. Roland also gave me a parang with a hornbill's beak handle and a blowpipe with a spear attached which had been used for hunting by one of the men. I still have all these presents, and to me they are priceless.

Our relief, four men of D Squadron, arrived at last: Sergeant A., two troopers and Captain X. We were having a two-day handover, which was luxurious by SAS standards – it was usually just a brief wave as we passed each other. Next day I took Sergeant A. and Captain X. to meet the headman at the longhouse. Straightaway Captain X. started promising to bring all sorts of things in for the villagers. I thought he was talking too much, so I gave him a good kick on the ankle and whispered to him to be careful as these people expected promises to be kept. All the trust and goodwill that Stan and I had painstakingly built up over such a long period could have evaporated in an instant. Before boarding the aircraft next day we shook hands and said goodbye to the headman, Mawan, Lian, Roland and the others. I confess that I had a big lump in my throat and had to look away quickly. These people had been loyal and genuine to us, and had become true friends, not just contacts who had helped us tremendously – which they undoubtedly had.

After I got back to Brunei I sent a badminton set to Roland for the school as a final parting gift.

Meanwhile back at the haunted house it was all hustle and bustle, writing reports and preparing to go home. Singapore was first stop, staying a night at Nee Soon transit camp, where, as we would be going through Calcutta, Bombay and Damascus on the way to the UK, we changed into civvies. I remembered how at Hereford a large group of our A Squadron blokes once went downtown to Vivian's Studio to get passport photographs taken. We were all in uniform except one man, who was sporting a civilian pullover. Mrs Vivian told us we had to be in civvies, and she was dead right, as in our passports we were marked as Government officials. Instead of taking the trouble to return to camp we solved the problem by each one of us in turn wearing that one bloke's pullover. I have often wondered since if any passport checker at Bombay or somewhere ever thought how popular that particular design of pullover was with British Government officials!

Anyway, I digress. I had no trouble getting my 6ft-long blowpipe on the civilian airliner – the stewardess very kindly put it up on the rack for me!

This hugely successful hearts and minds mission to win over the native populace took place in the first three months of SAS involvement in Borneo, right at the start of the bloody confrontation with Indonesia. At this stage, before the shooting war started, it was a key building-block to victory and a brilliant tactical manoeuvre in guerrilla warfare, cleverly exploited by the SAS, and it became a valued blueprint mission which was repeated in many future operations.

Next, however, I and a select few others were to become involved in one of the regiment's most daring and secret operations yet devised, again in the desert, but this time in the dry, dusty, searingly hot wastelands of the Yemen. I was briefed on my part in this truly cloak-and-dagger mission by none other than the founder and instigator of the Special Air Service Regiment himself, the legendary Lieutenant-Colonel David Stirling. This was to be a highly sensitive operation requiring some of the most experienced operators the SAS possessed. Yet after receiving our top secret orders from Stirling, all those involved accepted the mission with alacrity.

We knew instinctively that this one was going to be exciting – very exciting indeed . . .

Chapter 15

CLANDESTINE CAULDRON OF FIRE:
A SECRET MISSION TO THE YEMEN

After landing circumspectly and without fuss at Heathrow our SAS Squadron travelled in reflective mood back to base by coach. Approaching from the south on the A49 we caught our first glimpse of Hereford at the top of The Callow, a prominent hill about 3 miles out. After the heat and cloying humidity of Borneo the sight that was spread out before us was almost intoxicating. In the open, rolling countryside the fresh spring blossoms were out in a riot of colour – flowering cherries, apple blossom and daffodils framed by the familiar, welcoming sight of the city's cathedral tower standing out majestically in the distance. I must admit my stomach flipped right over with the nostalgic sight of it all. 'This *is* the most beautiful country of them all,' I thought to myself. The date was 29 April 1963, but the idyll of relaxation was to be all too brief. A new and far deadlier adventure was looming just around the corner, one in which SAS men were to be asked to risk their lives in foreign fields once again. But before we got wind of this vital mission we were given leave. I met up with Ann once more, though we drifted apart temporarily and I went out with another girl a couple of times. The regiment was then summoned to take part in another training exercise in Denmark on the same island as Copenhagen, but the event did not leave any lasting memories for me, dwarfed as it was by the news I was shortly to be given, of a momentous mission to follow in the Yemen.

Meanwhile, the regiment was on two weeks' leave, but being short of cash to maintain our high standard of living, I and another SAS sergeant, my good friend Dick Cooper, obtained employment temporarily as casual labourers, working for a local contractor named Paddy Lonnergan, whose main activity was laying tarmac on drives and car parks. It was hot, smelly and nasty work, and Paddy – a large, genial Irishman, and a stickler for detail – kept us hard at it. 'Make a tidy finish and you'll get a good name,' was his maxim. To help Paddy keep his good name we were paid the princely sum of £2 a day. Four or five days later I was enjoying a rest in my bunk (Paddy had laid us off for a day) when I received an order to report to the CO asap. Arriving at the CO's office a few minutes later I found two other lads waiting there, Taff Chidgey from D Squadron and Jimmy Catterall from A Squadron. Neither of them knew what it was about, and so I took a deep breath and knocked on the CO's door. We were called inside. Was this another rollicking for yet one more misdemeanour, or had the CO rumbled the clandestine tarmac-laying, I mused, my brain working at a frantic pace. Neither applied, actually, much to our relief.

The CO, Lieutenant-Colonel Woodhouse, asked us if we would consider going on a clandestine mission. This, I must stress, was not an official SAS mission. In fact, it was something completely different, but it soon became clear that it would be potentially hazardous to our health. Getting straight to the point the CO said, 'It will most probably be very dangerous, and the chances of you coming back are no better than fifty-fifty. I can't order you to go on this one; that's why I'm asking you to volunteer. I *can* tell you one thing, though,' the CO added. 'It will be for the good of our country.' John Woodhouse was, in my opinion, a fine officer and an absolute gentleman, so I knew he was giving it to us straight. 'Go away for a while and think about it,' he said. 'Then come back and let me know if you want to go.' Instant calculations went through my mind: fifty-fifty, even odds – that's not a bad bet for a horse race, but this wasn't a race and I was no horse. Even the great General Monty wouldn't attack unless he had a two-to-one superiority over the foe, and that was how I liked my odds as well. But it *was* John Woodhouse who was asking, and everyone in the regiment respected and trusted him. Anyway, fifty-fifty was, I guessed, considerably better odds for survival than most people had when crossing the road outside the City Arms in Hereford after a few drinks on a Saturday night when the pubs were turning out. At least I wouldn't have to risk life and limb doing that for a while. Without moving from the CO's office the three of us looked at each other. 'I'll go,' I said, and the others followed suit. 'OK,' said the CO. 'Wait along by the Ross Road at 1400 hr this afternoon and Johnny Cooper, who is in charge of the operation, will pick you up in his car.'

We all knew Johnny Cooper. He was one of the legendary SAS Originals who had been on the very first mission in the Western Desert and later been a Major, and the SAS A Squadron OC in Malaya and Oman in 1958–9 before leaving the Army in 1960 to join the Sultan of Oman's Special Forces. In fact Johnny had been a regular on most of the early wartime missions with David Stirling as one of the original members when the SAS was formed in 1941, the fledgling force being known then as L Detachment, Special Air Service. Later he also saw action in France and Germany as part of the massive post-D-Day SAS operations. 'JC', as he was popularly known, wrote an excellent book about his Army life and his work in Oman entitled *One of the Originals*, which was published in 1991.

Back in the present, parked out of town in a lay-by, JC gave us the gen, painting a vivid picture of what the mission entailed. It certainly sounded exciting and, I thought, very dicey. 'Right, do you still want to go?' he asked. Everyone assured him that they did. I vividly remember the exact words JC spoke next: 'OK, pack what you think you will need. No military kit. I'll pick you up tonight at eight.' JC then smiled and added, 'And, the nice bit is, you will be financially rewarded on return to the UK. But please, don't forget, this operation is top secret, so no idle chatter.' Back in camp we were issued with weapons from their special foreign weapons store. I selected a Carl Gustav SMG, Taff a German Schmeisser SMG and Jimmy a Walther P38 pistol. All the arms fired 9mm ammunition, which was the most commonly available, and we also took some fire-making materials, packed in separate bags for safety.

We were whisked off down to London that night and stayed for a few days in a flat owned by a friend of JC's. While there we received a fuller briefing and learned that the country we were to operate in was the Yemen. In 1962 the ruler, Imam Al Badr, had been overthrown by General Salal, the head of the country's army. Then, after Salal had declared the Yemen a republic, he was immediately given political and military support by Nasser, the president of Egypt. The military support included weapons and tanks, plus fighter and bomber aircraft, all crewed by Egyptians. Nasser was in turn supported by the Soviet Union, then NATO's enemy number one, which supplied most of his not inconsiderable weaponry. The Imam had made good his escape and fled into Saudi Arabia, from where, with the help of the Saudi king, who provided money and weapons, he had organised an army of loyal tribesmen known as Zeidi. The 'royalist' army, commanded by Prince Abdullah Bin Hassan, was concentrated in the mountains overlooking the Yemeni Capital, Sana'a. Our proposed task was to assist the Prince in the training of his forces and, secondly, to assess the extent of Egyptian ground and air support, and to stir up trouble if we had the opportunity.

Next day we were taken to meet David Stirling, the founding genius of the SAS, at his business premises – a film-editing studio. He was also involved in the operation but how, I didn't know then. I immediately took to him. I had heard a lot about him already and read the book *The Phantom Major*, written by Virginia Cowles in 1958, which describes Stirling's exploits from the earliest days when he formed the SAS in December 1941 until January 1943, when he was captured by the Germans in Tunisia and spent the rest of the war in the forbidding Colditz Castle. I observed that Stirling had a pleasant manner about him, with good, steady eyes and an undeniable charisma. I could clearly see how he had managed to gather around himself men who were willing to risk everything with his SAS in the desert. During our meeting Stirling drew me to one side and asked if, as the senior rank, I would be submitting a report on the operation to the SAS CO. I replied that I would most probably be required to do so. 'In that case,' he said, 'would you please confine your report to matters of reconnaissance and so on, leaving out any reference to killings of Egyptians should any battles take place?' I promised that I would do that. 'It's politically very sensitive,' Stirling added. 'We don't want any hot potatoes landing in our laps.' Returning to the flat we discovered that we were to have four Frenchmen going with us – two reporters, one from *Paris Match*, and two ex-Paratroopers.

The infamous John Profumo 'affair' came to light while we were in London waiting to go on our mission. Profumo, the Tory Secretary of State for War, resigned after it was disclosed that he had been involved with Christine Keeler, who was also the mistress of a Soviet naval attaché from the Russian Embassy. It was to become one of the biggest scandals of the twentieth century and almost brought down the Government of the day.

We left from Heathrow airport as scheduled. It was mid-afternoon when we took off. I had a window seat, and as I looked down at the beautiful, green English countryside already fading in the summer haze I wondered, as usual, what would be in store for me next. But soon my thoughts were on other things. I carried out a mental check on all my kit. Had I forgotten anything? No, we seemed to have covered everything. I can just imagine the commotion it would cause now at Heathrow if we tried to board an aircraft with what we had in our suitcases then – SMGs, fire-making materials and hundreds of rounds of ammunition, not to mention a quantity of PE. We were all well dressed in civvies. JC had bought us a new suit each, plus shirt, tie, shoes and socks. Also, from the Army and Navy Store, we had lightweight clothing and chukka boots to wear in the heat, plus water bottles, Silva compasses, sleeping bags, jack-knives and eating irons. JC had travelled by a different route, but we met up again at Tripoli airport in Libya, where we had to change flights. Almost catastrophically, one of our suitcases burst open in the baggage department there, and sticks of PE went rolling all over the floor. Luckily the airport staff didn't recognise it for what it was and very kindly gave us a hand to pick it all up again!

A BOAC Comet then took us on to Aden where, without leaving Khormaksa airport, we transferred to an old wartime Dakota which carried us on to Beihan near the border with the Yemen. Egyptian bombers had struck targets just over the border in the Yemen, and a British anti-aircraft unit was stationed near Beihan in case they strayed too far from their own territory. Some of the British officers there were intrigued by our presence and tried to find out who we were, but JC put them off by pretending to be French. JC could also speak fluent Arabic. A truck came and took us on to Nakoub, a village nearer again to the Yemeni border. There the local Arab sherif, who was also in on the job, put us up for the night. Next morning, having left our surplus kit with the sherif, we travelled on by truck again to RV with a royalist camel train which was assembling near the border. The camels, most of which were carrying supplies and weapons for the Prince, would be crossing the border that night, and our SAS contingent would be going with them. On the way to the RV we had to huddle in the bottom of the truck, covered with a tarpaulin, in case we were spotted by a British patrol which might have started asking awkward questions and possibly compromised the entire operation. At the RV we were allocated a group of camels, complete with drivers. Some of the animals we loaded up with our kit. I had a small suitcase in which I stuffed my sleeping bag and an assortment of goodies, such as a brew kit and a few odd tins and packets of food. The other camels were for riding. There must have been well over 100 camels to load and saddle, but eventually all was ready and we mounted up.

Fortunately I had ridden a camel before and knew what to expect, but to the uninitiated or unwary, getting onto a camel's back, followed by the animal rising to its feet, can be an embarrassing and often painful experience. From the kneeling position the sequence, if I remember correctly, of a camel getting to its feet is, first, part of its back rises suddenly. This is the moment when you are most likely to be thrown over the beast's head or backwards over its arse. Secondly, most of the front end comes up. If you didn't go over the front at first, but just leaned forward slightly, now is when the camel's head will rap you smartly between the eyes. Thirdly, the remainder of the camel's back-end lifts into position, usually with the effect of jolting you forward onto its neck. Fourthly, the last little bit of the front-end snaps up, so that if you did go onto the neck, you will feel as if you have just been kneed in the crotch by King Kong. Lastly, if you have managed to stay on, the camel will no doubt show its resentment by turning its head to spit at you and try to bite your leg! We all mounted OK except for one French bloke who, on the first move, performed a beautiful curving dive onto the desert floor. He let out a string of rapid French which I couldn't understand, but it sounded as if he was denouncing the camel, its ancestors and all the Arabs in sight, some of whom I noticed had hidden their mouths inside their robes, making a poor attempt to suppress hysterical laughter. Anyway, off we went, slowly and majestically. You don't rush a camel, and by travelling roughly westwards at a steady pace we crossed the Yemeni border just after last light. It is quite an experience riding on a camel in daylight, never mind at night, and that first night it was very dark. All I could make out was my mount's head and the faint outlines of the animals to the front and rear. Camels are very silent movers: their big, padded feet are practically noiseless, ideal for clandestine travel. The only sounds I heard from mine were the odd belly rumble, snort or fart, none of which would have been audible more than 5 yards away. Fully alert to the possibility of an ambush I had my loaded SMG slung on my shoulder in the ready position. It was a reasonable assumption that we had been observed moving off and that an enemy reception party was waiting for us. In the event of any trouble I was fully prepared to slide off the camel, hitting the ground on the side away from anyone shooting at us before opening fire myself. But I was knackered after a long day, and the gentle swaying of the ride was almost sending me to sleep. I had to fight hard to stay awake, not only to keep alert but also to avoid injury – it is possible to break your neck falling from the top of a camel's hump.

We plodded on all night with only brief halts. The Egyptians controlled the skies in their warplanes, so it was night movement only until we reached the high mountain area about 50 or 60 miles ahead. Distances covered each night varied between 5 and 15 miles, depending on the ground and how tactically we had to move. During daylight we hid underneath scrub or in small wadis. The camels were unloaded and left to graze, with the loads removed and hidden. We slept most of the time, or tried to, but it was very hot and clouds of marauding flies didn't help. Hunger and thirst kept waking me anyway. The brew kit and small supply of food we had taken in didn't last long, so we had to rely on the Arabs, who hadn't much to spare either. After the second day it was water and 'hubs', small cobs of Arab bread. The Arabs made hubs daily. Their method was to wrap a layer of unleavened dough around a tennis ball-sized pebble and bake it in the hot ashes of a fire, much the same way as we bake spuds in a bonfire on Guy Fawkes night. The reason for the pebble was to avoid having a soggy mess of uncooked dough in the middle. It was a tried and trusted method and didn't taste at all bad. At this stage we were not drastically short of water. The Arabs had brought quite a few goatskin bags full, but we still had to be careful. The daily ration was a full bottle, which was soon lost as sweat shortly after drinking, leaving us with a raging thirst most of the time.

During the daylight lying-up periods I had a chance to study our Arab companions. They were a rough-and-ready-looking bunch, seemingly resigned to their present way of life, which included clandestine journeys from border to mountains carrying supplies for the Prince, in between times 'duffing up' the Egyptians wherever possible. Most of them chewed the locally grown weed called 'quat'. Quat, or at least the stuff they were chewing on, was dark green and looked vile. It is, so I have been told, similar to cannabis in its effect on the brain, giving a feeling both of well-being and lassitude. Chewing the stuff certainly seemed to lessen the trauma caused by bullet and shrapnel wounds, as we soon found out. Later Taff Chidgey and I treated some of the wounded in the Prince's Army, and they didn't appear to be overly concerned about their injuries. I noticed at the time, though, that they all had great wads of quat to chew.

There was one very dicey bit of country to move through before reaching the relative safety of the mountains. We had to pass quite close to a village called Sirwah, where the Egyptian Army had a base. The ground we had to negotiate was also mined. Fortunately our guides knew a way through, although a narrow one, not much wider than a camel. On the night, with the leading Arabs on foot guiding the front camel, we threaded our way through, each keeping exactly behind the one in front. It was a particularly dark night, and extremely nerve-wracking, knowing that death lurked not more than a yard on either side. Not only would an exploding mine kill and maim, but the sound would bring the enemy running to investigate. Eventually we were through, and I had said goodbye to about ten pints of sweat from nervous tension! A short stop to make sure we hadn't lost anyone, and then on we went. Not long after that we entered the start of the mountain country where we were able to travel in daylight. The Egyptian forces up until then had not ventured from the safety of the low-lying ground, no doubt well aware that the hills were perfect ambush country. Also, for us, there was plenty of cover from possible air strikes.

One day we encountered a local sheikh accompanied by a small band of his men. They had ridden out on donkeys to meet us. All were heavily armed, and they appeared mean and businesslike. There was a water hole nearby, and as JC was talking to the sheikh, who was still mounted, I strolled over and got myself a mug of water to drink. I was just taking a sip when suddenly one of the sheikh's men started yelling at me and making threatening gestures. With my mug half-raised to my mouth I gazed at him in amazement. Coming closer, the man pointed to my mug, still shouting angrily. I looked at JC, who said, 'He's playing hell because you didn't offer the sheikh a drink first.' I turned to the sheikh, who was glaring at me. 'Get your own fucking water,' I said, throwing what was left in the mug onto the ground. If there had been a bit of politeness about it I would have given him a drink, but at the best of times I don't like being shouted at, never mind in our present situation. The sheikh, after glaring at me a bit longer, then spoke quietly to his man, who came over to me holding out his hand and saying something in Arabic. JC said, 'He's asking for a loan of the mug to give the sheikh a drink.' 'That's better,' I said and gave him the mug, which he filled and presented to his boss, afterwards handing it politely back to me. I suspect that the sheikh had realised that if he buggered us about, he might get it in the neck from the Prince. He might also have noticed that my finger was on the trigger guard of my SMG and my thumb ready on the safety catch. If they had started shooting, I would probably have gone out in a blaze of glory, but I would have taken him and his lackey with me.

By then my bum was feeling the effect of hours on a hard saddle, so I started to walk to ease my stiffness. The others were all in the same boat, except JC: his backside was already broken in!

During the mountain part of our trek we stayed in villages each night. We were made most welcome by the local sheikhs and were provided with meals of goat meat and rice, followed by tiny cups of sweet coffee or tea. Also, we were given rooms to sleep in, on mats. After flogging through the low desert region with little to eat and drink I could feel myself improving physically. It was also good for the morale to be walking in daylight rather than stumbling along in the dark. Onward and upwards we went, our final destination being a mountain area known as the Khowlan, which overlooked Sana'a. The Prince's royalist Fifth Army occupied the region, so we were among friends at last. At every village the men would turn out to greet us, and there would be a lot of shouting and firing of rifles into the air. When we finally reached the Prince's HQ area we were met by a crowd of about 2,000 men, all blasting away into the sky. I have often wondered how many of their own casualties were caused by falling bullets on those occasions. Every tribesman had a rifle or carbine of some sort, ranging from the old Martini-Henry single-shot carbines to ex-British Army .303 Lee Enfields and recently captured Russian AK47 assault rifles. Also, each man had an ornately sheathed ceremonial dagger stuck in his waistband. The more ornate they were, the more important the person was. Bandoliers of ammo were worn around the waist and shoulders, just like Mexican bandits. All wore turbans and djellabahs, a long flowing gown in various sizes, shapes, colours and states of cleanliness. Off-white seemed to be the favourite shade, having the advantage of providing good camouflage among the rocks and scrub! A pair of leather sandals completed their apparel. These mountain Arabs impressed me as being very hardy and fierce. They were not big men, most being shorter than me, but what they lacked in height was more than made up for in sinewy strength and toughness.

We met the Prince in his HQ, a cave in a steep-sided ravine. He was quite short and undistinguished-looking, not at all what I had imagined an Arab prince would look like. JC was accommodated in the Prince's cave while Taff, Jimmy and I occupied the cave next door. It was very cold in the Khowlan, a great contrast to the desert, and we were glad of our shelter from the wind. One good meal a day was provided, consisting of goat or mutton with rice. We used our eating irons but, as is their custom, the Arabs ate with their fingers – the left hand only, the right being considered unclean, as it was used in toilet ablutions. Belching, both during and after a meal, was regarded as a sign of appreciation and was usually answered with the words 'al hamdu lillah', pronounced 'humdilillah'. Farting, however, at any time, was looked upon as very bad manners and severely frowned upon. At times JC admonished us and whispered furiously, 'Silently, silently!' The trouble was, we were on an unaccustomed diet, and I for one just couldn't get it right. One thing I fully expected to have, living in rough conditions like this, was an abundance of lice, or 'crabs' as they are known in the ranks. Each day I gave myself a 'short arm inspection', that is a detailed look at my crotch, armpits and any other nook and cranny where unwelcome visitors might congregate. However, amazingly, I stayed free of them. Maybe I was too dirty even for crabs. If I had been a crab, I would definitely have hesitated before entering my underpants at that time.

For the first few days after arriving our group made a reconnaissance of the area. There was plenty of evidence of Egyptian bombing raids on the Khowlan villages, using not only HE but also chemical weapons, such as mustard gas and napalm, both of which leave tell-tale signs on the ground and their victims. Meanwhile the Frenchmen also carried out their own recce, part of which was selecting a DZ for a possible drop of paratroops. I would not have fancied doing a drop of that sort in that type of country, especially as it would have had to be carried out at night. Making some swift calculations I reckoned on 50 per cent casualties at least – an unthinkable prospect. After the SAS walkabout JC and Jimmy took the tribesmen on weapons training and taught them use of cover. Meanwhile Taff, a trained medic, and I went around treating some of the wounded from recent bombing raids and clashes with the Egyptian Army. There was plenty of work to do. The royalists had no medical kit at all, and so casualties were literally dying from treatable wounds. Unfortunately Taff had only a small supply of bandages and lotions, plus a few morphine syrettes (disposable syringes), so we concentrated on the worst cases. We came upon a group of wounded who were being looked after by their womenfolk. Most had minor limb or head wounds, but there was one man with a bullet hole in his chest, a sucking wound, one of the most feared to receive and the hardest to survive. Every time the man breathed in we could hear the distinctive whistling noise made by air entering the hole. He seemed very stoical and not at all worried, and neither were his comrades. 'For the Prince,' he said, indicating his wound. I understood that bit of the language and put his and their stoicism down largely to the quat which they were all chewing in huge amounts. There was no exit wound, and as Taff wasn't equipped with probes, all he could do was clean and dress the festering wound and hope for the best. Despite his injury, the bloke was still alive several weeks later, showing how tough and hardy some of these men were.

Egyptian fighter-bombers paid us a visit one day and began strafing up the line of our ravine. Almost immediately a man was brought to us with a mass of small wounds all over the front of his body. He was screaming in agony. It was too dark in the cave, so we laid the wounded man outside to treat him. Luckily we were partially protected from the air by a slight overhang. Taff injected a morphine syrette first, and then we set about picking the bits out of him. As we worked the enemy streaked in again and again, spraying heavy-calibre bullets and rockets in our direction. Most of the latter, fortunately, landed further up the ravine, but the bullets were ricocheting all over the place, several smacking into the rocks nearby, sending splinters whizzing noisily around our heads. Meanwhile JC and Jimmy had taken our LMG up onto the cliff top and were busy blasting away at the aircraft – an extremely brave action. The Prince, who couldn't have done anything anyway, very sensibly stayed in his cave. Finally, when we had treated the injured bloke as best we could and stopped his bleeding, the Egyptians decided to leave.

Shortly after that a young girl aged 6 or 7 was brought to us with a shattered hand. Removing the piece of gungy cloth her hand was wrapped in we could see that the bleeding had stopped, but her wounds were very dirty and the flesh was horribly splayed out. Apparently she and some other children had been playing with a grenade that the men had captured from the Egyptians. Before anyone could stop them one of the kids had pulled the pin, and it had gone off. Taff worked for hours on what remained of her fingers, cleaning, pulling splinters out and suturing where possible. I helped by passing instruments and holding her arm. Now and then I gave her a cuddle. She was a very brave little girl, not crying or anything, just making an occasional wince of agony. Many months later, after we had left, we learnt that the girl had retained the use of one finger and the thumb. We were also told that a doctor who went there with a medical team said Taff had done an excellent job. The day after treating the girl we witnessed Egyptian aircraft bombing a village with HE, mustard gas and napalm, and more casualties would inevitably have occurred among the helpless civilians.

During this time I was also busy trying to find a serviceable mortar and ammunition. The Prince's forces didn't have any of their own, and it wasn't until I had inspected several captured weapons that I found one that was suitable, together with about forty rounds of HE ammunition. We got the chance to use this to good effect later. Meanwhile we still had our fire-making kit and PE, but as things turned out we didn't get the chance to use either. It was a long way to Sana'a, where we had hoped to cause a bit of mayhem by blowing up the radio station there. The main problem was that to get there we would have had to travel through several different tribal areas. Each tribe, as is usual anywhere in the world, whatever name the tribe goes by, had a large amount of rivalry, jealousy and mistrust of its neighbours. This meant that, having been allowed to pass through one area, there was no guarantee of being able to proceed unhindered through the next, or even to return through the first. It was so complicated a prospect that the notion of an attack on Sana'a was postponed.

It is appropriate at this point to let Johnny Cooper tell in his own words what happened next. The following is an extract from his book, *One of the Originals*:

Having made our preliminary reconnaissance we decided that the time had come for action. Our plan was to lay a few mines, tickle up the opposition so that they would attack us, and then lead them into a prearranged killing ground. Little did we know what a big operation this was going to become. We had already started training the Yemenis on the weapons which we had brought in, concentrating on the Bren, which is one of the simplest firearms for use by guerrillas. We organised them into small groups of between five and seven men each, as gun sections or killing groups. Because of the language problem – the Yemeni hill dialects are very difficult even with a good knowledge of Arabic – we did not go into tactics at all. We restricted ourselves to showing them use of cover, how long to fire bursts and how to avoid overheating the barrel. Purely the basics of a first-time soldier. In fact, they were pretty good and knew how to keep their heads down and survive.

After that basic training, we set up an ambush in the Wadi Thoul to the east of Sana'a. This particular wadi narrowed down and then split into a 'Y' junction up a steep slope where there was a small area of level ground about fifty yards across. The arms of the 'Y' petered out into steep rocky escarpments and were unassailable. We positioned the gun sections in foxholes in three well-camouflaged spots protected by rocks, which overlooked the level area or killing ground. Each position had a 'funk hole' to the rear for when the real shit came in. At 0900 the Egyptians moved into the wadi in considerable strength with a parachute battalion leading, followed by T34 tanks and light artillery. They were unaware of our presence further up the valley, and about half way up, the tanks and artillery halted. The infantry, burdened with a lot of bulky kit and dragging Soviet heavy MGs on wheels, advanced shoulder to shoulder in tightly packed extended order. The Royalist gun sections held their fire until the Egyptians were well into the killing ground just below our positions which were on the steep-sided cliffs overlooking the wadi. We had piled up stone cairns in the killing ground beforehand to act as aiming and range markers. As the enemy reached the markers our men opened fire with devastating effect, knocking down the closely packed infantry like ninepins. Panic broke out in the ranks behind and the tanks started firing, not into our positions but among their own men. Then the light artillery opened up causing further carnage. For the rest of the day the Egyptians kept firing onto our positions, but we were well protected in foxholes. As night fell, they retreated back towards Sa'ana with a very bloody nose indeed. We counted 85 bodies which were left lying where they fell, remaining there for some two years before an agreement was reached to permit the Red Cross to collect skeletons. The weapons and equipment left behind by the Egyptians were collected up and given to the Royalist army quartermasters who stored them in the caves for future use.

Our next bout of action against the Egyptians was very different but equally successful. The SAS were informed that there was an enemy garrison of about two companies in strength, around 200–250 men, camped on a hill which was conveniently overlooked by higher ground. This well-dug-in camp base was supplied by helicopter, and the whole area was surrounded by barbed wire and mines. The enemy tents were well protected behind sangars which had been built up by the troops from material handily lying around. The whole area had such a defensive bias that it was obvious the Egyptian soldiers had no intention of venturing out from the safety of their camp to patrol the surrounding area and risk a guerrilla attack. Meanwhile our SAS men crept forward for a covert recce with field glasses and rapidly gauged that the encampment was a perfect soft target, just ideal for a mortar attack. As I was the mortar expert at the time Richardson, Jimmy Catterall and I were instructed to accompany Johnny Cooper in a daring attempt at a surprise attack, designed to cause mayhem and confusion. Three camels were loaded up with bombs and the mortar, and four Yemeni youngsters were taken along as interpreters in case the group ran into trouble with the local tribesmen. Our raiding group set out very early next morning in order to get into position by first light. On the way to our destination we encountered angry opposition from a group of locals who feared that if the SAS mortared the Egyptians, their villages would be bombed yet again. However, our trusty Arab guides managed to persuade the villagers that the Egyptians had to be taught a lesson, and there was no choice other than to attack the outpost.

Johnny Cooper continues, in *One of the Originals*:

When we reached the position we had selected, we put one man higher up on the hill above with a direction finder: a stick held up in one hand so that the mortar crew could get the line. The maps we had did not give us much idea of the range, but Doran was an expert and could use the man on the hill to give a line. We got the mortar set up and waited for dawn. The Egyptians were just getting out of bed all sleepy eyed when we opened fire. I think that it was the second round that landed inside their perimeter and then Doran banged away about thirty more bombs. Observed from the top, the panic was fantastic. It was obvious that the enemy thought that they had been attacked by a force of tribesmen as they started to blaze away in all directions. It was quite some time before their artillery started up, but by then we were three or four miles away. They were shelling the wrong place anyway and kept shelling the wrong place for the rest of the day. We had no idea how many casualties we caused, but the amount of confusion caused was worth it. When the bombs had all been used up, we packed the mortar onto the camels and headed back to base.

By now it was time to head for home, as the main object of our trip had been achieved: establishing that the Egyptians were heavily committed to supporting the 'illegal' regime. We three from the SAS had already outstayed our 'leave' and still had to walk out yet. A farewell feast was held for us in a nearby village when, being the guests of honour, we were offered the delicacies of the meal to eat. This unfortunately included the eyes and brains of sheep and goats, and also the sweetbreads! It would have been extremely bad manners to refuse these items once they had been offered and so, like it or not, down they went. It was a bit disconcerting, though, to see an eye looking at me from a handful of rice, I must admit.

Next day we set off on the return trek. Some of the Prince's men came with us as guides, and we also had a few camels, but as before I preferred to walk most of the time. We were not able to obtain much water this time, and when eventually we had reached a spot within an estimated day's march of the border we were all suffering terribly from thirst. I didn't feel hungry, even though we hadn't had much to eat; maybe my stomach had shrunk through lack of water. To make matters worse a really vicious sandstorm had blown up, and we had to take shelter among the scrub. As we lay there, me dreaming of ice-cold pints in the City Arms and resisting the temptation to finish off my last drop of water, I noticed a movement from the corner of my eye. I looked round and saw a hand reaching towards my water bottle. It was one of the Arabs. Without saying anything I lifted my SMG and aimed it at his face. He got the message and backed off. By this time my tongue was feeling like a lump of thick sandpaper, and I feared that if we were delayed much longer by this sandstorm it might be too late. The others appeared to be in a similar state.

Just then JC came along and told us that one of the Arabs had volunteered to go to the town of Marib, which we knew wasn't far away, and attempt to get our goatskin water bags filled. Marib had an Egyptian Army presence, so more than one man arriving would have aroused suspicion. I think our man was very brave to try. Off he went into the sandstorm, which was blowing harder than ever. By night-time the wind had dropped a little and, having drunk our last drops, we eagerly awaited the return of the waterman. Finally JC had to guide him in by firing pistol shots. I could have kissed that little Arab when he eventually staggered in with two full goatskins of water. As JC says in his book, 'The water was green and slimy', but to me it tasted like spring water! I was so thirsty that I would have been grateful for cold NAAFI tea. The Arabs attacked the water like maniacs, spilling it all over the place, but the camels didn't get any, as their ability to survive with little or no water for long periods is well known. After a long, steady drink I refilled my bottle and a canvas bag I had acquired, and then we settled down to sleep.

By next morning the sandstorm had blown itself out, and after climbing to the top of some high ground nearby we discovered that it was only a few more miles to the border. Later, after crossing the border at almost the same spot where we had come in, JC contacted the nearest Aden Federation Army post and sent a signal to the governor's office in Aden to inform him that we were out. The total distance of our trek to the Kowlan and back, taking in all the twists and turns to avoid the Egyptians, we estimated as at least 250 miles. After collecting our kit from the sherif's house we didn't have long to wait before an aircraft came to carry us down to Aden. We were sent to a part of Aden called the 'Crater', so named because it is indeed an old volcanic crater. Our troops spent a very relaxing two days in a discreet hotel there, during which time we gradually got our stomachs used to regular meals again. JC bought us all some new shoes and lightweight clothing to wear, so we could get rid of our other kit, which we had not had off since leaving London and which could now virtually stand up on its own. In the civilised surroundings of the comfortable hotel and in the relaxing bars and restaurants it was sometimes hard for me and the others to believe that we had so recently been involved in life-and-death actions and a vital mission of such international importance to Britain and to other countries – and governments – abroad. However, we did not dwell too long on that aspect of our situation. This loosely woven, almost clandestine way of operating was to be increasingly a fact of life for those of us who trained in the SAS Regiment and who were called upon to serve our country in many diverse theatres and locations in many diverse ways – and who will continue to do so in the future.

Chapter 16

TRAINING THE YOUNG LIONS OF THE SAS: THE INFAMOUS KILLING HOUSE

The beginning of August found me and my merry band of SAS comrades back on familiar territory in Hereford. As instructed I wrote my report on the special mission, remembering to honour my promise to David Stirling not to reveal any especially sensitive details concerning the operation. The CO, Lieutenant-Colonel John Woodhouse, thanked all three participants personally for our efforts, and we felt a special pride in a job well done. It was a very different mission from that which we were used to, somewhat similar in many ways to how the SAS worked with guerrilla forces in France, Italy and elsewhere in the Second World War, if much more politically sensitive. However, I was quietly pleased that my thorough SAS training and long experience, especially with the mortar detachment, had stood me – like the others – in good stead. I was very happy that we had done the job and earned the appreciation of the finest SAS officer I have ever known. The only annoying part of the affair happened a few months later, when John Woodhouse and I were interviewed by Special Branch (SB) in London. Special Branch's honk seemed to be that they hadn't known about our trip to the Yemen, and they appeared more than a little miffed. I suppose they had a point, but I came away from the interview feeling like some sort of criminal. Anyway I thought, tough shit, or, as they say in the French SAS, 'solide merde', and put that one down to experience!

Meanwhile I was sent on a short demolition course in camp run by Major 'Dolly' Edwardes. Explosives as used by the SAS then were in a constant state of experimentation. It was well known what PE could do, and it was a case of what could be achieved by the amount with which a man could parachute in and carry on his back. On our 'live' training at Sennybridge ranges in Wales

Dolly impressed me with his coolness. He was always last to take cover after we had lit the fuse. 'Walk to cover,' he would say, coolly. So we did, but our strides were invariably longer and faster than his! We would be down hugging the earth well before Dolly, and then, a second after he had crouched beside us, there would be a huge bang as the charge exploded, showering us with mud and stones. A device we experimented with at that time was a 'shape' charge, similar to more sophisticated devices currently being used by terrorists in Iraq to attack British and US Army vehicles and personnel. When detonated this device propelled a missile at very high speed – approximately 2,000 feet a second, we were told. Also, if the missile was made of glass it would melt into tiny hot globs, making a right mess of anyone on the receiving end. The night before we were due to go to Sennybridge to make shape charges I was having a curry in the Wing Hong restaurant in Hereford, and on my table was a round glass ashtray. That would make a perfect missile for a shape charge, I thought. Next day, on the ranges, it duly travelled at 2,000 feet a second. In recompense I gave the Chinese waiter an extra tip that night.

Dolly, meanwhile, had sussed out an old disused mine air shaft in Manchester for us to experiment on. The shaft had a fence with a locked metal gate, so the first job was to blow the lock off. We didn't intend to demolish the shaft, just pick at it with small amounts of PE to see the effects. Unfortunately several houses about 200 yards away suffered cracked windows after the first few explosions, even though we had taken the precaution of parking our vehicles in front to absorb the blast. To make matters worse the police, who apparently hadn't been informed of our intentions, arrived to find out what was going on, and we had to leave in a hurry. A visit to a local brewery had been laid on by Dolly, so we adjourned there to sample their wares and stuff ourselves with corned beef sandwiches. Meanwhile the press had got wind of our escapade at the air shaft and a report in the next day's *Daily Express* said something like, 'SAS fail to demolish mine shaft despite repeated tries.' I can't see how the reporter could have formed this opinion, as he wasn't there and didn't know what we were trying to do. A so-called explosives 'expert' also arrived on the scene and, wrongly assuming that we had been trying to demolish the shaft, said we were using the wrong method. Of course we hadn't been trying to demolish the bloody shaft at all! To do that would have required tamped ring charges exploded simultaneously.

Next day A Squadron motored up to Cultybraggan ranges in Scotland for training in the use of live ammunition. I had recently trained some new mortar teams, and this was an opportunity for them to do live firing. One exercise we did was a squadron attack with mortar fire in support. The classic method for this type of attack is for the troops to go in at right angles to the mortar's line of fire. This enables the troops to get closest to the target before the mortars have to stop firing. Before we started I agreed with the officer in charge that he would halt his troops by a hedge and wait until the mortars had finished their timed programme of firing before going on to the target. I had estimated the hedge to be just outside the safety limit. All went to plan, and we were blasting merrily away at the target, in sight of which I had placed the mortars for more interest. I watched the troops in their attack formation nearing the hedge where I expected them to stop. But they didn't! Through the hedge they went – running like hell. I yelled to the mortar crews to stop firing, but there were at least six bombs still on the way. The troops got to within 75 yards of the target as the last bomb fell. Fortunately the very high heather absorbed most of the shrapnel, and no one was hurt. Also, luckily I had applied the 'peace time' safety limit, twice the size of that used in a real attack. It was a near-tragedy, and I was absolutely furious. Back in camp I had a good ding-dong with the officer in charge over that one. About that time the term 'Rupert' was coined when referring to an SAS officer. Apparently a young officer in the regiment had made a cock-up of something and, turning to his troop, had said, 'Oh, I am a Rupert, aren't I?' The name stuck, but it was more irreverent than insubordinate. Little did I know at the time, but cruel fate was to intervene on my behalf to make this my last day in that particular Rupert's squadron.

It was the troop's last night at Cultybraggan, and the locals had laid on a farewell jig for us at the village hall in Comrie, not far away. All the SAS had a great time. The local girls taught the men how to do Scottish reels, and everyone was very friendly. Early next morning saw me and the boys on the road south back to base. I was travelling in a Land Rover with Budd, Jackie B. and Captain Larry Acre of the US Army, who was on an exchange visit from the Special Forces. They were towing a trailer full of kit. Just before midnight, as we entered the little village of Brimfield just north of Leominster, we knew we were almost home. Then, disaster! Going round a bend in the road we saw two sets of headlights next to each other coming towards us at high speed. Budd, who was taking his turn driving, had no choice but to steer to the left to avoid a head-on collision. Unfortunately for us we went straight into a wall that was part of a driveway to a house. I was sitting in the middle front seat, with Jackie on my left. Captain Acre was lying in the back. There were no seat belts then to save us, and the last thing I remember as I watched the wall coming at us was putting my hand up to protect my head from hitting the metal bar in the middle of the windscreen. Neither of the other two vehicles stopped, but luckily another of our Land Rovers came upon the scene a few moments later. I had been knocked unconscious and came to on the verge of the road with someone bending over me. I saw the beret on his head and realised it was a soldier. Training came to the fore: 'My field dressing's in my top left pocket,' I managed to croak, before passing out again. I had recognised the soldier bending over me looking so reassuringly concerned: it was John 'Taff' Prescott.

When I came to again I was in an ambulance on the way to Hereford General Hospital. Budd, Jackie and Captain Acre were also injured and taken to hospital. They were discharged the next day, but I was kept in for observation. I had partial loss of memory. I knew who I was but didn't recognise others and I couldn't remember where I had been. It took about four days before it all came back. Both my knees had smashed into the metal shelf which served as a glove compartment in the Rover, and X-rays showed that a chip had been taken out of the top of my right thigh bone. Also, what is commonly known as a 'slipped disc' in my lower vertebrae, from which I was already suffering, had been made worse. My head was OK, thanks again to my thick skull, but the hand I had put up to take the shock was very badly cut. My legs had been straddling the gear stick when we crashed, and I was fortunate not to have been castrated! I was discharged four days later with a limp and covered in plaster from waist to armpits.

That was to be the end of my career as an active Sabre Squadron soldier in the SAS. From then on, however, I was to be involved in admin and, especially, in training. It was the sort of routine work that was to provide me with some very interesting experiences. At the time I was extremely bitter, though, hating the person who had not only injured my body but had also deprived me of the job I loved. Fortunately at this excruciatingly difficult time I became reacquainted with Ann and realised she was the only girl for me. Why it took me so long to come to this fairly obvious conclusion I cannot quite fathom, but perhaps the bang on the head helped. She was a girl with a sense of humour and an easy smile – just a lovely person.

A couple of weeks later Herbie Hawkins and I were sent up to North Wales to the Snowdon area to man RVs for some young lads on the Duke of Edinburgh's Award Scheme, part of which involved marching and map-reading their way around the mountains for four days. It was actually an advantage having plaster on, because sleeping on the ground in a tent I couldn't feel the stones poking through! It was getting very itchy, though. I tried scratching with various things, but nothing worked. When the plaster finally came off I scratched for an hour, then had my first shower for two months. Sheer bliss. That October I bought Ann a signet ring with my initials on. We didn't see much sense in a fabulous diamond engagement ring costing a fortune. Then, in January 1964, I was sent to Netheravon for the Army's first course on the 81mm mortar. The 81mm, with greater range and accuracy, was replacing the old 3in weapon. Instructors were required from all units to spread the word, and I gained a 'pass' grade and proceeded to train new crews in the SAS Regiment. For my birthday that February Ann bought me a signet ring with her initials and the message LOVE inscribed on it. It was the start of an epic love affair which continues unabated to the present day.

In April that year I was part of a team sent to Malaya to train SAS recruits in jungle navigation and tactics. The Guards Parachute Company, due to serve in Borneo later, was also included in this programme. We had the use of a large area of jungle just north of Grik which we broke down into three sections: navigation, tactics and survival. The intention was to split the trainees into three groups, each spending a week in a different area, with a week's combined exercise at the end. Our CO, Lieutenant-Colonel Woodhouse, was in overall charge, with the 'Gloom' taking the tactics, me the navigation and Sergeant John Brunkhart, a Special Forces man on exchange, teaching the survival bit. John, an easy-going and cheerful man, became a good friend, and we spent many happy hours hunched over the bar together in the City Arms discussing life.

Before the trainees arrived we spent a week in preparation. I had three assistants, Pete, Terry and Rob, and together we established a basha area and carried out a detailed recce of all routes to be used. All went reasonably well. There were eight SAS recruits, five Other Ranks and three officers. The officers didn't impress me very much. One day one of them came into an RV where I was checking off names and sending them on. 'Sergeant Doran,' he said, 'this is not the correct location of the RV.' 'OK, sir,' I replied. 'Go and find the right spot and then tell me where it is.' About an hour later he came back looking rather sheepish. 'Er, yes, this is the place,' he admitted. The five rankers, Chalky White (later killed in Borneo), Ky, Mac, Mick and Norman, passed with flying colours, good men all. Of the Guardsmen 90 per cent were OK, although they were not very fit. There were about five Guards officers, I think, and if it had been a selection course, in my opinion all but one of them – who incidentally looked too short to be a Guardsman, but was full of go and had the right spirit – would have failed. One of them was so idle that one day I was stung into calling him – in front of everyone – 'a fucking lazy cunt'. I expected to be hauled to the gallows for that, but he didn't say anything at all. Fair comment, and I had plenty of witnesses. What had happened was that we had had an air drop, and the day after was free from training, so instead of letting them hang about doing nothing I set everyone the task of making a basha from natural materials. Most men worked hard, and some of the bashas were excellent, using rattan for fastening, split bamboo for floors and atap for the roofs. However, this particular officer hadn't done anything. When I asked him why, he just grunted, 'I didn't bother.' All this was in the hearing of other officers and men. What a fine example to the troops he was going to be!

Anyway, I had a little morale booster that night. Lying quietly, listening to the jungle noises, I heard an odd scraping sound. It was coming from our spare-ration store about 4 yards away. I reached for my torch with my left hand, parang in the other. Leaning on my left elbow I switched on, and there in the beam was a massive rat. He must have known exactly where in the ration pack the hard tack biscuits were located, because I had caught him in the very act of extracting a biscuit from a neat hole he had cut with his teeth. Rats with X-ray vision we didn't need. Keeping the beam on him I threw my parang, and it struck him on the shoulder. Off he shot, bleeding. I found his body nearby next morning. I was quite proud of that throw, as it was an instinctive one, made by torchlight from the lying position and at a range of around 4 yards.

For the final exercise week a company of Gurkhas under the command of Major 'Dolly' Edwardes came in to act as the 'enemy'. The Gurkhas worked well and did a good job. I hadn't been involved with Gurkhas before, and I found that they lived up to their reputation of being cheerful, likeable and hard-working soldiers. At the end of the exercise everyone, except myself and Dick Cooper, another Sergeant, made their way straight out to the road-head. Dick and I were given permission to go by a more circuitous route via the Sungie Kinta. Dick (ex-Suffolk Regiment), besides being an excellent and trustworthy soldier, was a good friend, easy-going and a pleasure to be with anywhere, especially as drinking partners in The Grapes pub in Hereford. (When I last heard of him he was gallivanting around Australia. Sheilas beware!) We had a very interesting walk and saw lots of wildlife. At one point we found ourselves in a sort of semi-clearing. It wasn't where trees had fallen, with secondary growth coming up; the trees were quite short, and the jungle floor was clear. There were many highly coloured birds fluttering around. Also, the foliage seemed to be brighter and let more light in from above. It was a magical place. All of a sudden we were back in ordinary jungle again, if such a place could be described as ordinary. Reaching the Kinta we followed it downstream, and at about 4 p.m. we came upon an aborigine longhouse, where we stopped to talk to the people. The headman invited us to dine with them and stay the night, which pleased us very much, not only because it saved putting up a shelter and cooking, but also because I liked the aborigines. I liked talking with them and watching them. They never had any hassle about doing anything, whether it be cooking, building a shelter, hunting or just walking along. Every task was performed in a cheerful, casual but efficient manner. We were given beautifully cooked chicken for dinner and then, next morning, after a good night's kip on the longhouse floor, disturbed only by the company of some large black bugs, we said goodbye to the headman and his people. A few hours later we arrived at the road-head. We enjoyed a couple of days' leave in Singapore before returning to the UK, and I was back with my lovely Annie by mid-June.

During the rest of 1964 and up to mid-1965 I worked in the Training Wing, helping to run the infamous SAS Selection Courses. Aspiring SAS men were, first of all, given a week's pre-selection training to polish up their navigation skills and get fit, but even this was too much for some. In that first week, out of an average course of 100, about 10 men would pack in. I remember one occasion when we had taken the recruits to the Malvern Hills, a long range east of Hereford with many ups and downs, and very steep in places. There the recruits started at the north end and made their way south to a big car park at a place called British Camp, crossing over the hills from side to side to check in at different RVs, a total distance of about 15 miles. Arriving at British Camp faces fell as the recruits were informed that there wasn't any transport available to carry them back to Hereford. Instead everyone, staff included, would be hoofing it back, alternately walking and running all the way. Just before they started off, however, one of the SAS Land

Rovers appeared, and the OC of the Training Wing told the recruits that if anyone didn't fancy walking, they could ride in the vehicle. I watched three or four men take up this invitation, but of course it was part of the harsh test, and once back in Hereford they were immediately given their marching orders.

The SAS Selection Course is widely recognised as arguably the most famous selection course anywhere in the world. Off we set, each of the staff with a group. On that stretch of road there is a pub called The Duke of Wellington, and after my group had gone a quarter of a mile past there I stopped them and asked if anyone could tell me the name of the pub. None could, so I ran them all the way back to see it again! 'Observe all round you all the time, no matter how knackered you are,' I told them. Further along the road one of our 4-ton trucks was parked. 'Everyone can't get on the truck,' I yelled. 'So we'll keep walking, but if anybody wants to pack in they can jump on.' When all groups had passed there were three or four bods who had taken up that offer. It was goodbye again. Then, just a few more miles down the road, all the trucks were waiting to take everyone back. That trick only worked on one more course before the word spread.

One of my favourite jobs was manning an RV up in the mountains checking recruits through. It was still the same procedure as when I did Selection. The recruits were given the map reference of the next RV and what it was, a road junction or whatever. That was all. There were no words of encouragement or advice, nor was there a glimmer of a hint as to the next RV – whether it was the final one or not. I used to study the men closely for any signs of distress. On one occasion a bloke looked all in and, much to his credit, he wanted to go on, but I made him stay with me to rest. He was RTU'd as unfit, but returned on a later Selection and passed. It is too easy to die up in the Welsh mountains, and several recruits have done just that. However, on this occasion I like to think that I saved a good man for the SAS.

By this time, despite the injuries received in the vehicle accident, I was reasonably fit again, although I had slowed up a lot. I could plod along, but only in second or bottom gear. I was nowhere near good enough to be in an active Sabre Squadron again. Besides that, I was developing very bad ear trouble. One of my jobs was helping to teach CQB (close-quarter battle), with pistol and SMG shooting. This involved me in a great deal of firing and also standing close to the firers being taught. We didn't have ear defenders in those days, just lumps of cotton wool which invariably fell out, hence the cumulative damage.

Another part of my CQB work was 'unarmed combat'. In my opinion this subject is overblown and of minimum practical value, simply because there are far too many imponderables in any given situation in real-life combat. All those magic throws and karate chops work well in a James Bond film, but the reality is somewhat different. It is never so clean cut. Nevertheless, I think it should still be taught because it sharpens the reflexes, is good physical exercise, gives confidence, is interesting practice and, lastly, you never know, it might just work some time!

Instead of standing and plugging away at paper targets all day we had built, to give a sense of reality, a special 'killing house' on the other side of the 30yd range wall near the camp. It had sandbag walls with (for safety) no windows. Inside it was divided into rooms with tables and chairs stuffed with dummies with face masks and different forms of dress, all placed in various positions. Each dummy had a role, 'friend' or 'foe', and some could be made to move by pulling on a lever. After a small approach exercise (which involved getting over barbed wire fences and silently killing a sentry) one man at a time, with an instructor behind him, would enter the house and proceed to eliminate all the enemy dummies. At first as many friends were shot as foes, but very quickly most blokes became tuned in. There was one lad, however, who always insisted on killing friends. I did think about having him arrested as a double agent! Some trainees would get really hyped up, and I remember one bloke, Pete, who, noticing me behind him, swung round and pointed his SMG at my guts. 'Pete,' I said, as calm as I could, 'it's me, Geordie – don't shoot.' He liked me, so he swung back round and carried on plugging dummies. That killing house was the start of all SAS training in that way, whose culmination in deadly reality was the famous siege of the Iranian Embassy by the SAS in London, in May 1980. Several members of the regiment instigated this type of training before I became involved, and all credit must go to them. One man in particular springs to mind: Alec, known affectionately as 'the Prune'. Alec became something of a legend in the SAS for the work he did in CQB shooting, unarmed combat and bodyguard training. Eventually the killing house became so shot up it had to be abandoned for safety's sake, and later, in the 1970s, a proper brick building was erected in camp to take its place.

Chapter 17

FIRST PINK PANTHER JEEP: DESERT TESTING WITH 22 SAS

A ll ranks in the SAS are encouraged to put forward new ideas on how to improve tactics, weapons and equipment. In fact one of the regiment's greatest strengths is its diversity of character, and the fact that SAS men are from every branch of the Army (and Marines) with many different skills and strong, independent minds. Lots of ideas are thrashed around, and although many never see the light of day, others are evaluated, tested and, if successful, taken on board and go on to prove themselves in action. 'Finger-poking' and 'Chinese parliaments' are a regular part of the SAS process and, in my opinion, help the men of the regiment to adapt to changes in the world around them. One of the subjects much under discussion in the early 1960s was a proposed SAS 'special fighting vehicle'. This vehicle, it was hoped, would be able to go virtually anywhere – over sand and rocks and through mud. It would have to operate in heat, cold, wet and snow, carry sufficient fuel for long journeys and be well enough armed with a variety of weapons so that, with a crew of three or four, it could make a damned nuisance of itself in just about any situation! The only vehicle available in the British Army at the time and thought to be up to the job – that is, big enough but not too big, considering the need for concealment – was the long-wheelbase, four-wheel-drive Land Rover (LWB Mk 9/1). In May 1965 I was part of a team from 22 SAS sent to Libya to carry out trials on the prototype 'SAS Armed Land Rover' (desert). It sounded very official, but we hoped it would prove itself to be, ultimately, highly practical.

Before we went the basic vehicles had to be extensively modified. The Ministry of Defence (MoD) had failed to produce six prototypes in time for the trials, and it therefore fell to Captain E., the officer in charge of the trials, to obtain authority for the vehicles to be modified in unit workshops at Hereford. A team under the command of Sergeant 'Gypsy' Smith (SAS) and Sergeant 'Robbo' (REME) worked many hours, day and night, making a total of thirty-five modifications to each vehicle. Much to their credit all were ready on time. The only thing that hadn't been decided upon was the colour of the vehicles. This came later, by accident. Our group was flown with our vehicles to RAF El Adem, just south of Tobruk, which was to be our base. We were joined there by a team of US Special Forces who were to accompany us into the desert; they had their own trucks for trials. The US vehicles were 2.5-tonners, commonly known as 'deuce and a halves', and the Americans were quite proud of them. Prior to that time most of the trucks used by the LRDG and SAS in the desert during the Second World War had been American and had almost become legends in their own right.

'You're not going to try to cross the desert in those things, are you?' they asked when they saw our Land Rovers. We did a couple of trial runs to make sure all was in working order. At that time we used sun compasses to steer by over deserts – just like the wartime LRDG – and an astro-navigation kit. This comprised theodolites, chronometers and star charts, to fix our ground position. As many troops found in the Western Desert in the Second World War, getting a star fix, called 'shooting the stars', was a very difficult and time-consuming business, especially if there were any clouds scudding about. A star's position had to be precisely timed in order to obtain a correct bearing, so if a cloud obscured it at the critical moment, the whole operation had to be repeated. During daylight we 'shot' the sun, a much easier task and far more accurate.

Two civilians from MoD research accompanied us on the trials – a Mr Plant, who evaluated different types of tyre, and Mr Lacey, doing the same job for clothing and equipment. There were around twenty SAS in our team, and the whole party, including the Special Forces, was under the command of Captain E., one of the best officers I have worked with. Captain E. was organised, down to earth, full of common sense, approachable and not a bit arrogant. But everyone knew he was in charge and wouldn't stand for any nonsense. In addition he was a thoroughly nice man, a gentleman.

On the main exercise, which lasted for three weeks, we headed roughly south, making for a certain point some 700 miles distant. For the first few days it was flattish desert, criss-crossed with wadis and covered with pebbles, rocks, camel scrub and dusty sand. A reasonable speed can be maintained over that type of terrain, sometimes as much as 40mph for long stretches. We kept in arrowhead formation where possible to minimise the amount of dust collected by those behind; it also made observation to the sides much easier. We took turns at point-duty navigating. My crew was joined by Mr Lacey, a jolly little plump chap who was really good company. He also did his fair share of work and driving. Each night we would form a circle, or laager, with the vehicles, a tactic used not only by the covered wagons in the Wild West, but also by the SAS and LRDG in the desert campaign of the Second World War. Cooking, checking vehicles and astro-fixing took a fair amount of time. Individual vehicle records had to be kept, along with mileage, bearings and breakdowns, and most nights we had a puncture to mend. Our Rover was fitted with huge balloon tyres, which were OK on sand but, because they had very little tread, were highly susceptible to penetration by camel scrub thorns and sharp rocks. After completing our tasks I would be more than ready for the old sack, but before that I liked to sit and ponder and gaze for a while with a brew of tea. The desert is a fantastic place – I mean the real desert, hundreds of miles from the nearest road. The crushing heat of the day, the freezing cold of the night, the beautiful sunrises and sunsets, and the uncanny silence. The stars were brighter, the moon was brighter and the sun was hotter than anywhere else I have ever been.

As we travelled further south it became warmer, and we were drinking water almost constantly during the day. A very popular piece of kit was the porous canvas water bags, or 'chuggles', we had hanging on the sides of the trucks. These kept the water nice and cool, especially when they had collected a coating of mud. We also carried plenty of water in jerrycans. When the exercise was over we discovered that there had been a party of Germans moving parallel to us but just over the border in Egypt. They had been travelling in ordinary Volkswagens and had run out of water, all of them tragically dying from thirst. If we had known about them, it would have been physically, though maybe not politically, possible for us to have reached and saved them.

It was on this stretch of the journey that our party discovered evidence of what the land must have been like thousands of years ago. We came across an area of fossilised wood where trees had once grown. After several hundred miles we entered the Kalansho Sand Sea, a vast area of dauntingly high sand dunes and relentless, blistering heat. Whereas on the flat plain there had been pebbles and scrub to relieve the eyes, here there was nothing, just sand. Driving became more difficult and sometimes, when the sun was high, we found it hard to focus on the ground in front. On those occasions, when there wasn't a horizon to fix the eyes upon, I couldn't tell whether our vehicle was travelling up, down or on the level. It was a weird sensation which fortunately didn't last very long. Usually we couldn't go around a sand dune, as they were mostly so very long. Some went on for miles, and the complications of plotting a series of different courses and altering our sun compasses were not worth the diversion. So, the method was straight over the top, the average height of a dune being between 50 and 250 feet. Anyway, it was all part of the trials we were engaged in – would our vehicles manage to get over the sand dunes, as the LRDG open trucks had done so successfully in the war?

Our direction of travel, south with a touch of east, was also, it appeared, the direction of the prevailing winds. This made it easier for us, because sand dunes nearly always have a steep and a shallow side, the latter being on the windward side where the loose sand is blown over, leaving a comparatively hard surface. So, facing the shallow side, we could, after making a good run at it, usually reach the top in one go. Once on the top it was politic to pause and survey the downward route before going on. Most of the dunes have a little curly bit at the top of the steep side, very like the shoreward side of a sea wave, so if a vehicle goes too far over it will collapse the curl and slide down. This made for a bit of excitement on the way up, because the driver had to judge the exact second when to stop accelerating in order to finish nicely perched on the crest. It was doubly exciting for the co-driver, whose right foot would instinctively stamp on an imaginary brake at the top! Of course things didn't always go to plan. If a dune was shelved, there would usually be patches of soft sand on the shelves in which a vehicle could easily get stuck. If it was on the up side, then the only solution was to dig out, go back down and try again. These were hot, sweaty and frustrating occasions. If the vehicle was down to the hubs, it was back-breaking spade work until the sand channels could be rammed under the wheels, followed by a lot of heaving and pushing. New swear words were invented, and some interesting variations on the old ones were wrought!

The 'certain point' we were aiming for was the Second World War crash site of a US Army Air Force Liberator bomber. The adopted name of the aircraft was *Lady Be Good*, the title of a popular American song of the time. It was a tragic tale. One night in April 1943, after carrying out a raid on German positions in Italy, the Liberator was returning to base near Benghazi. Apparently, as was discovered later, when the aircraft neared the Libyan coast there was some kind of navigational problem. Unable to find the airfield and running very low on fuel the captain decided to order everyone to bail out. Gauging that they had travelled southwards he thought that once they landed all they would have to do was walk north for a few miles, hit the coast road and then hitch a lift to Benghazi. Unfortunately they had travelled much further than they realised, and instead of a short distance from the coast they were hundreds of miles south. After the crew had bailed out their aircraft continued on in an almost straight line, slowly losing height and eventually making a near-perfect landing in the desert. The only major damage was to the tail section, which broke off at the end of the ground run.

The *Lady Be Good* was posted as missing with no survivors, and it was not until many years later, in 1958, that an oil exploration company discovered the wreckage and informed the US 'Wheelers' Air Force Base near Tripoli. Even then it was not until 1959 that any bodies were found. There had been nine members of the crew, and as the search parties methodically moved back along the estimated flight path they found a group of five decomposed bodies, including the captain and co-pilot, all lying together. Two more bodies were discovered a few miles further north, and later, a single body near to where it is thought the crew had landed. The ninth member of the crew has never been found. All the bodies were skeletal, but because of the exceptionally dry atmosphere complete decomposition hadn't taken place, according to the medics. A diary was found on the co-pilot, which is how it became known what had happened. We were asked to keep an eye out for the other body, but with so many dips and dunes we could easily have passed quite near it and not seen it. Also, drifting sand could well have covered all traces, so that finding it was impossible. Eventually, around noon one day, we estimated that we should have reached the crash site. We were in a relatively flat area, having left the big dunes behind, but there was no sign of the *Lady Be Good*. Captain E. decided to do an area search and sent each vehicle out in a different direction for a few miles. My instructions were to head for what appeared to be an abandoned 40-gallon oil drum about a quarter of a mile away, but the heat haze at that time of day was terrific. The whole horizon jumped and shivered. One moment I could have sworn there was a small lake ahead, next minute it would be gone and another would appear a bit further on. The 'oil drum' that we were making for danced and swam in the haze, but as we drew nearer it became more defined. It also looked too large for an oil drum as, gradually, the shape grew clearer and larger. Of course it wasn't one at all: it was the tail unit of an aircraft. By now several vehicles on either side were closing in, their crews having seen what it was. As we approached I experienced quite a spooky feeling. If I had believed in ghosts, I would have said that the American crew were all there, sitting around waiting for us. The rest of our vehicles had pulled in behind us now and had stopped just short of the aircraft. There was dead silence for a while as everyone gazed at the scene. I had the most extraordinary feeling about it all – partly, I think, a reaction to having finally reached our destination after travelling and navigating all that way, arriving on time and within sight of a virtual pinpoint on the ground. Also, the general atmosphere of the area, surrounded by this vast, empty desert, gave us all goosepimples.

Dismounting, we walked in closer. It was the *Lady Be Good* all right: there was the name by the cockpit for all of us to see. It was so dry, with practically no moisture in the air, that the aircraft was almost perfectly preserved. The only noticeable change was on the upper surfaces, which had been burnished by twenty-odd years of unrelenting sun. The whole machine had a pinkish hue, which was, I learned later, the colour used to camouflage most Allied planes in the desert during the war. Machine guns and radios etc. had been taken away by the Americans, who declared that everything had been in complete working order when they found the wreck. Survival kits with filled water containers were found intact, and there was coffee in the flasks. Exploring inside we discovered that there was surprisingly little damage. It was a hell of a thing to think that if the crew had remained on board some of them could well have survived and been able to send a radio signal for help. But of course they were not to know that, poor sods. On the fuselage, on the wings, all around on the ground and even inside the aeroplane there were hundreds of birds' skeletons. Apparently, migrating birds that fly over that region will land on anything sticking up from the desert floor, such as rock outcrops or anything similar. They need the extra height to make it easier for taking off again after having a rest. Some of the birds, having landed on the Liberator, had obviously been too exhausted to fly on and perished there. The only signs of life were the scurry and slither marks left by the tiny desert lizards and scorpions. Next day, about noontime, an RAF Twin Pioneer flew over. We were in touch with the pilot by radio, and he reported that he could see our vehicles OK but had difficulty picking out the *Lady Be Good*. After landing nearby the pilot came over to speak to us and inspect the wreckage.

The reason the bomber couldn't be seen easily, it was decided, was because of its pink colour. As that was the original intention of the camouflage it wasn't surprising. It was also later decided that pink would be the colour of the SAS (desert) 'fighting vehicle' we were testing. Pink wasn't perfect, but it was a definite improvement on the dreadful official khaki which was used previously. So the famed 'Pink Panther' was conceived on our trial, and the colour is still used on SAS and other fighting vehicles today, having been employed in both Gulf Wars, and doubtless it will be in other desert campaigns in future.

That night we took a resupply air drop, and next morning we set off on the return journey. There is a huge rock outcrop called 'Blockhouse Rock' to the north-east of the *Lady Be Good* where we paused for a while and 'shot' the sun. Turning north, we pursued our route over flattish, sandy desert, to the west of the Kalansho Sand Sea. Although not as difficult as the dune country it was still hard going, and I take my hat off to the men of the LRDG and SAS who passed this way during the desert campaign en route to cause chaos with their raids on Rommel's rear lines and airfields. They were hard men, well ahead of their time, and they also pioneered most of the techniques of desert travel we still use today.

We visited Gialo, often known as Jalo, a large oasis that lay on our line of travel, afterwards spending the night there, camping just outside the settlement. This particular oasis was one of several used as bases by the famous wartime soldiers of the LRDG and SAS. Just before leaving I sat with a brew of tea and viewed the oasis. The amazingly tall, ancient, reddish-brown mud-brick buildings, some of them reaching six or more storeys high, appeared very impressive, the colours accentuated by the morning sun, and surrounded as they were by waving palms. To complete the picture the scene was framed by the uncannily clear pale-blue sky beyond.

Next day, we passed by a burning oil-well installation that had, it was alleged, been sabotaged by raiders from Egypt. We had been asked to keep an eye out for any suspicious-looking bands of roving Arabs, but we did not see any. One night we were caught in the worst sandstorm I had ever experienced, and the only thing we could do was to batten down the hatches and wait it out. It was incredibly hot, noisy and gritty, and nothing could keep the sand from seeping through our shelter walls, while outside the wind howled like a million banshees. It was no wonder that some men lost their sanity when caught in the open in these frightening and highly claustrophobic, natural phenomena. Eventually, when it had abated, we reached the Jebel el Akhdar area south of Benghazi and stayed there for a few days to carry out trials on various weapons, including the vehicle-mounted machine guns and the American AR 15 carbine.

Moving on north through the foothills of the Jebel we went through many vineyards and so passed down to the coastal plain, where we came across evidence of the extremely heavy fighting in the area between Montgomery's 8th Army and Rommel's Afrika Korps, some of which involved the biggest battles of the Second World War in the Western Desert. There were wrecked tanks abandoned where they had been hit – a really forlorn sight. When we reached the coast road there was a little truck-stop café, all by itself, with not another building in sight. The only things to eat were boiled eggs and dates – the one guaranteed to bung you up and the other guaranteed to shift it! The dates looked pretty fierce to me, so I had a Coke and a boiled egg. The proprietor spun the egg on the counter before passing it over; apparently a wobbly spin meant a bad egg. Travelling on again eastwards we skirted Benghazi and then took the coast road through Bardia and Derna, stopping for a few hours to view the Roman ruins at Cyrene. Then it was on to the camp near Tobruk, where we had a few days' rest before returning to the UK. It had been a long, hard-working but very enjoyable trip. Incidently, during the journey I noticed that the American trucks broke down and got stuck in the sand much more often than did our Land Rovers. But they were a good set of blokes, and it had been a pleasure to travel with them.

I visited Tobruk one afternoon. It was a dusty, run-down-looking place. The town appeared as if it hadn't recovered much from the battering it took during the war, when Rommel tried for months to take the 'fortress' port and surrounds before eventually succeeding and forcing the British and Allied forces to retreat. There were a few grotty-looking bars, cafés and souvenir shops on the main street, catering mainly for the small British military presence in the area. The impressions I got from observing the local population's attitude towards us were a mixture of friendliness and hostility. We didn't know it then, but 'Colonel' Muammar al-Qaddafi's future revolution, involving the overthrow of King Idris in 1969, was already gathering momentum among the Libyan people. This must have accounted for the hostility shown. The friendliness came from the shops and bar owners, not surprisingly, as they knew that once the British servicemen and women had left, so would the bulk of their customers. Before leaving Libya we paid a visit to the British and Commonwealth military cemetery near Tobruk. Most of the dead buried there are from the desert campaigns of the Second World War. The cemetery appeared to be very well cared for, and everywhere was spick and span. I read the names on the gravestones: Private A., aged 22; Corporal D., aged 24; Sergeant M., aged 26; and so on and so on, row upon row of them, all just young lads. As I walked along a lump the size of a golf ball came into my throat and, I am not ashamed to admit, the tears began streaming down my cheeks. Now, when I see the youth of today, with their earrings, nose studs and ponytails, I think at first, 'What a bloody shower.' However, then I remember that Tobruk cemetery, and many more I have seen on my travels in many different countries, and I think again and say to myself, 'Don't be too critical, Geordie. Underneath they are still the same kind of men now as they were during that war and, what's more, some of them have been carving *their* names on military gravestones all around the world every year since the end of the Second World War – all in the cause of freedom for every one of us.'

Chapter 18

TRAINING WING QUARTERMASTER: 22 SAS REGIMENT

Arriving back in Hereford on Saturday 12 June 1965 my comrades and I had the Sunday off, which I spent with Ann. Needless to say it was a real pleasure to see 'my Annie' again and to hear her voice, but there was no rest for the wicked, or even the good guys. It was back to work on the Monday and back to the SAS grind. At that time I was still an instructor on Training Wing staff, and in the three months following the Libyan expedition I was fully occupied helping with the Selection Course, training more mortar crews and taking shooting parties on Ross rifle ranges near Hereford. Teaching CQB also came within my remit once more, plus the recognition and use of foreign weapons. The regiment had a sizeable collection of the latter, having inherited them from various parts of the world, and also the police had given us a fair amount from their haul of illegally held weapons after they were handed over by the public during a recent amnesty. What kept me happy in between times was courting my lovely Annie. We agreed to get married in February the following year, 1966, when she would be 21. We now travelled together a lot in my Morgan sportscar, parking out in the wilds somewhere and sleeping in a little tent. Evening meals would usually consist of a bottle of wine followed by curry and rice cooked by me in my mess tins on a hexamine stove.

In August I was told that I was being posted to the SAS forward base at Kuching in Borneo to work on Operations and Intelligence. The Borneo campaign was still rumbling on; in fact it still had another nine months or so to run. The soldiers of 22 SAS had been performing very well out there, and also in the Middle East in Aden and the Radfan, Southern Arabia. However, there were tragedies. Six SAS men were killed in Borneo, three in a helicopter crash and three by enemy action. Among the latter was Sergeant 'Buddha' Bexton, a good friend of mine, nicknamed Buddha because of his ever-genial smile and broad, heavy build. Two SAS had also been killed in the Radfan. Their bodies had to be left behind after the action and were, sadly, mutilated by the Arab enemy force, who cut off their heads and displayed them on poles. We had to accept such atrocities phlegmatically, as a brutal and humiliating demise was sometimes part of the risks accepted and taken as a fact of life by SAS men. This had been true from the time of the regiment's inauguration in the behind-the-lines cauldron of the Second World War right up to the present day. But acts such as this never failed to sicken, especially those who knew the victims personally, as we did.

Anyway, back to the present, and having bought Ann a Mini to drive herself to work as a nurse in Holme Lacy hospital, near Hereford, I went off to serve in Borneo once more, arriving in Kuching on 6 September 1965. The SAS base was in a large house on a hill just outside the city. The house was known as 'Pea-Green Palace', or PGP, named after the colour of SAS tropical dress uniform. I had at least half-a-dozen jobs at PGP and was kept busy until late into the night most evenings. It was essential but boring work. I volunteered a few times to go out on a short patrol but was turned down flat. These knock-backs were absolutely correct, as I was still unfit for active operations. My back was playing up, and my hip joint clicked and creaked constantly.

There is a small 'island' isthmus just off the coast at Kuching on which had been established a training cum rest camp for the SAS and Border Scouts, an indigenous unit that worked closely with the SAS. Some operations were mounted directly from the island, which meant that I had to make several trips out there with maps and other equipment. The island was reached by use of a rubber assault craft powered by an outboard motor. It was OK going down the calm water from Kuching, which was reputed to be inhabited by crocodiles, but we had to sail right round the island to get to the camp, and the sea could become quite rough, with high winds. Our flat-bottomed craft would almost take off from the top of a wave sometimes. The landing place was a little sandy beach in a sheltered cove, and just in from the beach was a longhouse which we used as accommodation. 'A desirable and secluded resort' is how a travel agent might have described the place. It was an ideal location for rest, recuperation and some retraining between operations.

There was at that time an SAS rear HQ situated on the island of Labuan, about 350 miles away. We received many signals from rear HQ, some of which seemed to be about nothing and were entirely surplus to requirements. Each signal had a reference number to be quoted on any reply which, in turn, also had a reference number. On replies to the 'nothing' signals we appended our ref, YPMO – meaning literally 'You piss me off!' I don't know if HQ ever figured out what YPMO stood for, but their 'nothings' kept coming, and I think we reached YPMO/30 by the time I left!

Christmas came and went, and on 4 January 1966 I was posted back home. Travelling via Singapore, where I had a day's leave, it was then the usual route to the UK, stopping at Calcutta, Bombay and Istanbul. I arrived back in Hereford on 6 January, and as soon as I got the chance I went to see Annie. We decided to get married on 26 February and so, back in Hereford, we took over a married quarters near camp. It was a horrible place. I hated it. The quarters were fairly new, with flat roofs, but were sarcastically likened to matchboxes, the larger ones being known as Swan Vestas. Naturally, with my luck, we lived in a Puck. Ann carried on nursing at Holme Lacy hospital, and I was still frigging about in HQ Squadron, but at the end of March I was ordered to Germany (BAOR) with four others to run a combat survival course in the Hartz Mountains, near the border with the then East Germany. The Hartz is very beautiful but very rough country, with vast forests and, at that time of year, enough snow on the high ground to ski. Our base, to which we moved a week in advance to get prepared, was in the Army ski school at Silberhütte, near a town named St Andreasburg. There we met up with Major X., an ex-SAS officer who was in overall command of the course. My four companions were Geordie L., who had been badly wounded in Borneo in an action (for which he was awarded the Military Medal) and who was just getting fit again; Mick Reeves, who was later to gain fame for the daring rescue of a parachutist trapped on the end of his static line (for which he was awarded the George Cross); Taff B., with whom I hadn't worked before; and Eddie Pickard. Eddie was to die tragically in a parachuting accident in Brunei in 1973. We dovetailed together without much fuss and made a good team – they were all good lads, and a pleasure to be with.

While making animal traps and personal shelters our group, with participants from various other regiments, had the use of an area of forest nearby. During our stay at Silberhütte we paid many visits to the pubs (*Gasthäuser*) in St Andreasburg. I loved the German beer, not least because it always had a good 'cheering effect' on me and never gave me a hangover. The locals were friendly, but nearby there were also some not-so-friendly neighbours. The East German border was quite close, and we SAS men would catch the occasional glimpse of one of their watchtowers, a grim reminder of an extremely vicious and repressive Communist regime.

To round off the survival course we held an exercise in which our trainees had to move across country in a survival situation and at the same time avoid capture by the West German border guards. Working in pairs the Brits had only meagre rations, including a live chicken for each pair. A couple of days before the exercise each man was issued with a length of hessian and some string with which to make a suit, footwear and a rucksack. They also had to cut themselves a long stave. Most of the suits were quite good, especially the outfit made by a resourceful RA bombardier. Perhaps not surprisingly the same man joined the SAS shortly afterwards. Earlier on we had carried out a recce on the local rubbish tip. There we found clothing, dirty and ragged, but serviceable; food, mouldy and squashy, but edible; material to make a shelter; cans to cook in; bottles to carry water; a railway timetable (still in date); some pieces of cutlery; and several well-thumbed pin-up books. I ordered the trainees to walk there to see if they could find anything that might be useful. Next time I looked most of the food was still there, but all the pin-up books had gone! The trainees had to make several RVs en route to their 'safe area', and I found out later that Major X. had revealed the RV locations to the border guards. Consequently it wasn't long before a lot of our men had been captured. The border guards were too late at one RV, though. I was sitting there at a track junction in a wood just before first light one morning. I had checked the last man through and was about to move off when a truck came roaring up the track and deposited two border guards. They took up position facing down the track, rifles at the ready. They hadn't seen me sitting a few yards away. Waiting quietly until it was light I rose and moved silently up behind them. Then, tapping the nearer one on the sole of his boot, I said, '*Guten Morgen.*' I've never seen anyone look so surprised! This was a salutary lesson for both sides: always check the area in question as much as possible before approaching an RV or establishing an ambush, and observe all round.

Back in Hereford at the end of April 1966, I was promoted to Staff Sergeant and told that I was to take over the duties as SQMS (Squadron Quartermaster Sergeant) of the Training Wing. There were three main tasks. First, the stores had to be complete, serviceable and ready for instant use.

Secondly, when Selection Course personnel moved to Brecon for the test fortnight I had to go there in advance to take over the accommodation at Dering Lines. Thirdly, I had to make sure that everyone, trainees and staff, were fed and also supplied with haversack rations to eat when out of camp. Taking over the accommodation at Dering Lines was an onerous business. However, this vital task was interrupted by unforeseen circumstances, as before I had a chance to take over the post I suffered a bout of serious back trouble. I had several slipped discs caused by my numerous parachute landings, many of which were on active service and on terrain of all types. Some of the landings were very hard indeed, and the effect was cumulative. I was at my mother-in-law's house when the attack occurred. All I could do was lie on the living-room floor and shout with the pain. I couldn't move. I couldn't even lift my head without suffering agonising pain. Ann called an ambulance, and when the medics saw me they just rolled me up in the carpet that I was lying on and took me to hospital. I was put in traction: ropes taped to my ankles were passed over small wheels at the end of the bed and attached to heavy weights. The foot-end of the bed was raised to prevent me being pulled onto the floor. The idea of traction, so I was told, was to pull the vertebrae slightly apart in order to allow the discs to go back into position between them. They had roughly the same thing in the olden days, only it was called a torture rack! After four days in traction I felt easily 3 or 4 inches taller. I left hospital in plaster from armpits to hips which I had to wear for three weeks.

So, finally, after a spot of sick leave I reported back for duty, plaster and all. The previous SQMS had left the Training Wing stores in a state of utter shambolication, and the bloke who had stood in for me while I was in hospital had made it even worse. There were heaps of unserviceable kit, and there were also lots of annoying deficiencies. However, Geordie Shipley, a Corporal from A Squadron, joined me as my assistant. He was a good worker, and between us we got stuck into the job. Within a few months we had restored some order and made up the deficiencies in kit. There wasn't much time to get bored, and I enjoyed it. The Second-in-Command of Training Wing, Captain Styles, was a decent bloke and a gentleman. Also the SSM, 'Sandy' Sandilands, was one of the nicest men I have ever met. He was generous and reliable, a fine soldier, being the holder of a well-earned Military Medal, and an extreme pleasure to work with. He had served in the Forces during the Second World War and in the 1950s won his Military

Medal with 22 SAS in Malaya for his bravery and tactical skill when leading jungle patrols on anti-terrorist missions over a period of a year, patrols that accounted for a number of enemy forces, some at his own hands.

Part of my duties as SQMS was to raise money for the Training Wing fund, and towards that end I used to sell various items to the recruits, such as tea and rolls at break time. Also, I had a range of clothing and equipment on offer, such as lightweight compasses, map cases, water-repellent woollen pullovers and lightweight waterproof anoraks known as cagoules. These were roomy, with big pockets, and could be rolled up tight and small. I flogged a fair amount of the other kit, but the cagoules were a touch on the expensive side and didn't sell. I decided that the best sales pitch for them would be up in the mountains when the recruits were plodding miserably around. So one day I motored out to a remote RV. The rain was lashing down, blown by a biting, cold wind. As each man checked in, wet and shivering, I offered him a cagoule, saying he could pay me later back at camp. I sold about ten that day!

It was around this time that Ann became pregnant with our first child. Two months into her pregnancy she developed appendicitis, which was initially diagnosed as indigestion. After an operation to remove her appendix Ann's condition deteriorated. She was moved to a bed near the ward door, which in those days usually meant you were hovering between life and death. She was semi-conscious for about four days. The only thing Ann can recall from that period was opening her eyes several times and seeing my worried, tear-stained face peering down at her. When she finally left hospital she had lost a lot of weight, but she and, as far anyone could tell, our baby, were both OK, miraculously. On 10 July 1967 our daughter Jacqueline was born, a fine healthy baby. The first time I held Jacqueline in my arms I cried my eyes out. I looked down at her and said, with feeling, 'Yes, bonny lass, I nearly lost you *and* your mother.'

At the end of August 1967 I handed over to my successor with everything in good order and no deficiencies. I was then promoted to WO2 (Warrant Officer second class) and posted as PSI (Permanent Staff Instructor) to 23 SAS (TA) at Birmingham. It was during my time with the Training Wing that the SAS, or rather those in charge, made one of the gravest mistakes in the regiment's history. A Guards SAS Squadron was formed of volunteers from the old Guards Parachute Company, the same one we had trained in jungle techniques in 1964. They just simply moved them in, complete with all their rank structure. We – that is, the rest of 22 SAS – were assured that those who held rank above trooper in the Guards Squadron would hold it only so long as they remained in the said squadron. But that arrangement went by the board after about a year, and 22 SAS found itself with senior NCOs from the Guards Squadron taking up appointments such as Sergeant Major, Regimental Quartermaster Sergeant and, on at least three occasions, Regimental Sergeant Major. This meant that genuine SAS men who had flogged their way through Selection and started as troopers were being left way behind. None of the initial members of the Guards Squadron had passed an SAS Selection Course, only those who arrived later as reinforcements, and many of those kept the rank they came with. Anyway, after a year or so the Guards Squadron couldn't keep its strength up from Guards recruits alone, and the whole idea was dropped. From then, out of the defunct Guards Squadron, 'G' Squadron was born, and recruits from all sources were put into it. However, the bad feeling created by this episode lasted for many years. One of the basic strengths of the regiment had been undermined: that is, the knowledge that everyone in 22 SAS had come in through the same door – Selection – and that all men, except officers, started off as troopers with equal opportunity for promotion. I knew a lot of those men from the Guards, and three-quarters of them, in my opinion, were OK and would probably have passed Selection anyway. However, the snag was they were *not* put through the test. Being on your own up in the Welsh mountains is a damned sight different from plodding along with others in a patrol, when a weaker-willed individual can be carried along. As a consequence a number of 'back-door merchants', some of whom were quite undesirable, went around with an SAS badge on their berets and SAS wings on their shoulders to which, in my opinion and the opinions of many others, they were definitely not entitled. This was a classic, perhaps inevitable but definitely embarrassing occupational hazard of being part of the finest Special Force the world has yet seen.

Chapter 19

PERMANENT STAFF INSTRUCTOR: 23 SAS REGIMENT

I was waiting to answer my next call of duty SAS-wise when I heard that I was due to be posted as a Permanent Staff Instructor (PSI) to the TA SAS, a vital role, and one that the powers-that-be thought was eminently suited to my wide experience. At first I was somewhat reluctant to leave behind my long-term colleagues and friends in the Regular SAS. Deep down I didn't want to go as an instructor to the TA – no one in 22 SAS did – but, looking back on it, I am very glad that I did go. It was a valuable experience, not only in military terms, but also in my other great interest – human nature. In addition I discovered that if a PSI did his job properly, it was extremely hard going and definitely not an easy ride. Having to work in Birmingham meant being away from Ann and our baby quite a lot, but that was hard luck and not so bad as the three- or four-month stretches of duty I would have undergone had I remained with 22 SAS.

Shortly after I started at 'Brum' Ann and I bought a small cottage just outside Hereford. It was situated on a hill overlooking the city and surrounding countryside. It was a very old place, 200 years at least, and had walls some 3 feet thick which were laid straight onto the underlying clay, with no foundations in the modern sense. It was a cosy cottage, although a bit primitive. Over the next few years we gradually improved the place. It was a beautiful, peaceful spot which we loved. We lived happily there until 1995.

My first job with 23 SAS was with A Squadron at Shirley, a suburb of south Birmingham through which ran the A34 road to Stratford-upon-Avon. There were two PSIs at Shirley drill hall, the other being my old friend and comrade-in-arms, Taff Taylor, who had been in D Squadron 22 SAS when I joined them in Malaya. Most of the men in A were Brummies and, with one or two exceptions, were a good bunch of blokes. There were three other Squadrons in 23 SAS: B at Leeds, C in Doncaster and D near Dundee in Scotland. They all had the same task in the event of war with the Eastern Bloc – that is, covert operations in support of British forces in Germany.

TA SAS men did most of their training on alternate weekends, plus one drill night during the week. Also there was a two-week period called 'annual camp' which was mainly spent abroad, usually in Germany. This didn't amount to a lot, so it took quite a long time to train a recruit from scratch to SAS soldier. To further complicate matters a TA Squadron usually had recruits at many different stages of training. This was because we couldn't regulate when people joined and had to grab them as they entered the drill hall door, quite literally. We couldn't hang about! New recruits would have an initial interview which, if satisfactory, would be followed by positive security vetting. The latter could take some time, and meanwhile the recruit would have a medical and be issued with kit. Then, if no vetting problems arose, they would start training for Selection.

TA SAS Selection did not last as long as the regular SAS process, but it was, in my opinion, equally tough. I started off as a PSI with a bit of a cynical opinion of TA men, thinking they were mostly motivated by the extra money. However, by the time I had finished my service I had great admiration for a good TA man, which the majority of 23 SAS were. A TA man, or woman in some units, is a civilian who, upon entering a drill hall, immediately has to switch from one world to another. It is not always an easy task, and it takes hard work and dedication to carry this out successfully. However, not all recruits lasted the pace. We had many fade away, never to return. Some decided that they couldn't give up sufficient time, others had family problems and quite a few found the going too hard. We summarily dismissed a number after discovering they were bad hats with murky pasts. Also, even though a bloke could be physically OK and with a spotless life, he just couldn't fit in mentally, that is, he couldn't get on with other people. Living a reasonably amicable life with your comrades is an essential attribute in the SAS.

Getting down to the nitty-gritty process of forming successful TA SAS soldiers, for some PSIs and senior ranks in the TA the technique for getting recruits trained up ready for Selection was to get them up in the hills with a rucksack on their back. Then it was head down and away. This was OK up to a point, but it didn't give the men enough to think about – not enough niggly snags. Whenever I was in charge of recruit training I used to give them extra problems and have them answer certain questions at each RV. It made them think about other things while they were marching and running instead of 'switching off and thinking about sex', as one grizzled old PSI told them to do. Thinking about sex is OK, but it might be your last thought in action when you have to be alert all the time, not only to your immediate surroundings but also the route that you have already covered: what lies ahead, and what the hell are you going to do if something happens unexpectedly? A thinking man is not only a better soldier but usually a happy one too, because he becomes more interested in what he is doing.

I also made sure that all recruits under my wing were given not only fitness and navigation training, but also that they covered as many other subjects as time allowed, such as training as medics, which included how to treat hypothermia and heatstroke. Hypothermia has killed numerous people up in the mountains, including some very fit SAS men. The Welsh mountains, for instance, appear quite benevolent when viewed from below on a nice sunny day but in winter especially they can be killers. This was as true for TA SAS soldiers as it was for the Regulars. Interestingly the pass rate for TA Selection then was the same as for 22 SAS: around 10 to 15 per cent.

After several months at A Squadron I was posted to the Regimental HQ at Kingstanding, north Birmingham, to take over as MTO. My job as MTO was shadowed by a TA officer. I was involved in recruit training, which I liked, and Ops Int (Operations/Intelligence), which I didn't. It wasn't the work I didn't like in Ops Int, it was the attitude of the officers there. They were all very pleasant types socially, but I'm afraid there wasn't a lot of extra spirit among them. No 'can we go always a little further'. I must admit that most of the Ops Int officers were extremely good at their basic job – but so they should have been, because that's all they ever did, as far as I could see, and many had been doing it for years. During the time I spent at Regimental HQ, from December 1967 to December 1970, I and other PSIs laid on numerous 'rough it' weekends, mainly in the Welsh mountains, for the boys. These were exercises not only for fitness but also to practise navigation, survival, escape and evasion, and living rough in any weather. I even organised a rally-type weekend when we all drove Land Rovers from South Wales to North Wales, RV-ing at odd locations on the way. However, very rarely did any officers turn up to take part, in fact none at all on most occasions. I tried to impress upon them that if we were at war, there was always the chance of being cut off and isolated. I reasoned that the priorities then would be evasion and survival, with the possibility of having to carry out offensive operations behind enemy lines. I emphasised that the only way to be ready for that eventuality was to train for it, but frustratingly I couldn't seem to get through. From my point of view there appeared to be a distinct lack of enthusiasm. One night in the drill hall during one of my 'trying to impress upon them' sessions, when I was met as usual with solid indifference from a group of these officers, I lost my temper and told them off in no uncertain manner. All I got were blank looks. One of them accused me of being 'cynical'. Cynical, be damned! If a Russian tank commander had been looking down his barrel at that officer, the word would have died on his lips – quite literally, I believe.

I didn't have a lot of backing from the upstairs hierarchy either. Both COs during my time were non-SAS and seemed quite unconcerned. Similarly the second-in-command, who was supposed to be SAS, also appeared to be untroubled by the situation. In fact Major Roy Ball, who had worked his way up through the ranks and arrived from 22 SAS in December 1970 as training major, was the only officer at Regimental HQ during that period who managed to move TA arses around. But I didn't see the results, because that month I was told that I was to move to a place called Prudhoe in Northumberland to start a new Squadron.

In 1968, during my time at Regimental HQ, the Regimental Sergeant Major (RSM), Paddy Nugent, died suddenly. I had known Paddy from the time when he was a permanent fixture on the staff after doing my Selection at Brecon. He was a marvellous man, steady as a rock and extremely witty. It is difficult to find sufficient words to do justice to the man, his ability, resourcefulness and wide experience. Paddy's main job had been training recruits and running the vital Selection Courses in Wales – and that's where he died, ironically, of a heart attack in bed, at Dering Lines Camp. While the SAS mourned Paddy the inevitable question arose: 'Who's going to be RSM now?' I knew it wouldn't be me, as I had not yet acquired sufficient seniority and, it has to be admitted, I had told too many officers exactly what I thought of them. Everyone expected a veteran SAS man to appear as the next RSM, but they were to receive an unsavoury surprise.

What happened next was that a Guards Squadron was formed to be assimilated into the ranks of the SAS. There was nothing particularly unusual in the move at the time and, as previously described, the men were assured that those who arrived with rank in the Guards Squadron would hold that rank only so long as they remained in that squadron. However, when the squadron folded through lack of Guards recruits and became G Squadron SAS some of the newcomers' senior ranks started to get posts, in their original rank, throughout 22 SAS – just as some of the regular SAS veterans had feared all along. The SSM of the Guards Squadron, who had been appointed RQMS of 22 SAS, now appeared as RSM 23. He was a nice enough bloke and I always got on well with him, but he had never been through SAS Selection, never been on SAS operations and came into the SAS already as WO2. So here he was, the senior NCO of an SAS operational unit! He was now expected to teach recruits the ways of the SAS and was also supposed to command and guide myself and the other PSIs, all of whom had passed Selection, sweated our way up after starting off as troopers on the bottom rung of the ladder and been on numerous SAS operations. This strange and baffling set of circumstances meant that a regular SAS man in our midst had been deprived of the fruits of his labour and a post that should, logically, have been his by right and the laws of common sense. Eventually the same man became Quartermaster of 23 SAS, but at least that made way for a genuine SAS man to come in as RSM. That was Bill M., a good steady choice. Bill had been in the regiment for a long time and knew the ropes.

Meanwhile, on the domestic front, my wife presented me with a second daughter, Frances, another great cause for celebration!

Training went on relentlessly at 23 SAS HQ. I attended two courses. The first, in the autumn of 1969, was the Nuclear, Biological and Chemical (NBC) warfare course at Winterbourne Gunner and Porton Down near Salisbury. This course, which I found interesting and extremely well taught by the staff, was intended to turn out unit instructors who could pass on what they had learned to other SAS men. Part of our daily training was carried out in a bunker representing an HQ set-up. Dressed in NBC suits complete with rubber gloves and respirators, we found that writing and talking to each other was difficult, and, to make sure no one cheated, the bunker was kept constantly filled with CS gas. The special clothing had to be used repeatedly. As soon as it was disturbed while we were changing little pockets of CS gas would be released and start everyone off sneezing like mad. It was a small price to pay for the chance of staying alive in a real-life emergency, however. The other training given was a medical orderly course. A couple of weeks' instruction at Hereford was followed by a month's attachment at a hospital casualty department, in my case at the Radcliffe Infirmary at Oxford. The final few days of the course were spent in London to visit the Wellcome Foundation medical museum. Three of us went to the Radcliffe; we stayed in digs and travelled to work on the bus. One of our number was a large Irishman known as 'Danny the Ditch'.

Danny was a favourite with the nurses because his size meant security for them when, at weekends especially, a lot of violent drunks and druggies were brought in for treatment. I think the size of Danny's boots alone would have frightened off any potential troublemakers! Our task in the casualty department was to gain experience in dressing and suturing wounds, plus giving injections of local anaesthetics and antibiotics. We also watched surgeons in the operating theatre performing on patients with broken bones and large areas of skin laceration. No one came in with bullet wounds while we were there, but I had helped treat some of those in the shape of fellow soldiers before, anyway, especially in the Yemen. Autopsies I didn't like, but they were an important part of the instruction, because we could see what the inside of the human body actually looked like, as opposed to studying diagrams.

My first patient was a young girl with a cut hand. She was as calm as you like, but I was very nervous. After managing to get the local anaesthetic in more or less the correct place, I succeeded, at my third attempt, to suture the cut. The last procedure needed was an antibiotic jab on the bum. For the latter I always called in a female nurse to witness, but I remember once a young woman coming in with a cut leg, and just as I reached the antibiotic jab part of her treatment her husband, who had been present up until then, went out for some reason. I couldn't wait for him to return – the needle was ready and other patients were waiting – so I said to her, 'Pull your skirt up, please. I want to give you an injection in the rear.' 'What?' she cried, looking around startled. 'Antibiotics,' I hastened to explain. 'Oh,' and up went her skirt. She had on the flimsiest, frilliest, sexiest knickers I'd ever seen in my life. She pulled one side down exposing a buttock, and just at that moment in walked her husband, but before he could say anything I gave her cheek a hard smack and plunged the needle in. Battle training was never as embarrassing as this!

A few drunks and druggies came in at times, usually with wounds from falling down or getting punched. However, we didn't have any trouble. Maybe the sight of Danny looming over them did the trick. There's one thing about druggies: most of them didn't need local anaesthetic, they didn't seem to feel the suturing needle going in and they didn't bleed a lot either, unless it was a deep cut. At the end of our time at the Radcliffe we were getting quite slick – clean, stitch, jab; clean, stitch, jab. However, I learned a lot more besides, not least about human nature, which added to the rich store of experience of life that I had already accumulated.

Chapter 20

Up North with the SAS
Terriers: Forming a Sabre
Squadron from Scratch

I now arrived at one of the most fulfilling parts of my SAS training duties, when I was ordered to start a new Territorial Squadron at Prudhoe in Northumberland. As I have often said since, the TA, or 'Terriers', often produce some excellent soldiers for the SAS, many going on to train and be selected for the Regular SAS after their TA training. The TA has always been a popular attraction in north-east England, and so I didn't visualise any great difficulty in getting enough recruits. The basic ingredients were already there – moulding them into fighting soldiers was our job. I was to be accompanied up north by my old friend Taff Taylor, who was by then a Staff Sergeant. In point of fact it was not just a new SAS Squadron but the rebirth of C Squadron, which had been based in Rotherham and Doncaster. I cannot recall the exact reasons, but the original C Squadron had been disbanded, the survivors being given the choice of joining either B at Leeds or the new C now being established at Prudhoe.

Taff and I travelled up to Prudhoe a few weeks before Christmas 1970 to recce the drill hall and also see the training areas at Otterburn in Northumberland. We had the use of a Land Rover ambulance part of the time, which was very handy because it made a good mobile home when up in the hills. We found the drill hall, which was in a little side street just uphill from the centre of town. There was a large church directly opposite – to which, I thought to myself with a touch of wry humour, I might have to go sometimes to pray for guidance! Ever the realist, I knew that a lot of hard work lay ahead to lick the recruits – those who survived the process – into shape. Wise words of encouragement came from Lieutenant-Colonel 'Dare' Wilson, one-time CO of 22 SAS, who was proud of the fact that he had started his Army career in the Royal Northumberland Fusiliers at Prudhoe drill hall just before the Second World War. At Otterburn we checked into the camp and met a very friendly WO2 there in charge of training and range allocations. A recce of the training ground was next. It proved very hilly with broken ground and plenty of streams to wade through. That, along with the area having a reputation for heavy rainfall, made it a perfect place in which to train our recruits in cross-country navigation, test their endurance and at the same time get them physically fit. The whole area was roughly triangular, about 10 miles long each side, stretching from a little village called Alwinton on the River Coquet in the south to the Cheviot Hills on the Scottish border in the north. It was a wild and beautiful piece of country. We prayed that our recruit intake would not be too wild and be a little more malleable to our instructions! Once we had planned everything on our maps Taff and I set off to prove the various theories by walking over every inch of the proposed routes, including night marches and checking meticulously on times and viability. After we had completed that task, which took us a week or more, we had to make contact with the TA Association HQ office in Durham. The TA Association supervised the administration of drill halls, including personnel such as caretakers and so on. That done, we headed back to Hereford for Christmas.

One morning after the Christmas break, in January 1971, Taff came to collect me to go back up to Prudhoe. We had had a heavy snowfall the night before, and I really didn't feel like going anywhere, hoping instead that Taff was snowbound at home so we could have an extra day's leave. No such luck! Taff arrived on the dot, all smiles and in four-wheel-drive mode, both mechanically and mentally. He was a great bloke, who sadly died a few years ago of lung cancer. Anyway, off we went! It was a fact that not many people have been given the task of starting an SAS Sabre Squadron, albeit TA, from square one – it was a daunting prospect. At Prudhoe the drill hall was empty, as no furniture had been delivered. We did have a caretaker, however: Tom Williams, whom I had interviewed for the job before Christmas. He and his family were already in residence. Tom, an ex-wartime Paratrooper, had been captured in North Africa, afterwards escaping from the POW cage in Italy. He was a good man, one of the best, and an excellent worker.

We also needed a secretary and a vehicle mechanic. The local Labour Exchange (Job Centre) was just down the road, so I went along to vet some likely candidates. I told the man there what was required and jokingly said, 'The secretary must be able to type, etc., also she must be blonde and beautiful. The mechanic need not be beautiful, but he must be able to make engines talk and sing.' 'I've got just the people you want,' replied the bloke. 'A husband and wife called Bill and Christine Rollingson. She's just finished typing school and needs a job. He's just been made redundant from his mechanic's job with the Co-op.' Bill and Christine lived not far away, so I went to see them and liked what I saw, so I recommended them for the jobs. Christine was a beautiful blonde (she still is) and a very good typist. Bill, although not beautiful (he still isn't), could definitely make engines talk and sing! They proved to be good workers and lovely people with it. Furniture now arrived, enabling a lecture room and canteen to be set up. Stores, including weapons and equipment for the recruits, came shortly afterwards, accompanied by a storeman in the shape of 'Paddy' from the RE. Paddy was quite a character, with a thoroughly 'lived-in' face, the kind that crumpled into pieces in the night, then in the morning he'd put it back together again with the help of a fag and a cup of tea. The squadron was ready for business at last, and within days the first recruits came in. Most of them, I discovered, had deserted another TA unit – a Parachute Regiment company based at Gateshead – to join the TA SAS.

During the next couple of weeks, as more recruits flowed in, we were busy with documentation and arranging medicals, plus initial training – mainly lectures on navigation. Then, almost inevitably, over the first few months several misfits attempted to join. Some lasted a month or so but most faded away within weeks. I recall that one bloke strode through the drill hall doorway with a pistol strapped to his side – the perfect picture of 'Death or Glory'. Naturally I took his gun off him straight away. He stayed just two weeks. Another recruit, an ex-SAS man actually, left after a while, moaning that the blokes weren't the same as when he was in the regiment in Malaya! What he didn't seem to realise was that those lads were just recruits, and if he had stayed on, he would have found them eventually every bit as good as, and in some cases much better than, his old comrades. One big plus was that I was delighted to be surrounded by Geordie accents again. All those 'wey-ayes' and 'howay mans' were music to my ears! Three TA SAS men came to join us from B Squadron. They lived nearer to Prudhoe and so simply transferred over. They were Corporal Colin White, a trained medic and rugby player who was capped at least once for England; Corporal Dave Moorat, a nurse by profession and a nice quiet, steady, reliable bloke; and Corporal Dick Graham, a coal miner nicknamed 'Dick the pit', another good, steady character. They were three excellent men who each proved to be a valuable asset to the squadron, which was growing in assurance and confidence almost daily, though much hard work and training lay ahead. The training programme that Taff and I had agreed on provided for a drill night on Tuesdays from 7 p.m. to 10 p.m. and alternate weekends from 7 p.m. Friday to noon on Sunday. Regular exercises at Otterburn meant a 6 a.m. start on Saturday. All exercise briefings and other talks were given on Friday evenings and, as the SAS doesn't have reveilles, it was left to each individual to get himself up and be ready to move on time.

Saturday 23 January 1971 was our first day on the training area. We had more than twenty recruits, all full of theory and raring to go. It's usually a long, hard winter up around the Cheviots, with plenty of deep snow, but that day we were lucky; it was extremely cold and icy, but with only flurries of snow. The place I chose to park the trucks and start walking from was a road-track junction with a little stream nearby which ran under a bridge. I picked that spot because there was plenty of space to park vehicles and level ground to pitch a tent on if needed, plus water nearby for making brews and cooking. Also, it would be an easy place to find in an emergency. All anyone would have to do was walk downhill from almost any direction and they would find it. I used the same location every time we trained at Otterburn, and it eventually became known among the SAS as 'Geordie's RV'. It still is today. Before starting I split the recruits into two groups, one for me and one for Taff. Our first walk, by different routes, was a gentle 'warm-up' to the Scottish border to a spot known as Windy Gyle, where there is a trig point and a huge stone cairn. It was a round trip of about 12 miles. The day before, on the Friday, a TA officer from Regimental HQ in London had appeared at the drill hall. I knew him, but I didn't have a clue what he had come for, and he was definitely not needed. That night he gave a lecture to the recruits in which he particularly emphasised that to be SAS you must be a 'self-starter'. When we set off on our walk the Regimental HQ officer went with Taff's group. Taff told me afterwards that the officer hadn't gone far, just 2 or 3 miles, before he turned back to the RV. He had his own transport and left immediately. We never saw him again – so much for self-starting in his case!

My group had a nice steep hill, Barrow Law, to start with, and one or two blokes had a good spew on the way up with all the effort, but everyone made it to the top. Marching in single file, each recruit taking a turn at leading, I made sure everyone was following the route on their map and noting their surroundings. I also got them to identify visible features, including woods on the map, and describe, without looking, the ground already covered. It taught them to observe the country all round at all times. That night at base RV the recruits slept in a big shelter which I had brought out, and everyone cooked their own meals from individual ration packs. There were a few late-rising sleepy-heads next morning, which qualified them for a bollocking from me and extra miles to walk to remind them of their error. The weekend was a great success, and we had set the pattern. After that it wasn't long before most recruits were good enough to go out as individuals, though on one weekend when the weather was so bad, with rain and sleet moving horizontally with the strong wind, I thought some might pack it in, but they didn't. We had taken shelter for a while in a barn at Usaway Ford farm near the Scottish border. 'OK, saddle up!' I ordered. 'First pair to go.' The weather was so severe I didn't want to risk men taking part as individuals. One of the men looked outside, tentatively. 'You're not sending us out in that, are you?' he asked, looking worried. 'I certainly am,' I replied. 'And I'll be right behind you, so keep moving!'

Six months passed. Some of the initial recruits had succeeded in passing Selection. Also, many more came in and were fast catching up. In the first couple of months three ready-made officers joined, two from the Parachute Regiment TA and one ex-21 SAS. One of the Para TA officers and the 21 SAS man faded away after a while, but Peter Newton, the one remaining officer, stuck it out, eventually becoming Squadron Officer Commanding. In my humble and seasoned opinion Peter was every bit as good as any 22 SAS officer and a damned sight better than most. Predictably the Para TA made a hell of a fuss about the transfer, as they didn't want such a good officer to go.

There was a fourth officer, whom I shall call Major T. He came from B Squadron at Leeds to take over as C Squadron OC. He seemed quite content to allow Taff and me to handle all the squadron administration and training arrangements. It was a tremendous amount of work, with requests for training areas, ranges and parachute jumps that had to be booked months and sometimes years ahead. We even had to be on the ball getting a decent disco group for the squadron parties when letting off steam! I was very fortunate in having Taff as assistant PSI, but even then I would be working late most nights. A certain PSI, who had been with the old C Squadron when it was disbanded, was heard to say that 'Everybody and his uncle went to Prudhoe to help.' That simply wasn't true. Only one man came to give specific assistance, and that was Sergeant Tim Holt, a PSI with B Squadron at Leeds. Tim came on several occasions to instruct on the general purpose machine gun (GPMG). Everyone else who went to Prudhoe was either doing their own job or taking part in exercises. I will admit we had many visitors, but most of them did nothing useful and were quite unnecessary, really. One visitor we didn't get was the CO. This quite surprised me at the time, as I thought the CO would have liked to see how we were doing. If the Eastern Bloc had started a shooting match, he would have been commanding us on active service, so it seemed an odd omission. Neither did we have a visit from the padre – another typical SAS tradition begun on active service in the Second World War and involving, notably, the much-loved, late and lamented Reverend J. Fraser McCluskey MC, who parachuted in with 1st SAS into the forests of France, lived rough with the men behind the lines in their covert camps, and regularly held church services for the troopers in the midst of a countryside teeming with bloodthirsty SS and Gestapo, who were intent on hunting the SAS men down before torturing and executing them. Maybe our padre thought that we were all good boys and not in need of spiritual guidance. If so, he was dead right: 'C' stood for 'chaste'! I admired our padre, though, as he was a good bloke, the only holy man I have known who swore and carried a gun! He liked his pint as well. However, for all that, I think he was closer to his God than some sanctimonious vicars I've come across. Personally, my religion is 'Live and let live'.

During my time at Prudhoe I tried to make friends with the Sergeant Major PSI at Gateshead Para Company. I hoped that exercises could be arranged involving both units but, frustratingly, he didn't want to know. For some unknown reason, professional jealousy perhaps, a lot of other units, both regular and TA, had a dislike of the SAS that sometimes bordered on hatred. I discovered later that the Para PSI hadn't been there long and that the previous PSI, who had left just before I arrived at Prudhoe, was none other than my old friend Freddy Blake, with whom I had served in 1 Para mortar platoon in 1956–7. If Freddy had still been at Gateshead, things would have been totally different. In fact technically I was still in the Parachute Regiment myself. In those days most SAS men remained on the strength of their parent unit, serving consecutive three-year attachments to the SAS. Now and then I would receive from Para HQ a seniority list showing the positions of senior NCOs in the regiment. I noted that as I gained promotion in the SAS I was automatically given the same grade in the Paras. Towards the end of my service, perhaps not surprisingly given my experience and seniority, I found myself to be one of the senior WO2s on the list.

Despite all the activity I managed to get home to Hereford every other weekend. We were still not on mains water, so I would arrive at our cottage late at night with a Land Rover loaded full of water jerrycans. The water used to last two weeks. I always travelled in a Land Rover because of the need to pick up stores from 22 SAS or Regimental HQ in Birmingham. The IRA had just started operating on mainland Britain then, and all drivers of military vehicles had to keep a sharp look-out. This was a problem, because the volume of traffic on the roads made it virtually impossible to know if some vehicle behind or about to overtake was packed with IRA terrorists intent on filling you with lead. However, with typical phlegmatism I just ignored it all, apart from the obvious precaution of not picking up any hitch-hikers.

Another problem afflicting the country at the time was the 'rent-a-mob' demonstrators. They were mostly young, with a lot of students among their ranks, and these people, a motley collection of Marxists, anarchists, dopey liberals and general dickheads, went around supporting such things as 'wild-cat' strikes, CND and other causes. They were anti-British Army, pro-IRA and pro-Communist, both Soviet- and Chinese-style. I warned the squadron men that if any 'demonstrators' were to gather around our drill hall, they should not try to antagonise them or start a punch-up, however tempting it might be. That was precisely what those people wanted to be – martyrs. I visualised the headlines in the *Morning Star*, the British Communist newspaper: 'Brutal SAS beat up innocent and peaceful demonstrators', or suchlike. Anyway, none appeared and we were spared the trouble. There was one tricky incident, though, which took place during the first few weeks at Prudhoe. I had obtained permission to stage a recruiting demonstration in the main square of a nearby town. We parked an SAS armed Land Rover with several of our men on it and around it, dressed in combat gear and armed with rifles. Also two general purpose machine guns (GPMGs) were mounted on the truck. At the time there was a postal workers' strike on, and we had positioned ourselves, unwittingly, only 20 or so yards from the post office, outside of which there was a strikers' picket. When they observed our arrival, parking nearby and looking very tough and businesslike, they started muttering among themselves in an animated manner. After a while one of them came over and said, 'They won't break the bluddy strike this way, you know, sending in the bluddy Army!' For a minute we didn't comprehend. Then, when it dawned on us, we burst out laughing, as we were only there on a recruiting drive. The picket man seemed a bit nonplussed, so I explained, and he went off laughing to tell his mates, who also appeared to be amused, and not a little relieved. Talk about getting a hammer to crack a nut!

Later on, in the summer, we had a recruiting stand at the Newcastle Fair on the Town Moor and took an SAS armed Land Rover and a display board covered in photographs. I also released a load of helium balloons with recruiting leaflets tied on them, but no one that I know of ever joined as a result of finding an airborne leaflet. I suspect they all landed in Norway, where they would undoubtedly have been taken as advertising for the Scandinavian Air Services (SAS)!

Shortly afterwards the squadron had a 'field firing' weekend at Otterburn, including firing the GPMG from the SAS Land Rover. At the time there was a ban on night firing, so when it became dark we did a runner down to the nearest pub. There we met some men from a TA Company of the Royal Northumberland Fusiliers (NF). Their OC was with them, and during our conversation I arranged with him a joint weekend exercise at Otterburn, with the NF playing the 'enemy' to C Squadron. I planned the exercise in detail, later giving each side specific tasks. At last we had another unit to work with! If all went to plan, I thought, it should be very interesting and would surely improve our skills, but alas, my optimism was short-lived. When I contacted the NF with my plan, which meant starting Friday night, they said, 'Oh, no, we don't even report to our drill hall until Saturday mid-day.' 'OK,' I replied. 'We can hold a shortened exercise from 6 p.m. on Saturday until 6 a.m. Sunday.' 'No fear,' came the answer to that. 'We always knock off at ten or eleven on Saturday nights so we can have a drink in the club at Otterburn camp. Then we clean our weapons on Sunday morning.' At that rate, I wondered, how the hell did they manage to get them dirty in the first place? Eventually we held the exercise for four hours on the Saturday night, during which time all C Squadron tasks were performed successfully. It was better than nothing, but only just. The NF were, all of them, very nice blokes, but I considered it would be a waste of time working with them any more. They didn't get in touch with us again either. I suspect we kept too many unreasonable hours for their liking.

At that time in the TA SAS everyone had to attend a certain number of 'obligatory' days, plus an annual camp training fortnight, in order to earn an extra bounty payment. Bounty night meant a good piss-up in the drill hall bar. We had, by this time, a fantastic bar, as a few of the lads had donated their spare time and 'knotty-pined' the walls, plus they had put up a beamed ceiling from which hung all sorts of Army memorabilia. The bar had a tiled roof and, to complete the decor, we had been given some old bench seats from a closed-down pub. It was an ideal place to relax in after a hard weekend on training. Unfortunately, some years after I left, the then reigning PSI had it all ripped out. 'Fire hazard,' he said stubbornly, but when I paid visits later, it just wasn't the same – more like a NAAFI.

By Christmas 1971 the new C Squadron was progressing nicely. There were around twenty-five to thirty men who had passed Selection and were parachute-trained. The squadron as a whole was also well advanced on SAS-type training. The lads didn't do much drill, like marching and saluting, which is expected in some units where a certain amount of blind obedience is called for. During SAS ops, however, the men have to operate in small groups and very often alone, so self-discipline is essential. It has to be, because usually the commander of a four-man patrol is a junior NCO, and very often it is the senior trooper. In my first few months in Malaya with the SAS our troop was commanded by Corporal 'Archie' Archer, and a damned good job he made of it too.

Otterburn, although ideal for recruit training, was becoming too familiar to the older members of the squadron. There is a vast amount of hilly moorland in Durham and Northumberland where I held some of our more advanced exercises, strictly unofficially, but as we only moved at night no one ever knew we had been there. We also spent a lot of weekends in the Wensleydale area of North Yorkshire, a beautiful piece of country to train in and to look at. I loved the hills and moorlands, and my favourite part is on the Cheviots. I remember one crisp Sunday morning at the end of May on SAS exercise. It was about 9 a.m.; the sky was blue, and all was still and quiet. The odd snow drift, as yet unmelted, lay underneath hummocks facing north. I breathed in the cold, clear air and just stood for a while marvelling at it all – the emerald-green hills, the blue sky. I didn't want to be anywhere else at that moment, and I had seen some incredible sights the world over!

Meanwhile time was passing quicker and ever quicker. I was due to leave the Army on 30 September 1972. I knew I was entitled to two months' leave before then, so I went to see the chief clerk at Regimental HQ in Birmingham and gained the necessary permission.

In the July I did my final parachute jump. The Paras at Gateshead had laid on a balloon jump programme on the Town Moor at Newcastle one Saturday, and the RAF insisted that all other airborne units in the area also take part. The Paras had turned the event into a PR stunt as well, having invited the Lord Mayor of Gateshead and other dignitaries along to watch. It was to turn into a momentous occasion for me, and a significant milestone in a long and varied career in the SAS. I remember the event as though it happened yesterday. I duly arrived on the Moor at the appointed time with a truckload of C Squadron men. The RAF team issued parachutes, and while we were fitting them on, the Lord Mayor, complete with big chain of office, looked on. Also, a photographer from the local *Gateshead Post* was busy snapping away. My turn in the balloon cage eventually came. At 800 feet the despatcher gave me a tap on the shoulder, and away I went for the very last time. About halfway down I was floating nicely and admiring the view when I suddenly thought, 'Bloody hell, I'd make a good target for an IRA sniper up here!' It was the first time I had wished for a faster descent. Anyway, I had a lovely soft landing, handed in my chute and, finding the Para OC sitting in the RAF control vehicle, I decided to have a chat and make friends. No way! Old rivalries surfaced once more. We were talking amicably when in burst their Sergeant Major. 'Them bluddy SAS blokes are trying to recruit our men!' he yelled indignantly. 'What do you mean?' queried the OC, clearly stirred to action. 'Well,' growled the Sergeant Major, his face suffused with rage, 'as one of our blokes lands, an SAS man is running up to him and shoving an SAS recruiting leaflet into his hand. It's not bluddy on.' The OC looked at me. 'I don't know anything about this, sir,' I said, biting my lip to stop laughing as I dashed outside. On the DZ I discovered the chief culprit was Tommy Butler, who together with several others was doing exactly what the Sergeant Major had accused them of. I congratulated Tom on his initiative. Then, finding that all our lads had completed their jumps, I hurriedly ordered them onto the truck and left for Prudhoe. I believe C Squadron had a few recruits from the Paras as a result of this very exercise shortly afterwards! To make matters worse, when the *Gateshead Post* published the story and photographs there, for all the world to see just behind the Mayor, was yours truly, face on to the camera, fitting my parachute. There were two Paras in the picture, but their badges weren't showing, and, to rub it in, I had on my SAS beret with badge prominently displayed. It really rubbed salt into the wound!

The squadron was due to go to Kenya in August for training. I was really sorry to miss that one, and I knew I would miss the squadron like hell, too. I had seen it start from nothing and now there it was, nearly full strength and ready for its role in war. It had been a difficult job for both Taff and myself, but the results made it worthwhile. They were a great bunch of lads. I would have been confident and proud to have gone to war with them anywhere in the world. At a farewell party just before I left Prudhoe I was presented with a silver-topped wine decanter, which still sits in pride of place in our living-room. I left behind the bar a wooden hand with two fingers giving the V sign. My message to go with that was, 'Every time you, as an SAS soldier, assume you've done enough training and think you can't get any better, just look at those two fingers and think again!' A famous Russian Field Marshal and opponent of Napoleon, Count Alexander V. Suvorov (1729–1800), once said, 'Train hard and fight easy.' It has become a famous Army quotation, often repeated. He got it spot on, especially where the SAS is concerned.

Before going on end-of-service leave I had to hand in all my Army kit, less boots and socks. One item that I was pleased to get rid of was my No. 2 Dress, the infamous walking-out and ceremonial uniform. Whoever designed the No. 2 Dress must have wanted British soldiers to appear ridiculous. No one that I knew of looked good or comfortable in it. And even tailoring didn't seem to make any difference. My waistline always ended up under my armpits, and everyone's trousers were as baggy as hell around the arse. But as I gazed down at my uniform on the Quartermaster's counter I saw for the last time the SAS wings and brass collar badges, and I thought, yes, it was bloody hard work getting into the SAS and bloody hard work while in it, but it was worth every minute. Then, for no apparent reason, I remembered all the service people whom I had met and heard of who had pretended that they had been in the SAS but hadn't. I have talked to men from a number of different units who have claimed membership of either 22 SAS or TA SAS, but close questioning has always easily revealed their claims to be false. I cannot fathom why those people should have faked anything. They were, in my opinion, already doing a good, if unglamorous, job in their own regiment or corps. The SAS isn't the 'be-all and end-all' that they think it is, anyway. Without the work of such units as Ordnance, the REME, Medics, etc. the SAS simply could not exist.

On 1 October 1972 I was a civilian once more, this time for good. I never did make it to Field Marshal, as I often kidded myself (with my tongue-in-cheek sense of humour) I would. However, I was quite satisfied with attaining the rank of WO2: it meant still being 100 per cent involved with the lower ranks, the real nitty-gritty part of the Army and the SAS. I didn't come through without a scratch, as the saying goes, although most of my injuries were caused by accident, vehicle crashes and parachuting. Still, I did have one small wound from enemy action, but it was so slight that I didn't fully realise what it was until about five years after I left the Army! Caught outside by enemy mortar fire one day in Korea I felt something strike the inside of my left thigh. When I examined my leg later I assumed a small stone had been hurled up by the blast of the bomb that hit me. I merely stuck a piece of rifle cleaning flannelette on to stop the bleeding and thought no more of it. However, the skin never quite healed properly, and it felt lumpy underneath. 'Scar tissue,' suggested one medic when I showed it to him about ten years later. Then in 1977, while having a bath one night I felt a sharp edge sticking out from the wound. I pulled at it with tweezers, and a thin piece of metal about 1 inch long came out. It was black through being in my leg for so many years. I fully intended to mount it in a glass case and display it on the mantlepiece, but just as I was getting out of the bath I jogged my elbow and the tweezers fell from my grasp into the water. Catastrophically, I had already pulled out the plug, and despite frantic efforts I was unable to rescue my prized bit of ancient shrapnel before it disappeared rapidly and unstoppably down the drain!

The loss was almost symbolic. It seemed as though the fates were telling me loud and clear that it was high time I moved on to a brand new phase in my life, leaving behind an adventurous SAS career, and many good and courageous comrades, in the not always smooth waters of my wake. However, this is not quite the end of my story, which I have tried to tell honestly and with down-to-earth candour. There are still one or two surprising twists in my tale, as will be revealed in the final chapter.

Chapter 21

SAS Stores Supremo: The
Iranian Embassy Siege and a
Final Farewell

ithin a few weeks of leaving the Army I bumped into the then
RSM of 22 SAS in Hereford and was offered a very tempting job
in the Middle East. I was fascinated with the top-secret scheme
but reluctantly turned it down, even though the pay would have been
excellent and it was an exciting mission. It would, however, have meant
being away from home for two or three months at a stretch, far from my
wife and young family. At first I tried a few civvy jobs around Hereford, the
home of the SAS, including work as a salesman delivering bread door to door.
But this type of work just didn't appeal – I couldn't bear to be tied down
to factory work. I had had enough of that up north. But at least the bread
round meant I was on my own, with no one looking over my shoulder all
the time. Inevitably it did not last long before I packed it in and tried an office
worker's course at Hereford Technical College, where I was taught typing,
book-keeping, use of English and office machinery. It was a well-put-together,
three-month course, and much to my surprise I found I had quite an aptitude
for typing and was managing, towards the end of the course, to rattle off
at least thirty words a minute. I also did pretty well on the book-keeping,
and as a result I landed a job in a fruit and veg canning factory in Hereford,
where I was put to work in an office keeping a daily production ledger. It was
the early 1970s, and it seemed that the SAS and I would never cross paths
again. However, just before Christmas 1973 I met the Quartermaster (QM)
of 22 SAS at a reunion and asked him if there were any civilian jobs going
in camp. 'I'll let you know,' he promised and, true to his word, a few months
later I received a letter from him asking if I was interested in working in the
QM stores. It was manna from heaven! I was rescued at the last gasp from

the clutches of humdrum civilian working life. I jumped at the chance and started my final role on 4 March 1974, remaining in the job for the next twelve years! During this time I met and got to know many of the famous names of the modern SAS, including the members of the world-famous, though anonymous, team that broke the Iranian Embassy siege in May 1980.

The QM stores was mostly known then as the 'G-ten' stores. This was a reference to Army Form G 1098, the document that laid down the scale and quantity of stores to be held by any unit or establishment. In those days the QM's storeman was an all-powerful individual, sitting as he did not far from the right hand of God, who is known to us on earth as the Quartermaster. During my time in the Army it was generally acknowledged that QM's storemen knew everything – or thought they did. They were the fount of most of the important and latest gen within a unit. They were also the source of many rumours. 'I've just had the OG (olive-green) kit in, so we'll be off to the Far East before long,' was a typical comment someone might hear the QM's storeman whisper loudly to the Post Corporal in the NAAFI. 'Yes, I'm getting ready to redirect all mail,' the postie would reply. Within a couple of hours the whole camp would be agog with the news. Actually the top brass were probably very grateful to QM's storemen for keeping a lot of units on their toes in an almost permanent state of mental readiness.

So here I was, about to occupy that exalted position myself, although with somewhat shared power, as nowadays the amount of stores held, especially in the SAS, is so great that several stores are needed. The G-ten, where I was, contains all the hardware such as spades and ropes and all the climbing gear, and many more items too numerous to mention. I was reminded of two items of kit with which I was issued when first joining the Army and which I neglected to mention earlier. The first is the holdall, an item similar to a tool roll, which was used to carry cutlery, shaving kit and toothbrush. The second was the ubiquitous housewife – a small, white cotton pouch in which was kept a repair kit, needles, thread and buttons. It was a modest but indispensable piece of gear for every SAS soldier. I thoroughly enjoyed my time in the G-ten stores. It was interesting, varied and worthwhile. I got on well with 99 per cent of the other staff, and also with my SAS 'customers', most of whom I knew already. And I tried very hard not to spread rumours!

A Hereford branch of the SAS Regimental Association was formed in 1975, and in January 1977 I was elected branch secretary. There was a lot of work involved in laying on events, such as open days for families and gigs in the camp canteen, the Paludrine Club, It was worth the effort, because we managed to raise funds to provide assistance for members down on their luck. In October 1978 I had to go into hospital for an operation called 'spinal fusion' – a legacy of my para jumps on all terrains. This involved my bottom five vertebrae being fused together with bone from the pelvis. It cured the back pain OK, but the price was great difficulty in putting shoes and socks on, and from then on, when taking a bath, I had to clean between my toes with a long-handled bottle brush. But it was a small price to pay for so many years' SAS service, many on active duty. Many of my best mates had paid the ultimate price, so I counted myself lucky. I was out of action for a long time after the operation. I wasn't supposed to sit down for three months, only lie down or stand up. Standing for very long was out of the question, so I spent most of my time lying down. As the duties of branch secretary were impossible to carry out from the supine position I handed over to someone else. Meanwhile back in the stores everything was being looked after very splendidly by my good friend and colleague, Vince Lane.

After six months' convalescence it was back to work. I immediately noticed a new sound disturbing the even tenor of our reasonably peaceful existence in the QM department. It was the noise of gunfire! As I have mentioned earlier, a new, brick-built 'killing house' was erected at Hereford, not far from the QM department, to replace the old and battered sandbag effort behind the 30-yard range. It had the same sort of set-up as the previous house but on a much larger and more organised scale. So we now had the almost daily rattle of pistol and SMG fire to listen to as the anti-terrorist teams carried out their training. Little did we realise it then, but it wasn't to be long before those same men were to perform for real. In May 1980 the now famous Iranian Embassy siege took place. It turned out to be a brilliantly successful operation and put the SAS, though somewhat unwillingly on our part, right into the public eye. There was only one sour note. During the siege one man at the rear of the embassy was hung up when his abseil rope somehow became snagged. For a while it looked as if he was in danger of being burnt alive by the flames, because by then the building was burning quite fiercely at the back. In the event he was badly hurt and put out of action. Several days later Vince and I were asked – I say asked, but it appeared to be almost an accusation at the time – if it was possible that a faulty rope had been issued from the G-ten stores. I banged that one on the head straight away! Each abseil rope issued from the stores was either new or accompanied by a record card filled in by the previous user showing the number of abseils done, with a permitted maximum of 40. I explained that upon issue each user should have checked the condition of his rope, and if there had been the slightest doubt, then a replacement would have been issued immediately. After that we heard no more about it.

The next 'bit of excitement' to come the way of the SAS and other key elements of Britain's Armed Forces arrived with a veritable bang in Easter 1982, when the Argentinians invaded the Falkland Islands. Two SAS Squadrons were immediately despatched to the South Atlantic. It was quite an emotional experience for me and the other ex-SAS Regiment men working in the Quartermaster's to be issuing stores to the troopers and watching the soldiers, some of whom we knew well, packing up to go to war. In May we were absolutely devastated when we heard that a helicopter had crashed into the sea on its way between two ships. Nineteen men were lost, mostly SAS but also several attached personnel. Among them was Corporal John Newton, REME, brother of my favourite TA officer, Pete Newton, of C Squadron 23 SAS. This was a tragic event still remembered by the regiment to this day. That same year the old wartime huts of Bradbury Lines were finally, after a long rebuild, replaced by new ones, and the camp was renamed Stirling Lines in honour of David Stirling, founder of the SAS. In June 1983 a regimental open day was held to celebrate this event, at which I met a lot of old comrades whom I hadn't seen for years. I also shook hands with the great man himself, David Stirling, and he remembered me instantly from the time when I had first met him in London just before my secret trip to the Yemen in 1963.

In March 1986 I went into hospital to have a hip replacement operation, the direct result of the injuries received when I was involved in the vehicle accident in 1963 that I described earlier. The fairly gruelling operation finally put paid to my working life in any connection with the SAS. After a period of convalescence it became obvious that I couldn't carry on with my stores job, so I was given an honourable early 'medical' retirement. However, I consoled myself with the knowledge that I would now have far more time for other things, such as touring Europe and further-flung places with Ann in our battered, old – but faithful – VW camper tourer, which I still use today for trips around Britain and to attend SAS Regimental reunions in York and London.

In summary, I honestly do not regret a single minute of my many years' service in the Army, the Paras and the world's elite special force, the SAS. Now, I can look back with satisfaction on a highly eventful life, both as a civilian and a soldier. As I said, I never did make it to Field Marshal, but I didn't do so bad! I might have climbed a few more rungs up the ladder if I hadn't been so ready to argue with, and question, my superiors. But rightly or wrongly I'm glad it turned out that way. I remained true to myself, true to the ideals of the north-east where I was born in hardship and fierce comradeship, and true to the loyalty that I feel for Britain, a country that I love deeply and for which no SAS soldier or serviceman or woman of any of the branches of the Armed Forces should flinch from fighting and – if necessary – paying the ultimate price, as many of my good friends did in trouble spots the world over. For me, it is their memory that is the lasting legacy – the memory of their courage, which marks them out as the true heroes of the SAS.

A SHORT HISTORY OF THE SAS

Britain's famous Special Air Service Regiment, often copied but never equalled, was the brainchild of the gifted military genius Lieutenant-Colonel David Stirling. His ground-breaking behind-the-lines unit, the SAS, burst spectacularly onto the scene in the North African Desert in 1941, and the world regularly reverberates with its successes right up to the present day.

After the regiment's first parachuting mission to destroy German warplanes on the ground at airfields was wrecked by a gale, they were transported covertly to their targets in the trucks of the Long Range Desert Group (LRDG). Soon Stirling's small force of well-trained, well-armed and determined men operated at will deep behind enemy lines, achieving damage and destruction way out of proportion to their unit's size and destroying – on the ground – more than 400 of the enemy's best warplanes. The SAS obtained its own heavily armed jeeps to use on missions and tied up thousands of enemy troops who were engaged in a constant but futile attempt to wipe out the lethal raiding force, the activities of which made a significant contribution to victory in the Desert War.

Later on in the assault on Italy they parachuted into action, or used landing craft in lightning naval assaults, as part of the temporarily renamed Special Raiding Squadron. Broadening their devastating hit-and-run tactics with variations such as attacks on troops, trains, ammunition dumps, installations and communications, this successful formula was repeated throughout the war in various areas of conflict, including north-west Europe after D-Day and Germany itself for the final victory. The SAS used their own famous transport, their feared armoured jeeps – bristling with deadly Vickers K and Browning machine guns – to devastating effect in all theatres of war.

Each SAS soldier, and those of its sister force the Special Boat Squadron, was part of a hand-picked elite, and Stirling's crack regiment spawned some of the greatest fighting soldiers of all time, including the legendary

Lieutenant-Colonel Paddy Mayne (DSO and three bars), Major Roy Farran (DSO, MC and two bars) and Major Anders Lassen (VC, MC and two bars).

After a shock – and, many believe, ill-considered – disbandment at the end of the Second World War by the top brass, the SAS was urgently recalled to active service in Malaya in 1950, initially via volunteers of the Malayan Scouts (SAS). This force was later reinforced to found the new 22 SAS Regiment. The SAS has been at the centre of hot spots the world over ever since, often using helicopters to go into action, but more often than not relying on clandestine, long and gruelling marches to targets, backed by a host of hi-tech specialist equipment, weapons and navigational aids.

The SAS roll of campaign honours reads like a *Who's Who* of key Special Forces action, including Borneo, Oman, the Yemen, the Falklands, Northern Ireland, the Iranian Embassy siege, both Gulf Wars, Sierra Leone and, currently, secret operations in Afghanistan and Libya. Undoubtedly many more active operations will be added in future to this impressive list. However, though intense public interest in its activities continues to dog the SAS and its members via associated fame, military experts are agreed on one salient fact: the regiment is as relevant, effective and feared today as the day it was conceived.

There is no finer tribute to Stirling's uncanny foresight and courage.

MIKE MORGAN

INDEX

Lightning Source UK Ltd.
Milton Keynes UK
UKOW06f0003010316

269334UK00006B/55/P